Letts

revise GCSE

Steven Croft

English and English Literature

Contents

This book and your GCSE course   4

Preparing for the examination   6

Five ways to improve your grade   7

Coursework   8

1 Writing to argue, persuade, advise

1.1 Arguing a case   9

1.2 Persuasive writing   14

1.3 Writing to advise   19

Sample GCSE questions   23

Exam practice questions   24

2 Writing to imagine, explore, entertain

2.1 Imaginative writing   25

2.2 Writing to explore   31

2.3 Writing to entertain   33

Sample GCSE questions   35

Exam practice questions   36

3 Writing to analyse, review and comment

3.1 Writing to analyse   37

3.2 Writing to review   43

3.3 Writing your own reviews   46

3.4 Commenting on texts and ideas   49

Sample GCSE questions   51

Exam practice questions   52

4 Writing to inform, explain, describe

4.1 Writing to inform   53

4.2 Writing to explain   57

4.3 Writing to describe   61

Sample GCSE questions   63

Exam practice questions   64

5 Media and the moving image

5.1 Examining newspapers   65

5.2 Looking at advertising   71

5.3 Film and television   78

Sample GCSE questions   86

Exam practice questions   88

6 Non-fiction texts

6.1 Approaching non-fiction texts   89

6.2 Magazine articles   90

6.3 Biographies and autobiographies   93

6.4 Travel writing   95

6.5 Documentary writing   96

6.6 Literary non-fiction   98

Sample GCSE questions   101

Exam practice questions   103

7 Reading Shakespeare

7.1 Types of play	105
7.2 Plot and structure	107
7.3 Opening scenes	109
7.4 Presenting characters	113
7.5 Shakespeare's language	115
7.6 Endings	120
Sample GCSE questions	122
Exam practice questions	123

8 Studying drama texts (pre- and post-1914)

8.1 Approaching the text	124
8.2 Opening scenes	125
8.3 Presenting characters	127
8.4 Issues and themes	130
Sample GCSE questions	135
Exam practice questions	136

9 Studying novels and short stories (pre- and post-1914)

9.1 Approaching novels and short stories	137
9.2 Openings	139
9.3 Developing characters	142
9.4 Setting and context	146
9.5 Exploring themes	151
Sample GCSE questions	153
Exam practice questions	154

10 Studying poetry

10.1 Reading poetry	155
10.2 Features of poetry	157
10.3 Poetry in context	163
10.4 Modern poetry	166
10.5 Poems from different cultures	168
10.6 Comparing poems	171
Sample GCSE questions	173
Exam practice questions	174
Exam practice answers	175
Mock examination papers	176
Index	200

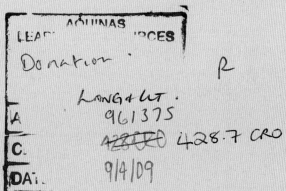

This book and your GCSE course

GCSE English AQA Specification A.

What your course will cover.

The aims of the AQA Specification cover three main areas:

a) **Speaking and Listening:** this will involve you in talking about your ideas in various ways. You will need to show that you can adapt your speech to suit different situations. You will also need to show that you are able to listen, understand and respond appropriately to other people. Where necessary you should be able to show that you can use standard English. Finally, you will need to take part in drama activities of some kind.

b) **Reading:** you will need to show that you can read accurately and fluently. Your work will involve you understanding and responding to literature of various kinds including a Shakespeare play and literature from different cultures and traditions. You will also need to analyse and evaluate different kinds of texts including non-fiction and media texts.

c) **Writing:** this will involve showing that you can communicate your ideas through writing using a wide range of vocabulary and effective style. You will need to use grammatically correct English, accurate punctuation, correct spelling and clear handwriting. You will be expected to write in different ways to suit different situations.

How you will be assessed

You will be assessed through two written exam papers and coursework which will include both oral and written work.

Written Paper 1	1 hour 45 minutes	30% of total marks
	Section A	A multi-part question on reading of unseen non-fiction and media texts.
	Section B	A choice of one from three or more questions testing writing to argue, persuade or advise.
Written Paper 2	1 hour 30 minutes	30% of total marks
	Section A	Choice of 1 from 2 questions based on a cluster of poetry drawn from different cultures and traditions in the AQA *Anthology*.
	Section B	A choice of 1 from 3 or more questions testing writing to inform, explain or describe.
Coursework		40% of total marks (divided up as follows)
Speaking and Listening		20%
Reading.	Shakespeare*	5%
	Prose Study*	5%
Writing.	Media	5%
	Original writing	5%

Coursework pieces marked * can also be used as coursework for GCSE English Literature.

How you will be assessed

You will be assessed through two written exam papers and written coursework which will include both oral and written work.

STAY YOUR COURSE!

Use these pages to get to know your course

● *Know how your course is assessed:*
  – *What format are the papers?*
  – *How is coursework assessed?*
  – *How many papers are there?*

GCSE English Literature AQA Specification A.

What your course will cover.

The aims of the AQA Specification cover three main areas:

a) **Analysis:** you will need to read, understand and respond to a wide range of literary texts and show that you appreciate the ways in which the writers achieve their effects. You will need to develop all the skills that are necessary for studying literature, learn about the techniques that writers use, analyse various literary texts and use evidence from the texts to support your ideas

b) **Context and different interpretations:** as part of your study of literature you will learn about the social, historical and cultural contexts that can influence works of literature and look at the ways in which texts can be interpreted in more than one way.

c) **Comparison of texts:** you will also need to explore comparisons between literary texts, evaluating them using relevant material to support the points you make.

How you will be assessed

You will be assessed through one written exam paper and written coursework.

Written Paper   1 hour 45 minutes   70% of marks

       Section A   One question based on post-1914 prose. There will be a choice of questions.

                        30% of marks.

       Section B   One question based on pre- and post-1914 poetry from the *Anthology*. There will be a choice of questions.

                        40% of marks.

Coursework   30% of marks

Three assignments are required:

1. Drama (pre-1914) (*Shakespeare if you are using a piece from GCSE English as a Cross-over piece for your English Literature course.) 10% of marks

2. Prose (pre-1914) (*If you are also doing GCSE English your piece on prose for that course can also be submitted for your English Literature coursework). 10% of marks

3. Drama (post-1914)   10% of marks

Preparing for the examination

Planning your study

The final three months before taking your GCSE examination are very important in achieving your best grade. However, a good grade also depends on you **following an organised approach** throughout your course.

- After completing a topic in school or college, go through the topic again in the *Letts Revise AQA GCSE English Study Guide*. Copy out the main points again on a sheet of paper, or use a **highlighter pen** to emphasise them.
- A couple of days later, try to **write out these ideas and key points** from memory. Check **differences** between what you wrote originally and what you wrote later.
- If you have written your notes on a piece of paper, keep this for revision later.
- **Try some questions** in the book and **check your answers**.
- Decide whether you have fully **mastered the topic** and write down any weaknesses you think you have.

Preparing a revision programme

In the last three months before the final examination, go through the list of topics in your Examination Board's specification to **identify those topics you feel the need to concentrate on**. It is tempting to spend valuable revision time on the areas you already know well, but balance this with time spent improving your knowledge of the topics about which you feel least confident.

When you feel confident about all the topics, spend time studying and **trying past exam questions**. Each time, check your answers with those given. In the final couple of weeks, go back and **re-read your summary sheets, notes or previous answers** (or your highlighting in the book).

How this book will help you

Letts Revise AQA GCSE English Study Guide will help you because:

- it contains the **essential content** for your GCSE course without the extra material that will not be examined
- it contains **Progress Checks** and GCSE questions to help you confirm your understanding
- it gives **sample GCSE questions** with summary answers and advice from an examiner on how to improve the answer
- **comments in the margin** and **highlighted key points** will draw your attention to important points you might miss otherwise

Five ways to improve your grade

1   Practise the kinds of questions you will need to answer

As part of your preparation for the exams, you should **make sure you are completely clear about the kinds of questions you will need to answer**. You should have practised writing answers to these kinds of questions, both throughout the course and as part of your revision programme.

2   Read the question carefully

Many students fail to answer the actual question set. Perhaps they misread the question, or answer a similar one they have studied during revision. To avoid doing this, **read the question once right through**, then **re-read it more slowly**. Some students <u>underline</u> or **highlight** key words as they read through the question. Questions set for AQA GCSE English often ask you to give your own views on a topic. **Make sure you express your ideas clearly** and, where necessary, **support your ideas with appropriate references and evidence**.

3   Plan your answer

Planning what you are going to write is a very important part of answering the question. Essays written without any form of planning are usually poorly structured and rambling and, consequently, score low marks. Don't think that time spent planning your work is wasted – **careful planning will mean that you produce a much better answer**.

4   Write accurately

Make sure your responses are written as clearly and as accurately as you can. Poor spelling, punctuation and grammar will mean that you will not score as highly as you might and can interfere with the clarity of what you want to say. Try to **leave time to check through your work** before the end of the exam.

5   Keep a check on the time

Time is a major factor in writing an examination answer. In the AQA GCSE English and English Literature exams, you will have about 45 minutes to answer a question. In order to ensure you say all you want to say in the time and do not have to leave the essay unfinished, **you need to time yourself carefully**.

Coursework

As part of your AQA (Specification A) GCSE English and English Literature course you will need to produce coursework.

Here's what you will need to do.

GCSE English

Your coursework will carry 40% of the total marks on which your final grade will be based. It is divided up as follows:

Speaking and Listening   20%

An assignment on:

1. a Shakespeare play
2. a prose text (novel or collection of short stories)
3. some aspect of the media
4. a piece of original writing   20%

(Note: your assignments on Shakespeare and the prose text can also be used as part of your coursework for AQA GCSE English Literature (Specification A))

GCSE English Literature

Your coursework will carry 30% of the total marks. You will need to produce an assignment on:

1. a play (pre-1914)
2. a novel or collection of short stories (pre-1914)
3. a play (post-1014)

Coursework gives you the chance to spend more time making sure your assignments are the best you can produce but in order to achieve this you should:

- make sure you understand what the assignment asks you to do and make sure your **response** fulfils this

- be aware of the assessment **objectives** that your assignment covers

- **plan your work** carefully and structure your ideas effectively

- make sure your work is focused in terms of the **purpose** and **audience** it is aimed at

- if you are given **word limits** or **guidelines**, stick to the general length indicated for the assignment

- do a first draft and then work through this correcting, altering or adding to your ideas in order to **improve your work**

- produce a **final draft** that represents the best work you can produce – this should be as error-free as you can make it

Remember that, although your teacher can't do your coursework for you, he or she will be able to offer you **advice**.

Writing to argue, persuade, advise

The following topics are included in this chapter:

- ● *Writing to argue a case*
- ● *Writing to advise*
- ● *Persuasive writing*

1.1 Arguing a case

LEARNING SUMMARY

After studying this section you should be able to understand:

- ● *how to plan an argument*
- ● *how to use different approaches and techniques to develop your ideas effectively*
- ● *how to begin your argument*
- ● *how to end your argument*

How to plan an argument

There are many types of argument and they can be about almost anything. They can be **formal** or **informal**, written or spoken and structured in all kinds of ways. For the purposes of studying GCSE English, though, it is likely that you will be given the topic on which to construct your argument and you will be assessed on your ability to write this argument effectively.

When presented with the topic on which to base your argument, your aim is to present and develop your point of view as clearly and effectively as possible.

In order to do this, you must first establish what your ideas on the given topic are and what your view is. To establish this, it can help to '**brainstorm**' your ideas. Try to think not only about points to support your view but also about those that do not agree with it.

From this, you need to decide what particular points you want to make and in what order you want to make them. It is important that you support your ideas with **evidence** to add weight to your case. When you have developed your case, you then need to draw your argument to a close with an effective **conclusion**.

Here is one way you can plan your argument:

1. Think about the topic you have been given.
2. Work out what you think.
3. Brainstorm ideas both for and against the view you have taken.
4. Decide which points you want to make and the order.
5. Develop your ideas on each point.
6. Decide on the evidence that you will give to support your ideas.
7. End your argument with an effective conclusion.

In an exam, time spent on ordering your thoughts is never wasted.

KEY POINT   **Careful planning is the secret to writing an effective argument.**

Now look at each of these stages in more detail.

Beginning your argument

Here is an example of a question that requires you to write an argument as a response.

'Write an argument either supporting or opposing the view that skateboarding should be banned in town and city centres.'

Having decided on what view you wish to take, you would now brainstorm your ideas. Here are some points that a student made in response to this question.

For skateboarding:

A range of points is listed.

- Town centres are for the use of all groups.
- It is good exercise.
- It develops skills.
- Skateboarders use the architecture for a purpose.
- Some cities encourage skateboarders.
- Skateboarding can be viewed as a 'performance art'.
- It gives youngsters something useful to do.
- There are few areas provided by councils where skateboarders can go.
- Support for local businesses selling skateboarding equipment.

Against skateboarding:

- Damage to architecture.
- Danger to the public.
- Nuisance to shoppers.
- Elderly people feel intimidated.
- Irritating for nearby shops.
- Skateboarders are hooligans.
- There are other places for them to go.

There are quite a few points here both for and against the view that skateboarding should be banned in town centres.

Fact and opinion

Some of these points are **facts** and some of them are **opinions**. Most arguments are a mixture of fact and opinion and it is important to bear this in mind when planning your argument.

For example, 'Skateboarders are hooligans' is an opinion and not a fact. On the other hand, 'Skateboarding provides exercise' is a fact as it is a strenuous activity.

Some points may be partially true, for example, 'Skateboarding is irritating for nearby shopkeepers'. It may well be that some nearby shopkeepers are irritated by skateboarders but others may not be.

You may think there are too many points here to develop fully and use in your response (particularly if you are working under the time constraints of an exam) and you may choose not to use some of them. You will need to decide which points you consider important enough to use in your argument.

The opening paragraph

The **opening paragraph** of your argument is very important. This is where you have the chance to capture your reader's interest and make clear which point of view you will argue from.

Here is how the student begins his argument on skateboarding:

> In recent years, skateboarders have become a familiar sight in our towns and cities but their presence has provoked a good deal of criticism from various members of the public. However, I would argue that much of this criticism is unjustified and that we should show more tolerance towards their use of the town and city centre environment to pursue their hobby.

Notice how the student begins the argument with a **statement of fact** that cannot be disputed. He then uses the word 'however' to change the direction of his writing and allow him to state clearly the view he takes and the line that his argument will follow.

 KEY POINT Your opening paragraph should capture the reader's interest and state your viewpoint.

Developing your ideas

Avoid the type of approach where you impartially put all the points in favour of a view, then all the points against and then end with a brief 'What I think' type of paragraph.

Having written your opening paragraph, you then need to develop your argument in more detail. This is where the **key points** that you identified earlier come in. There are a number of ways that you can develop the main part of your argument. Here are two possible approaches:

- You can **develop** your response by initially stating the view that you are opposing and outlining why people might hold this view, and then countering this view by putting forward the arguments that you support.
- You can write your argument totally from one viewpoint but, throughout the response, you make reference to alternative views where appropriate.

The student who wrote on skateboarding chose the second kind of approach. Here's how he began to develop his ideas:

> At a time when we hear a lot in the news about young people today taking less exercise and being less fit than in the past, skateboarding offers an enjoyable and demanding way of taking exercise. **The problem for some** is that this exercise often takes place in the pedestrian precinct of a town centre. **Some people believe that** groups such as skateboarders should be kept out of town centres but it can be argued that town centres should be able to cope with the demands of different groups of people. **In contrast to this** view that skateboarders are simply a nuisance, some towns and cities in other countries actually welcome them as just one element that makes up the varied life of a town or city. Barcelona, **for example**, takes the view that skateboarders and different groups, such as shoppers and tourists, can co-exist in harmony.

Notice how the student is clearly arguing the case for skateboarding being allowed in town centres. He also brings in other commonly held **opposing views** so that he can counter them with his own arguments.

Later, the student brings in other ideas.

Using opposing views

Personal experience

Rhetorical question

Presents an example of a different attitude

> Many say that there are plenty of other places that skateboarders can go to skate but this is simply not true. Skateboard parks are few and far between and very often they are situated in out of the way places. In my own town there is one very small area in a large park on the outskirts of town for skateboarders to use. Surely this is not good enough. The facilities are poor, the park has no lighting and it is situated in a secluded area. This is certainly not a safe or attractive environment even in daytime and after dark it is virtually a 'no-go' zone. **Is this the kind of facility that we want to encourage our young people to go to?**
> On the other hand, in some countries such as the USA and some continental countries, excellent facilities are provided in safe and central locations.

Notice again how the student uses a commonly held view in order to present the **counter-argument**. It is also worth noting how he uses examples from his **own experience** and **factual information** about the contrasting situation in other countries to support his ideas.

> **KEY POINT** A range of techniques and approaches should be employed to present the argument.

Ending the argument

The ending of the argument is just as important as the beginning and so you should make your final paragraph as convincing as possible. Here is how the student ended his essay on skateboarding:

Signals that the argument is being drawn to a close

Emphasises the key point being made

> In conclusion, then, while some of the concerns raised by those who oppose skateboarding in town centres are legitimate, I do not believe that the answer is a blanket ban. Perhaps the most important point is our towns and cities are there to serve the needs of many different groups of people, and there must be a way of co-operating and living together with tolerance and accommodating the needs of all – including those of the skateboarders.

Note how **reasonably in tone** this conclusion is. The student recognises the validity of some of the concerns, which actually gives strength to his view that skateboarding should not be banned. The appeal at the end for tolerance and co-operation again helps to convince the reader of the reasonable position of the writer, as well as re-stating the position taken.

Using different approaches and techniques

You can make your argument more effective by using **different techniques**. For example, there are various words and phrases that you can use when discussing different points of view and ideas. Some of these have been used by the student writing about skateboarding and have been highlighted.

- However…
- The problem for some…
- Some people believe that…
- In contrast to this…

- On the other hand…
- In conclusion…
- Perhaps the most important point is…

Here are some other useful words and phrases that you might use:

- Alternatively…
- Nevertheless…

- Similarly…
- This suggests that…

 KEY POINT   **Using key words and phrases can help you to make your argument more effective.**

As well as using particular words and phrases to add power to your argument, there are also other techniques you can use. Here are some ideas:

The rhetorical question

These are questions that are used to create an effect as opposed to those that require an answer. They raise questions in the reader's mind and perhaps appeal to the **emotions** and **involve** the reader in the argument. The student uses this technique when he says, '*Is this the kind of facility that we want to encourage our young people to go to?*' It is designed to make the reader feel 'No it isn't – this isn't good enough'.

Personal experience and anecdotes

It can add weight to your argument if you include some reference to your own experience. The student does this to some extent when he mentions the situation in his own town: '*In my own town there is one very small area...*' Such references based on personal experience or short personal stories or accounts can help to prove your points and give your writing an air of authority.

Using opposing views

Predicting or anticipating what someone who does not hold the same view as you might say, and then answering it, can also be an effective technique.

 KEY POINT There is a variety of techniques that you can use to make your argument more effective in presenting, developing and convincing the reader that your view is right.

 PROGRESS CHECK Write down the key stages you would go through in preparing to write an argument on a given topic.

1.2 Persuasive writing

 LEARNING SUMMARY

After studying this section you should be able to understand:
- *the purpose of persuasive writing*
- *the techniques you can employ in order to write persuasively*
- *ways of structuring a persuasive essay*

The purpose of persuasive writing

In your examination or as part of your coursework, you might be asked to write a response in which you **persuade** your reader of something. When you are writing to persuade, your aim is to try to make your reader do something or believe something. In many ways, this can be very similar to writing to argue a point but there can be some differences too.

When writing to persuade you might:
- be more **subjective** in giving your personal view
- try to **appeal** to your reader's **emotions** as much as their reason

In our everyday lives, we constantly see language used in various ways to try to persuade us to do something, believe something, buy something or act in a particular way. For example:
- Advertisements use persuasive language all the time to try to persuade us to buy the product they are selling.
- Charity appeals use persuasive language to try to persuade us to give donations to good causes.

- Public service information uses persuasive language to try to persuade us to behave in particular ways – for example, stop smoking, eat lower fat foods, don't drink and drive.

Below and on the next page is an example of a leaflet that uses persuasive language to try to persuade us to donate money. Look at it carefully and make a note of any points you notice about how it uses **language** persuasively.

Here are some ideas:

- Two rhetorical questions are asked that make the reader think about the value of the 'great outdoors'. The second question gives the impression that £2 is a fairly small sum to give to help protect the natural environment.
- The language of the opening paragraph stresses the lengths that Greenpeace campaigners are prepared to go to in order to protect the environment.
- The quotation from Mahatma Ghandi, and the fact that it is in bold type, draws attention to the importance of the non-violent aspect of their work
- The language addresses the reader as someone who believes in the things that Greenpeace believes in – note the use of '...*you doubtless understand...*', '*That's why we're asking you...*'.
- The use of specific details, such as the campaigner tying herself to the bow of the ship and the equipment and training needed, stresses the importance of funding.
- The images created of walking in an unspoilt world appeal to what the reader might find important.
- The references to developing climate-friendly systems and renewable energy are again designed to appeal to the reader's sense of helping to preserve our environment.
- The stress on the value of the '*relatively* small amount, like £2 a month' gives the feeling that this is an amount that almost anyone could afford but, by giving it, they would be helping to protect the environment.

[Front page of leaflet]

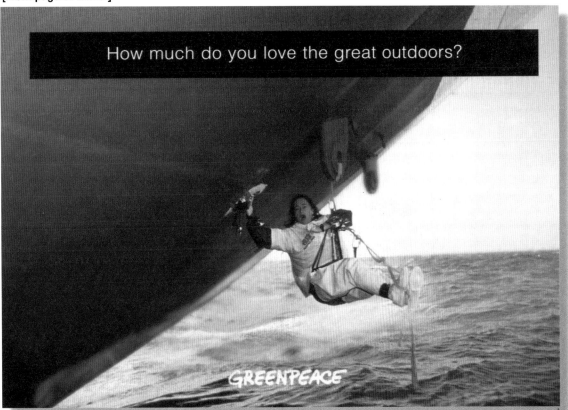

Enough to give £2 a month to protect it?

Greenpeace campaigners really love the natural world. In fact, we love it so much that we're prepared to go to almost any lengths to protect it. Over the years, we've been threatened, shot at and even bombed in the course of defending nature. We won't let that stand in our way.

"Non-violence is a weapon of the strong"

Mahatma Gandhi

As someone who also loves the great outdoors, you doubtless understand our campaigners' determination to protect the natural world. But determination alone will not defend the environment. For that, we need money too. Greenpeace can only ever be as strong as the men and women who support us, because we depend on donations from individuals. That's why we're asking you to join us today.

Obviously, we don't pass a collecting tin around before we embark on every single non-violent direct action. But we do have to ensure we have the money we need to see it through, no matter what it takes. That's why we need your support today.

If the joy of walking through unspoilt forest, the thrill of climbing ancient rocks, the adventure of diving in unpolluted seas, or even the simple pleasure of watching wildlife in its own habitat really moves you then you share Greenpeace's view of the world. Please turn that view into concrete support today.

Everything we do costs money. Take the action on the front of this leaflet. Before our campaigner could tie herself to the bow of the Exxon Valdez, just metres above the crashing waves, to highlight the threat oil poses to the environment, Greenpeace had to buy the ropes, harness, karabiners and survival suit. To say nothing of the training she needed to keep herself safe and confident. And before we could do that, we had to raise the funds to pay for it all.

It's a story that's repeated around the world every time Greenpeace takes non-violent direct action to stop environmental destruction. Because it is vital for our campaigns that we remain totally independent, we never solicit donations from companies or governments, so we depend entirely on support from individuals like you.

Is £2 a month too much to ask?

Even a relatively small amount, like £2 a month, will soon build up into an immensely valuable contribution to protecting the natural world we love so much. And 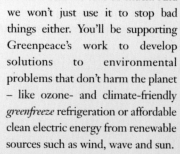 we won't just use it to stop bad things either. You'll be supporting Greenpeace's work to develop solutions to environmental problems that don't harm the planet – like ozone- and climate-friendly *greenfreeze* refrigeration or affordable clean electric energy from renewable sources such as wind, wave and sun.

Think about it another way. If you want a future where you can continue to do the things you love in the great outdoors, you need to make sure you've got a great outdoors to do them in. Giving Greenpeace your support is one way you can do that. And that's got to be worth £2 a month.

Will you give us your support today?

To turn the panel below into an envelope, please detach from rest of leaflet at perforation, enclose cheque if appropriate and seal along gummed edges.

Photos: Greenpeace/Grace, Greenpeace/Jongens, © Robert and Visser, Indrich/Greenpeace.

Recycled paper

[See previous page for front of this leaflet.]

Question types

Questions that ask you to **persuade** can be either quite **formal**, requiring a formal style of reply, or they can be more **informal**.

Here is an example of a more formal question.

'Write a letter to your MP to persuade him/her of the importance of improving public transport in your region.'

A question requiring a less formal response might be:

'Write a speech aimed at a group of friends whom you wish to persuade to help you organise a "fun-run" to raise money for charity.'

> **KEY POINT**
>
> **Whatever type of question you get, you need to use language in such a way as to persuade the reader or listener to your view.**

Approaching the question

As with writing an argument, clear planning of what you are going to write is essential if you are to write persuasively and convince your reader to your way of thinking. In order to do this you should:

- write down the aim you wish to achieve (how you wish to persuade your audience)
- write down all the points you want to make
- write down the ideas you will use to support your points
- organise your points and ideas into a logical order – the order that you are going to write about them

Now you are ready to begin.

The opening

An **effective** opening is one that immediately **captures the reader's attention** and this is exactly what you should do when writing persuasively.

Here is how two students began their responses on the following title:

'Write an information leaflet designed to persuade people to visit your home town.'

Read each of these opening paragraphs:

 Many people still think of Halifax as a grimy, northern industrial town but they are wrong. Halifax is an interesting town with a lot of places to go and things to see. For example, there is the Piece Hall, which is an interesting old building, there is a good museum and the moors are not far away either if you like walking in the countryside.

 What picture comes into your mind when you hear the name Halifax? A grimy, boring northern mill-town? You couldn't be more wrong. Halifax is a town steeped in history and culture with a wealth of features to interest any visitor. For example, there is the magnificent Piece Hall, the only example of an eighteenth century cloth market in Europe, there is the nationally famous Eureka science museum for young people and, of course, the awesome beauty of the hills and dales of the nearby Pennine uplands.

Which of these openings do you think is more likely to persuade you to visit Halifax?

The answer would seem to be clearly the second one, but why? Think about this and note down your ideas.

Here are some possible points:

- The first sentence seems rather **boring** and **uninspiring**.
- The second sentence describing Halifax as an '*interesting*' town with '*…a lot of places to go*' doesn't sound very exciting.
- Examples are listed but they do not sound very exciting either.

- The piece opens with two **rhetorical questions** that capture the reader's interest right from the start.
- The third sentence **challenges** the possible assumption that the town has little to offer, again catching the reader's attention.
- The language used to describe the town is designed to **appeal** to the reader's imagination and create a positive effect, for example '*steeped in history*', '*a wealth of features*'.
- The examples that are given include lots of **positive adjectives** to make the reader want to see the things described, for example '*magnificent Piece Hall*', '*nationally famous Eureka*', '*awesome beauty of the hills*'.

> **To make your writing more persuasive use:**
> - emotive language
> - rhetorical language
> - visual imagery

The ending

Having developed your ideas and put them forward as persuasively as you can, just as in writing an argument, you need to find a way to end your piece of persuasive writing effectively. How exactly a piece of persuasive writing should end depends very much on the specific details of the task but there are two basic ways to bring the writing to a close:

- Sum up what you have said or the points you have made.
- Find a final, particularly persuasive note on which to end.

Here is how two students ended their piece on promoting their town:

> So the next time you want to visit somewhere, think of Halifax – you'll have everything you want from stimulating museums, superb restaurants, a wide variety of shops, a sense of history, all set within the stunning beauty of the Yorkshire Pennines.

> And if all this has not managed to persuade you, then this might – anyone booking a winter break weekend at one of our superb hotels any time between January and March (inclusive) will be entitled to a further two nights (including breakfast and dinner) for two, absolutely free. You can take these two nights at any time and the offer is valid for 12 months.

The first student concludes his piece by summing up the **key points** of his piece. The second student, however, opts for a different approach by bringing in a completely new, persuasive selling point.

KEY POINT Make sure that your ending is powerful and persuasive.

Techniques for making your writing more persuasive

Many of the techniques used in persuasive writing are the same as or similar to those you might employ in writing an argument.

Here are some ideas:

- Use **emotive language** to influence the reader's feelings, for example 'stunning beauty', 'superb restaurants'.
- **Rhetorical questions** involve the reader, arouse interest and make them think.
- **Repetition** of words and phrases can make them have more impact.
- **Exaggeration** can be used to make a point more persuasively (be careful not to over-exaggerate though as this can make your points appear silly).
- **Humour** can help to make your points more persuasive.

PROGRESS CHECK What is the purpose of persuasive writing and what techniques could you use if you were asked to write persuasively?

1.3 Writing to advise

LEARNING SUMMARY

After studying this section you should be able to understand:

- *how language and layout make advice clear and easy to understand*
- *how language is chosen to suit the audience and purpose*
- *how to approach your task*

Language and layout

Advice comes in many forms and we are constantly being given or seeking advice of one kind or another. It may be advice on diet, fashion, money, what to see at the cinema, career options and so on. The list is almost endless. Advice can also be presented in different ways. There is verbal advice given by a friend or relative or that we hear on the television or radio, but much of the advice that we encounter will be written. It may be in a magazine, a pamphlet, on the Internet, in a newspaper, book, poster or any other form. Whatever kind of advice is being given, though, the writing is likely to have particular features that it is useful to be aware of.

Here is some advice about what to do if there is a fire, published by the government.

Make your plan. Get out alive.

FIRE KILLS

YOU CAN PREVENT IT

Important fire safety information for you to keep

What to do if there's a fire

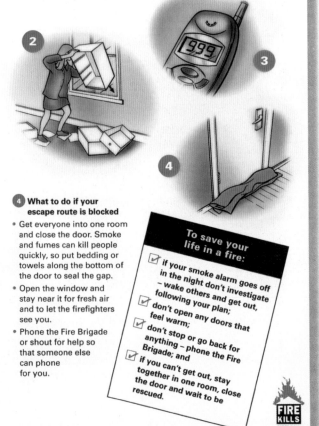

1 Raise the alarm

- If your smoke alarm goes off while you are asleep, don't investigate to see if there is a fire. Shout to wake everyone up, get everyone together, follow your plan and get out.
- Check doors with the back of your hand – if they are warm, do not open them – the fire is on the other side.
- If there is a lot of smoke, crawl along with your nose near the floor where the air will be cleaner.

2 Escaping from a window

- If you are on the ground floor or first floor you may be able to escape from a window. If you

have to break the window, cover the jagged glass with towels or thick bedding.

- Throw some more bedding out of the window to break your fall. Don't jump out of the window – lower yourself down to arm's length and drop to the ground.
- If you have any children or elderly or disabled people with you, plan the order you will escape in so that you can help them down.

3 Don't go back inside your home

- Call the Fire Brigade from a mobile phone, a neighbour's house or a phone box. Give the address of the fire.
- Don't stop or go back for anything.

4 What to do if your escape route is blocked

- Get everyone into one room and close the door. Smoke and fumes can kill people quickly, so put bedding or towels along the bottom of the door to seal the gap.
- Open the window and stay near it for fresh air and to let the firefighters see you.
- Phone the Fire Brigade or shout for help so that someone else can phone for you.

To save your life in a fire:

☑ if your smoke alarm goes off in the night don't investigate – wake others and get out, following your plan;

☑ don't open any doors that feel warm;

☑ don't stop or go back for anything – phone the Fire Brigade; and

☑ if you can't get out, stay together in one room, close the door and wait to be rescued.

FIRE KILLS YOU CAN PREVENT IT

What do you notice about the way that this advice is presented?

You might have noted the following points:

- The language is clear and simple.
- It is divided up into clear sections, each dealing with a particular point
- Bullet points are used to make each specific piece of advice stand out clearly.
- It ends with a checklist of the key points to remember.
- In this case, the illustrations help to reinforce the point.

In lots of ways, this example contains many of the key features of effective, written advice bearing in mind its main **purpose** is to communicate its ideas **clearly** and **effectively**.

- The language is simple and clear.
- The layout helps make the points clear and straightforward.
- The checklist/summary re-emphasises the key ideas.

Audience and purpose

Thousands of mobile phones are being stolen by street robbers every month and young people are especially vulnerable. By taking a few simple steps you can reduce your risk of becoming a victim of mobile phone theft.

What you can do:

By providing the police with some basic information about your phone, you can make it more difficult for a thief to use it. Please record the details requested on this leaflet and keep the leaflet in a safe place.

These details may be needed by the police if you report your phone stolen. The 15-digit serial or IMEI number helps to identify your phone and can be accessed by keying *#06# into most phones or by looking behind the battery of your phone. This number could help the police to trace ownership quickly.

- Always use your phone's security lock code or PIN number.

Protect your PHONE

- Security mark (in permanent form) the battery and phone with your postcode and street number or the first two letters of your house name. For more information on security marking, contact the crime prevention officer at your local police station.
- Register your phone with the operator. If you report your phone stolen, the operator should then be able to bar the SIM card.
- When using your phone, remain aware of your surroundings and do not use it in crowded areas or where you feel unsafe.
- Avoid displaying your phone where it is in public view. Keep it with you at all times and do not leave it unattended.

Street robbers are cowards, help us catch a coward

If you know who has taken your mobile phone, or have any information about anyone involved in criminal activity, please call Crimestoppers anonymously.

Call anonymously with information about crime

You could get a cash reward

CRIMESTOPPERS
0800 555 111
Uniting against crime

As with most forms of writing, one of the key points to bear in mind when writing to advise is to use language in an appropriate way to address and communicate your ideas to your audience. When writing to advise, then, it is important that you:

- understand the task set
- understand the **purpose** of the advice
- understand the **audience** it is aimed at
- use language appropriately

Now look at the example here and the one on the next page:

2

HAND HELD?
HAND OVER.

If it's expensive and cool
don't take it to school.

Always register your stuff with
www.immobilise.com

think safe, be safe

www.avonandsomerset.police.uk

RELENTLESS

PROGRESS CHECK

What is the main purpose of the advice given in each? Who do you think the intended audience is? What features do you note about each text?

- PURPOSE: To give advice on protecting your mobile phone from theft.
- AUDIENCE: Text 1 – General audience, perhaps a little older than the target audience for Text 2. Text 2 – Young people, school students.
- TEXT 1: Combined use of blocks of text and bullet points to present information. Technical language e.g. *'IMEI number'*, *'bar the SIM card'*.
- TEXT 2: Eye-catching design. Little text but the message is clear. Use of vocabulary aimed at young people e.g. *'cool'*, *'your stuff'*.

Sample GCSE questions

Writing to argue

Spend about 45 minutes on this question. Leave enough time to read through and check what you have written.

Write a letter to your headteacher in which you argue that the ICT facilities in the school should be upgraded and increased.

2 Orchard Lane
Topton
Great Standing

1.5.02

Dear Mrs Maloney,

I am writing to you to express my concern about the poor state of the I.T. facilities. It has become clear that we have reached a point where, I believe, students are being educationally disadvantaged by the current facilities provided in school and I ask that you look at the possibility of improving them as a matter of urgency.

> *Purpose of letter is clearly stated, the problem highlighted and a desired outcome mentioned.*

Together with a group of concerned students, I have looked carefully at the situation and several issues have emerged. Firstly, the machines that we have are very outdated now. They are extremely slow when downloading information and the number of machines out of action is increasing by the week.

> *The first point is explained in some detail.*

Secondly, the networked systems that we use have become increasingly unreliable and many students have taken to doing work at home on their own equipment because it is not possible for them to do it in school as very often the facilities are not available.

> *The second point is explained and an important issue raised.*

> *Important use of connectives.*

Thirdly, because of the lack of terminals available in the learning centre, access to the research facilities provided by the Internet is very restricted. Again, students are being forced to use their own equipment. Unfortunately, though, not all students are lucky enough to have their own machines at home.

> *A third point is developed.*

I have conducted a survey of all students in Years 10 and 11 and 98% of them feel disadvantaged by the lack of facilities. I would be happy to give you copies of the survey if you feel it would help you argue the case for more funding for this with the governors.

> *The writer provides evidence to support the arguments.*

I know that funding is a problem and that you have little available at the moment but I have discussed this with many students and the general feeling is that they would be more than willing to help with fund-raising. Many suggestions have been made, including a sponsored swim, fun-run and sponsored spell. Students also feel that their parents would be willing to help and I am sure that the Parents' Association would help too.

> *Shows an appreciation of the financial constraints on the head and makes some constructive suggestions that will help the situation.*

It would be useful to discuss these ideas and I would be happy to arrange for a small group of interested students to meet with you.

> *Ends with a constructive suggestion.*

I look forward to hearing your views on this topic.

Yours sincerely,
Tracy Seaton (Form TS11)

Exam practice questions

Write an information leaflet for people who are taking up a particular hobby for the first time, explaining what the hobby involves. The hobby can be anything you wish.

You might write about:

- what the hobby involves
- what equipment you need
- any specialist clothing required
- any special training required
- any special problems to watch out for
- clubs or societies catering for the hobby

....

....

....

....

....

....

....

....

....

....

....

....

....

....

....

2 Writing to imagine, explore, entertain

The following topics are included in this chapter:

- *Imaginative writing*
- *Writing to explore*
- *Writing to entertain*

2.1 Imaginative writing

LEARNING SUMMARY

After studying this section you should be able to understand:

- **some important features of imaginative writing**
- **the importance of the plot and setting**
- **how openings can be made effective**
- **how to develop characters**
- **how to make a start on your own writing**

Features of imaginative writing

Often, imaginative writing takes the form of some kind of 'story' – this is sometimes called a **narrative**. To 'write a story' sounds a fairly simple task but stories can be quite complex pieces of writing and they are made up of various features.

PROGRESS CHECK

Think about a story you have read and write down as many features as you can that help to make the story effective or memorable in some way.

You might have noted some or all of the following:

- the plot or structure
- the characters
- the setting and atmosphere
- the style it is written in
- the themes or ideas it contains

 KEY POINT

The plot, characters and setting are aspects you need to think about carefully when planning your imaginative writing.

Plot and setting

In very basic terms, stories usually have a beginning, a middle and an end, and the **plot** consists of the series of events that occur and the experiences the characters go through as the story moves from its beginning, through its middle to its conclusion. The plot, therefore, is concerned with the specific details of the **events that occur** in the story.

 KEY POINT

In order to write a successful story you need to:
- **plan your storyline carefully**
- **capture and maintain your reader's interest**

The **setting** of a story is closely related to the plot. Obviously, the setting depends on what kind of story it is. Many stories are set against the background of everyday life that we are all familiar with but even these familiar '**realistic**' backgrounds can be many and varied. For example, a story could be set against a background of home or work, in a town or city or in the countryside, or any combination of the whole range of settings that form the background to our lives. Other settings may depend more on the writer's imagination. Science fiction stories, for example, are often set against backgrounds that are totally the product of the writer's imagination. Alternatively, the story may be set in a different time and historical background.

> Careful planning is essential if you are to write an effective story.

 KEY POINT

Whatever the setting of the story, it must remain convincing to the reader.

Openings

The opening of a story or piece of imaginative writing is extremely important because this is where the writer must capture the attention and interest of the reader.

 KEY POINT

You must open your story in such a way as to make your reader want to continue reading.

Read the following openings carefully and think about the effects they create in your mind.

Lemona's Tale by Ken Saro-Wiwa

Lemona. Lemona. Beautiful woman. Exquisite. She'll be hanged tomorrow. You know that, don't you? And you insist on seeing her? Well, I have no objection personally. But I don't know if she'll agree to see you. That's the problem. That woman is an enigma. In all my thirty years in service, I haven't met a prisoner like her. She doesn't talk to anyone, she's not had a personal visitor that I can remember. It's like she's not of this world. Even at her age, she remains very attractive. A beauty queen. I wish she could be saved. She shouldn't die. But she'll be hanged tomorrow at dawn. The warrant has finally been signed and delivered to me. It's tragic. A real tragedy.

Brave New World by Aldous Huxley

A squat grey building of only thirty-four storeys. Over the main entrance the words, CENTRAL LONDON HATCHERY AND CONDITIONING CENTRE, and, in a shield, the World State's motto, COMMUNITY, IDENTITY, STABILITY.

The enormous room on the ground floor faced towards the north. Cold for all the summer beyond the panes, for all the tropical heat of the room itself, a harsh thin light glared through the windows, hungrily seeking some draped lay figure, some pallid shape of academic goose-flesh, but finding only the glass and nickel and bleakly shining porcelain of a laboratory. Wintriness responding to wintriness. The overalls of the workers were white, their hands gloved with a pale corpse-coloured rubber. The light was frozen dead, a ghost. Only from the yellow barrels of the microscopes did it borrow a certain rich and living substance, lying along the polished tubes like butter, streak after luscious streak in long recession down the work tables.

A Christmas Carol by Charles Dickens

Marley was dead: to begin with. There is no doubt whatever about that. The register of his burial was signed by the clergyman, the clerk, the undertaker, and the chief mourner. Scrooge signed it: and Scrooge's name was good upon change, for anything he chose to put his hand to. Old Marley was as dead as a door-nail.

Here are some points you might have noted:

- The description of Lemona immediately captures the reader's attention.
- The **information** that she will be hanged tomorrow ensures that the interest is maintained. (Note that the reader is given all the information in the first three sentences.)
- The further **description** of Lemona, stressing the fact that she is different, intrigues the reader.
- The sense of the tragedy of the situation is emphasised.

- The description of the building immediately captures the reader's attention – the building is described as '*squat*' and '*only*' thirty-four storeys high.
- The unusual terminology, e.g. '*CENTRAL LONDON HATCHERY AND CONDITIONING CENTRE*' and the reference to the '*World State*'.
- The description of the room with the emphasis on the cold, clinical atmosphere makes the reader want to read on to find out what it is for.
- The use of words associated with death – '*corpse-coloured*', '*frozen*', '*dead*', '*a ghost*' add to this effect.

- The opening sentence – '*Marley was dead*' immediately captures the reader's attention.
- Scrooge is introduced (he is the central character).
- There is an element of humour introduced e.g. the play on the idea of '*door-nail*'/coffin nail.

> **KEY POINT** A variety of techniques can be used to capture the interest of your reader.

PROGRESS CHECK

From the examples you have examined, make a list of the ways in which you can make your opening interesting and capture the attention of your reader.

- vivid description
- unusual names or terminology
- intriguing situations
- surprising first sentences
- the introduction of the central character
- creation of an effective atmosphere
- the use of humour
- the creation of a sense that something is going to happen next

Developing characters

Characters are a very important element in any story. In fact, a story wouldn't be a story without characters of some description and you will need to think carefully about them as the action of your plot will hinge on them. If your story is to be effective, it is essential that your characters are **convincing**. Look carefully at the following two extracts.

Of Mice And Men by John Steinbeck

At that moment a young man came into the bunkhouse; a thin young man with a brown face, with brown eyes and a head of tightly curled hair. He wore a work glove on his left hand, and, like the boss, he wore high-heeled boots. "Seen my old man?" he asked.

The swamper said: "He was here jus' a minute ago, Curley. Went over to the cook-house, I think."

"I'll try to catch him," said Curley. His eyes passed over the new men and he stopped. He glanced coldly at George and then at Lennie. His arms gradually bent at the elbows and his hands closed into fists. He stiffened and went into a slight crouch. His glance was at once calculating and pugnacious. Lennie squirmed under the look and shifted his feet nervously. Curley stepped gingerly close to him. "You the new guys the old man was waitin' for?"

"We just come in," said George.

"Let the big guy talk."

Lennie twisted with embarrassment.

George said: "S'pose he don't want to talk?"

Curley lashed his body around. "By Christ, he's gotta talk when he's spoke to. What the hell are you gettin' into it for?"

"We travel together," said George coldly.

"Oh, so it's that way."

George was tense and motionless. "Yeah, it's that way."

Lennie was looking helplessly to George for instruction.

"An' you won't let the big guy talk, is that it?"

"He can talk if he wants to tell you anything." He nodded slightly to Lennie.

"We jus' come in," said Lennie softly.

Curley stared levelly at him. "Well, nex' time you answer when you're spoke to." He turned towards the door and walked out, and his elbows were still bent out a little.

Hard Times by Charles Dickens

He was a rich man: banker, merchant, manufacturer, and what not. A big, loud man, with a store and a metallic laugh. A man made out of a course material, which seemed to have been stretched to make so much of him. A man with a great puffed head and forehead, swelled veins in his temples, and such a strained skin to his face that it seemed to hold his eyes open and lift his eyebrows up. A man with a pervading appearance on him of being inflated like a balloon, and ready to start. A man who could never sufficiently vaunt himself a self-made man. A man who was always proclaiming, through that brassy speaking-trumpet of a voice of his, his old ignorance and his old poverty. A man who was the Bully of humility.

A year or two younger than his eminently practical friend, Mr Bounderby looked older; his seven or eight and forty might have had the seven or eight added to it again, without surprising anybody. He had not much hair. One might have fancied he had talked it off; and that what was left, all standing up in disorder, was in that condition from being constantly blown about by his windy boastfulness.

How do we learn about the characters in these extracts?

You might have noticed that Steinbeck uses several techniques to create an impression of Curley.

- He describes his physical appearance.
- He describes some of the things he wears.
- We are told how he looks at other characters – *'glanced coldly', 'calculating and pugnacious'.*
- His arms bending and hands closing into fists further suggest his aggressive nature.
- The way he speaks and what he says add to this impression.

Now look at how Dickens gives us an impression of Mr Bounderby.

- He gives us details of Bounderby's occupation and status.
- He describes his physical appearance.
- His nature and attitudes are indicated.
- He uses imagery and humour to make his description more entertaining and effective.

> **Your choice of words is very important because it gives the reader clues about the character.**

KEY POINT You can use a variety of techniques to create an impression of your characters.

 PROGRESS CHECK

Summarise the ways you can show your reader what your characters are like.

- what they look like
- what they say
- how they say it
- how they behave
- how they feel

Making a start

When you are given a title that requires you to write imaginatively, there are certain points to remember when planning your work.

The opening

We have already seen how important it is to open your story in a **lively and interesting** way. You need to **capture your reader's interest** right from the start. There are various ways to do this. For example:

- You can give your reader information about the characters, background, setting etc.
- Begin with some kind of action that plunges your reader straight into the story and fill in the background information later.
- Starting with dialogue can make your opening more interesting.

Developing your ideas

Do not have too many characters in your story – you don't have the time or space to develop many characters in detail.

Having captured your reader's interest and attention, your next task is to **maintain** it throughout your story. You need to do this by:

- keeping the action moving
- developing your characters and making them convincing
- using dialogue to bring the narrative to life
- using vivid description – but be careful not to overdo it

 KEY POINT Use a variety of techniques to keep your narrative interesting and maintain the interest of your reader.

A strong ending

The ending of a story is obviously very important. Often it is the thing that keeps the reader reading – they want to know what is going to happen at the end.

Here are some points to think about:

- The ending should develop naturally from what has happened before.
- It should be powerful.
- It should have some kind of impact.

 KEY POINT Think carefully about how you are going to end your story and make sure that it is a strong ending.

PROGRESS CHECK

Read these two endings and explain which you find most effective and why.

1 The creature was gaining on me all the time. I knew in my mind that there was no escape. I tripped and turned to see the claws descending on me and then I woke up and it was all a dream.

2 By the time I had reached the top of the lane, the only lane leading out of the village, the air had started to chill with the onset of night. I turned and allowed myself one final look. The village, still visible, looked small and insignificant perched on a small plateau of land between the folds of the rolling moor. The view that I had at that moment had always been the same. It, like the village, like the people who lived there, would never change. If I'd had any doubts before, I knew then I had made the right decision – it was time for me to move on. I turned and faced the darkening lane ahead. I wasn't sure where it would lead me; I only knew that it was in the right direction.

2.2 *Writing to explore*

LEARNING SUMMARY

After studying this section you should be able to understand:

- ● *some forms of writing to explore*
- ● *how to approach exploratory writing*

Forms of writing that 'explore'

Writing to explore can take many forms. Exploring ideas can be a part of imaginative writing but some kinds of writing explore ideas in a more explicit way.

Here are some examples where writers explore their ideas, feelings, relationships and so on:

- ● autobiography
- ● journalism
- ● poetry
- ● travel writing

In the following extract from Martin Kemp's autobiography, the actor explores how he felt when he learned he had got the part in *EastEnders*.

> It was on the following Friday that Derek called me and told me I had got the part.
> I can't tell you the relief an actor goes through when he hears those incredible words coming from his agent... THEY WANT YOU!... it's like a giant weight being lifted from off your back; all your anxiety and stress immediately turn into joy and elation, and a smile finds its way on to your face that only seconds earlier had been filled with worry. Your stomach unties itself and your stiff neck starts to loosen as he reassures you that you did actually make a good job of that casting, when by now you've convinced yourself and everyone around you that you were crap.

I was no different. I was as pleased to get the part as I was relieved that I didn't have to tell people that I didn't. This was my mum and dad's favourite show, and by now word had spread through the whole of the family that I was possibly going to work on Albert Square. Even my aunts and uncles in deepest Islington were waiting for that phone call, waiting to see if they were going to watch me on television three times a week. The pressure had been enormous, but after Derek's phone call it was time to relax and enjoy the congratulations that came with it, before starting work three weeks later.

PROGRESS CHECK

What ideas does Martin Kemp explore here?

- He explores the circumstances surrounding the experience.
- He explores his feelings on hearing he had got the part.
- He explores how he reacts and responds.
- He explores the effects on others.

Now read the following poem by Gillian Clarke.

BABY-SITTING

I am sitting in a strange room listening
For the wrong baby. I don't love
This baby. She is sleeping a snuffly
Roseate, bubbling sleep; she is fair;
She is a perfectly acceptable child.
I am afraid of her. If she wakes
She will hate me. She will shout
Her hot midnight rage, her nose
Will stream disgustingly and the perfume
Of her breath will fail to enchant me.

To her I will represent absolute
Abandonment. For her it will be worse
Than for the lover cold in lonely
Sheets; worse than for the woman who waits
A moment to collect her dignity
Beside the bleached bone in the terminal ward.
As she rises sobbing from the monstrous land
Stretching for milk-familiar comforting,
She will find me and between use two
It will not come. It will not come.

What ideas does Clarke explore through the poem?

The poem is an explanation of Clarke's feelings as she looks after someone else's baby for them. She thinks about how she feels out of place sitting in a strange room and how the baby is strange to her. Her emotions towards the baby are mixed and she wonders how the baby will respond to her. She thinks about how the baby will look for comfort but there is no bond between them.

KEY POINT   There are many different ways in which writing can explore.

Approaching 'writing to explore'

Writing to explore can take many forms and often it is interlinked with other purposes. For example, much imaginative writing also 'explores' ideas and feelings. Similarly writing that may, primarily, set out to 'entertain' will probably also 'explore'.

However, you might be set a task that specifically asks you to 'explore'. For example:

- Explore your feelings at a particular moment in your life or when something has happened.
- Explore a particular emotion you have experienced.
- Explore your thoughts on a particular theme or issue.

When tackling a question:

1. Read it through carefully.
2. Identify what exactly that question is asking you to explore.
3. Be clear in your mind what your feelings/ideas etc. are on the topic.
4. Order your thoughts coherently.
5. Plan your answer carefully.

> When writing to explore, it is important that you structure your ideas clearly before starting to write your answer.

2.3 *Writing to entertain*

LEARNING SUMMARY

After studying this section you should be able to understand:

- *ways in which writing entertains*
- *how some examples of 'entertaining writing' work*

Many kinds of writing can be said to 'entertain'. For example, the vast majority of imaginative writing is designed to 'entertain' the reader, as well as exploring ideas, telling a story etc. 'Writing to entertain' often overlaps with other kinds of writing. However, some is written with the primary purpose of entertaining, like in the following poem by Wendy Cope:

> *Valentine*
>
> *My heart has made its mind up*
> *And I'm afraid it's you.*
> *Whatever you've got lined up,*
> *My heart has made its mind up*
> *And if you can't be signed up*
> *This year, next year will do.*
> *My heart has made its mind up*
> *And I'm afraid it's you.*
>
> Wendy Cope

Although the poem undoubtedly explores an aspect of human nature, its primary aim could be seen as being to **entertain** the reader with its humour.

A good deal of writing that entertains does so by using humour. Read this extract by Bill Bryson.

I come from Des Moines. Somebody had to.

When you come from Des Moines you either accept the fact without question and settle down with a local girl named Bobbi and get a job at the Firestone factory and live there for ever and ever, or you spend your adolescence moaning at length about what a dump it is and how you can't wait to get out, and then you settle down with a local girl named Bobbi and get a job at the Firestone factory and live there for ever and ever.

Hardly anyone ever leaves. This is because Des Moines is the most powerful hypnotic known to man. Outside town there is a big sign that says WELCOME TO DES MOINES. THIS IS WHAT DEATH IS LIKE. There isn't really. I just made that up. But the place does get a grip on you. People who have nothing to do with Des Moines drive in off the interstate, looking for gas or hamburgers, and stay for ever.

From *The Lost Continent* by Bill Bryson

PROGRESS CHECK

How does Bryson 'entertain' here?
- through the use of humour
- creating amusing stereotypes
- through exaggeration

Other methods that writers use to entertain their readers include:

- the creation of tension
- exploration of ideas
- intrigue and mystery
- characterisation
- interesting plot

When writing to entertain, make sure you are clear about your task and the methods you intend to use to complete it.

Sample GCSE questions

As part of your coursework for AQA English Specification A you will need to produce a piece of Original Writing that involves writing to imagine, explore or entertain.

Explore your thoughts and feelings on the value of friendships and the things that affect them.

Speaking from my past experience, it is very difficult to find good friends that you can trust but once you have found them, they are worth keeping! Therefore, I think friendship is the most important relationship that anybody could have.

Focuses on the question right from the start. View of friendship made clear and a strong sense of personal voice.

The qualities I look for in a friend are a good sense of humour but sensitivity when it matters. Also that friend would have to be strong minded and highly spirited. I think that these qualities are the key qualities to look for in a good friend.

Clear assessment of essential qualities.

However, even the strongest friends can still have arguments, although usually about more serious topics, rather than the usual teenage childish arguments. For example, drugs can seriously affect a friendship. If one of your friends started experimenting with harmful and dangerous drugs, what would you do? A good friend would try to help as much as possible, whereas a bad example of a friend would simply shrug and turn a blind eye.

Develops ideas introducing possible problems that will test friendship.

Sometimes the sex of a friend can affect a good friendship. Again, from past experience, drink can have a bad influence on a friendship. For example, if you caught your friend and your boyfriend/girlfriend doing things that they should not do together, then in my mind that person obviously was not a friend that you can trust and rely upon.

Further problem areas discussed. Fluent writing.

However, not only the bad things affect friendship - good activities do too. Such as bonding with one another, not just by going out on a night with them, but by spending quality time with them and talking to each other, which indicates a good ability to communicate. This is a key aspect of a good friendship.

Examines the positive aspects of friendship.

Good friends do not always have to be in the same age group as you. I have a good friend and she is 47 years old and I am 16.

Sums up ideas in conclusion.

Unfortunately, some people lose contact with their friends as they grow older, which is a sad way to lose a good friend.

I think friendship is one of the most important things in life because if you have no friends you will have no happiness.

Overall a fluent and accurately written response focused on the question and covering relevant areas of discussion.

Exam practice questions

Choose one of the following titles and write an imaginative essay on it.

The quality of your writing is more important than its length. As a guide, think about writing between one and two sides (or, for a poem, a minimum of 12 lines).

a)   Write the opening of a short story entitled '*The Cage*'.

b)   Write a story that ends with the line '*and I laughed all the way to the bank*'.

c)   Write a story that involves three characters, a dog and a river.

d)   Write a poem on the topic of 'memories'.

e)   Write a story that opens with the line '*The storm clouds were gathering as I turned and looked back*'.

Writing to analyse, review and comment

The following topics are included in this chapter:

- **Writing to analyse**
- **Writing to review**
- **Writing your own reviews**
- **Commenting on texts and ideas**

3.1 Writing to analyse

After studying this section you should be able to understand:

- **how to analyse ideas and issues**
- **how to analyse a text**

Writing to analyse an issue

One of the things you may be asked to do as part of your GCSE English course is to analyse particular ideas or issues that you are presented with. You might also be asked to analyse your own thoughts and ideas on a particular issue. These ideas or issues may be presented in a variety of forms.

For example, you might be given:

- a topic to think about
- a newspaper article exploring a particular topic
- an article from a magazine or journal
- an extract from a book
- an information leaflet
- information from a website

Your analysis of the given topic or material can take three basic forms:

1. An analysis of the **content, ideas, issues** etc. that the text explores
2. An analysis of the ways in which **language** is used to express the ideas
3. An analysis of your own **thoughts and ideas** on the issue

Read the following article from the RSPCA's website.

The RSPCA's wildlife department seeks to improve the welfare provision for wild animals. The aims of the department are achieved through research, the promotion of an awareness of the requirements of animals, and an emphasis on a precautionary and humane approach to human interactions with wild animal species.

Wildlife care and rehabilitation

Through the work of the three wildlife hospitals and a wildlife unit, the department continues to support and co-ordinate the rehabilitation work of the Society to maximise the successful integration of wildlife casualties back into the wild.

Management and control of wildlife

Whenever the taking or killing of animals is being considered, the wildlife department continues to promote the use of alternative solutions. The humane killing of an animal should only be contemplated where there is serious damage and all alternative control methods have been ineffective or impractical.

Zoo and circus animals

Based on an opposition to any degree of confinement likely to cause distress or suffering, the RSPCA campaigns against the display of animals by circuses and promotes an ethical, welfare-based approach to all zoo activities. Through the Zoos Forum the wildlife department was involved at the highest level in the major review of the Secretary of State's Standards of modern zoo practice based on five principles to improve animal welfare.

Trade in wildlife

The department continues to monitor and influence the decisions taken through the Convention on the International Trade in Endangered Species (CITES); striving to improve the welfare of wild animals traded internationally and promoting public awareness of the suffering endured by the exotic animals that are kept as pets in the UK.

Marine issues

As well as campaigning against commercial whaling, a major campaign was launched in 2000 to call for an immediate reduction in the incidental capture of harbour porpoises and other small cetaceans in fishing nets.

Firstly, think about the content of this article. What are the **key points** that it makes?

Analysis of content

- It states its position as aiming to improve welfare provision for wild animals.
- It highlights the rehabilitation work the society undertakes.
- It advocates alternatives to killing as a way of controlling wildlife where possible.
- It states its opposition to circuses.
- It monitors the situation regarding trade in endangered species.
- It raises public awareness of the problems of keeping exotic animals as pets.
- It campaigns against whaling and the accidental catching of porpoises and other marine mammals.

Now think about the ways in which **language** is used here to convey the message of the article to the reader.

Analysis of language and style

Here are the notes that one student made in preparation for writing about how this article uses language:

2
'*Aims*' are listed making clear how this is to be achieved

3
'*promotion of awareness*', '*humane approach*' emphasises the importance of changing views

1
'*seeks to improve*' clearly states RSPCA viewpoint

4
'*Support*', '*co-ordination*' stresses role of RSPCA

10
Reference is made to official reports and to international bodies

5
'*alternative solutions*' to the killing of animals suggests such killing should only be as a last resort

WILDLIFE

6
When it is the only solution '*humane killing*' again places the emphasis on the caring element

9
The language used is clear and generally straightforward but some technical terms are used

8
The article is clearly structured with the use of sub-headings with a paragraph of explanation on each

7
'*opposition to... confinement*', '*distress and suffering*', '*campaigns against*' highlight the society's opposition to animal suffering and their active involvement in trying to prevent it

An analysis of your own thoughts and ideas

Another kind of analysis that you could be asked to carry out involves analysing your own thoughts and ideas on an issue. For example, you might be asked to analyse your own views on the issue of improving the welfare of wild animals and write an essay exploring your views on the subject.

KEY POINT   **Analysis can take a number of forms.**

Analysing a text

It is very likely that, as part of your course, you will need to analyse a text or texts. This may include:

- analysing **what** is being said in the text
- analysing how it is being said – how **language** is used
- analysing the **effects** created by the particular use of language
- supporting your ideas with specific references from the text
- drawing conclusions about the effectiveness of the writing

Read the following article carefully.

It's high noon for Britain's gum slingers

Clean-up tackles £150m litter crisis on streets

by Juliette Jowit

Environment Editor

BUS SEATS, school desks and suede boots will have something to celebrate this week, with a nationwide crackdown on their greatest scourge: chewing gum.

Manchester United manager Alex Ferguson is known for spitting out his chewing gum, but he is not alone: half the population – 28 million – are regular gum-chewers. The popularity of gum has resulted in about 3.5 billion bits being spat out on to Britain's streets in the last century. The problem is not just unsightly and annoying – especially when the gum sticks to shoes, clothes and even hair – but expensive, too. Councils say they spend about £4.5m a year to clear up just some of the gum as to do the job properly would cost £150m.

Tomorrow every council in Britain will be sent a guide on how to tackle the sticky problem – from advertisements telling people to dispose of their gum carefully, to 'pouches' for used gum. There will also be an 'awareness campaign' about new fines of up to £75. The gum manufacturer Wrigley's has put up £600,000 to fund the drive.

'All local authorities have a problem with chewing gum,' Environment Minister Ben Bradshaw told *The Observer*. 'We really hope to help local authorities reduce gum litter, reduce the money they spend on cleaning it up and, in turn, help increase the pride people have in their communities.'

The nationwide push to get tough on gum-dropping is being led by the Chewing Gum Action Group, set up last year by government, Wrigley's and the Keep Britain Tidy charity. Gum takes five years to biodegrade. The gum that is trodden into pavements is removed with high-powered cleaning hoses – each piece takes 10 seconds to clean and costs 10p. Some councils spend £200,000 a year each on the problem – equivalent to six teachers' salaries.

Last May saw the launch of three pilot schemes in Preston, Manchester and Maidstone, where councils spent £180,000 on advertising, free plastic pouches for putting used gum in, and wardens to enforce fines for litter dropping. In Preston, the only city with figures available, gum dropping was reduced by 80 per cent, though only one person was fined for gum dropping.

The Department for the Environment, Food and Rural Affairs is considering applications from another 12 councils to join the scheme, and will exhort all authorities to join the nationwide crackdown. The principal aim is to change attitudes, said Peter Gibson, Keep Britain Tidy's spokesman. 'People have this almost psychological view: "It's

The government aims to stop the dropping of gum on the pavements.   Getty Images

FACTS TO CHEW ON

- Each year, 560,00 tonnes of gum is produced, worth $5bn
- The most popular flavours are cinnamon, spearmint and peppermint
- Wrigley's is the leading manufacturer, with 90 per cent of the British market
- The biggest gum bubble was recorded in California in 1994 at 23in wide
- Collectors of chewing gum wrappers have their own internet magazine, *The Gum Wrapper Times*

a small item of litter, it doesn't matter." But our most prevalent forms of litter are cigarette ends and chewing gum – they still need removing, and that costs money,' he said. More drastic measures, like the ban adopted by Singapore and a tax favoured by some British councils, were rejected. Bans would be 'disproportionate' and a tax may encourage people to discard gum because they would feel 'less guilty' having paid for the clean-up, a department spokesman said.

Meanwhile, scientists are working on finding the surest solution: non-stick chewing gum.

Approaching the text

When preparing to write analytically about a text you need to adopt a **structured** approach to examining what the text has to say and how it says it.

Here's one possible way of approaching a text.

Stage 1

1. A preliminary read to get a general idea of what the text is about.
2. Re-read the text, this time making a note of the key points.

Carry out these first two stages on the text above.

Key ideas

- Discarded chewing gum can create a nuisance.
- Many people spit their chewing gum out on the streets.
- This not only looks unsightly but can cause a problem for others if they get it stuck on their shoes or clothing.
- It can be expensive to clean up.
- Councils are to be issued with guidance on how to tackle the problem.

PROGRESS CHECK

Stage 2

Having established the **content** of the text, now you need to think about its **purpose** (what the writer wants it to achieve) and the **audience** it is aimed at (who the writer intends to read it).

What are your ideas on the purpose and audience for this particular article?

Here are some ideas:

Purpose	Audience
To inform the reader about the problem of chewing gum being spat out on the streets	A general readership
To use statistics to shock the reader into understanding the scale of the problem	Those interested in combating litter and with a sense of the community
To inform the reader of the range of measures being used to deal with it	Those interested in learning more about the scale of the problem
To give the reader some facts about chewing gum	Those interested in the measures being taken to deal with the problem

Stage 3

Having established the links between content/audience/purpose, the next stage is to look at how language is used to suit the particular audience and achieve the particular purpose.

 KEY POINT

Adopt a logical approach to your analysis: Think about:
           PURPOSE – AUDIENCE – CONTENT
and answer WHAT?   WHO?   HOW?

When you are analysing a text, it is important to support your points with evidence and then comment on it.

For example, look at how this student began her analysis of this article.

makes a point ┈┈┈➤ The writer begins the article by explaining the various ways in which chewing gum can

quotes to support point ┈┈➤ be a nuisance to us. She quotes several things that chewing gum often. gets stuck to,

"Bus seats, school desks and suede boots" and creates an element of humour by

comments on a technique used ┈┈➤ personifying these things, saying they "will have something to celebrate." The writer

goes on to give an indication of the size of the problem, informing us that "about 3.5

makes another point ┈┈➤ billion bits" were "spat out on to Britain's streets in the last century". This is an amazing

quotes evidence to support the point ┈┈┈➤ amount but the writer follows up with another staggering statistic as "Councils spend

about 4.5 million pounds a year" clearing up gum. However, for this amount they can

makes a comment ┈┈┈➤ only clean up some of the gum. To clean up all the gum would cost £150m

This method of **point – evidence – comment** can help you structure your analysis of your text and also help you to avoid describing what the text is saying.

KEY POINT

It is **essential** that you support the points you make with specific examples and evidence from the text, and comment on the meaning or significance of the examples you have quoted.

PROGRESS CHECK

Now try writing your own response to the question: 'How does the writer use language in this article to explore his ideas and influence the audience?'

3.2 Writing to review

LEARNING SUMMARY

After studying this section you should be able to understand:

* *what a review is*
* *writing about reviews*
* *writing your own review*

What is a review?

A review examines something and gives an opinion or assessment of it. We come across reviews all the time in our everyday lives and they can be about a wide range of things, for example films, books, plays, television programmes, music albums, art exhibitions and consumer products.

The purpose of a review is to put forward a view of the thing being reviewed and to give the reviewer's opinion of it.

Work on reviews can take two forms:

1. Reading reviews written by others and analysing or assessing them.
2. Writing your own review.

Reading and writing about reviews

When reading a review it is important to remember that the review will probably contain some **facts** about the thing being reviewed but it will also contain some opinions too. These **opinions** represent the reviewer's view but they may not be the only views that it is possible to have. For example, one reviewer might say that a particular film is very good, while another might think that it is poor.

Look at these reviews of the film *King Kong*.

A **Reviewed by:** guest

Reviewed on: 1 Jan 2006

An awesome rollercoaster of a movie with a great cast, a great script and beautifully shot, with the most intense and thrilling plot to boot. Romantic, heart-stopping and moving; fantastic.

B **Reviewed by:** nick

Reviewed on: 12 Jan 2006

Terrible, terrible, terrible! This is not one of the worst films I have seen: I have seen some very bad films; but, it was twice as long as most of them. Boring, self-indulgent; the constant use of sweeping strings made me want to kill. Has he heard of editing?

C **Reviewed by:** lei B

Reviewed on: Jan 2006

King Kong is possibly one of the worst films I have ever seen. The acting isn't that bad and there are some good scenes where King Kong smashes things and throws people around but apart from that, it is all so dull. There's only so many looking-off-into-the-sunset-with-a-tear-in-the-eye scenes that a film can take before it becomes drained of any drama.

PROGRESS CHECK

What view does each of these reviewers have on the film?

Reviewer A gave a very favourable review. He thought the film was 'fantastic'.

Reviewer B is very negative about the film and thinks that it is boring and self-indulgent.

Reviewer C didn't like the film but does feel that the acting wasn't bad and there were some good scenes.

Here are two more extended reviews of the film. Read each through carefully.
- Identify each reviewer's opinion of the film
- How do the reviewers use language to convey their views of the film?

A   **Reviewed by:** demonicawe@yahoo.com

Reviewed on: 8 Jan 2006

Having read the other 'reader reviews' before writing mine I am surprised that so many people have been disappointed by this film. Don't get me wrong, I can get bored of special-effects just like anyone, in fact I felt the second Lord of the Rings movie was a tad tedious for that very reason. King Kong is a very different kettle of fish though. By the end of the movie I was in a daze. Wow! Mr Jackson has done the original film proud, introduced new twists to make the movie watchable for a broad-range, modern audience – agewise and culturewise. The other reviewers who thought the movie corny, wooden, and boring just didn't 'get it'. Jackson has really enhanced the beauty/beast message with the special-effects. In the end the film reminded me a little of the film Moulin Rouge – very over the top, trying things never done before while finding new formulae for old chestnuts. I cried in this film, very unusual for me, and I would go and see it again. SMASHING!

B   **Reviewed by:** TxB

Reviewed on: 19 Dec 2005

Despite all the advances in technology, I prefer the original Kong to this one. The ape seems to be a half-baked politically correct gorilla. You can see how the creators tried to incorporate real gorilla behaviour and modelled Kong on actual Gorillas, but as with most things PC this is a most uninteresting ape. Note to director: before betting your movie on an ape, watch the Disney animated film Tarzan to see how to make ape behaviour appear genuine and interesting. Spiderman 2 did the same thing very well, with a robotic exoskeleton that was credible as it embraced the NY building in its crushing grip. This 5 ton 10 m ape climbs the Empire State Building and doesn't leave so much as a fingerprint. It's as if the director used the same sub-standard game engine (sold alongside the movie) in which we have a creature with a very limited (and un-credible) repertoire of moves, an environment with a few token objects which are (easily) destructible and the rest is immutable texture. It's not believable and it does not engage.

Writing about a review will mean **analysing** it (see previous section) and perhaps **commenting** on it (see next section). When analysing a review it is essential to:

- identify what view the reviewer is putting forward
- identify how the reviewer uses language to convey that view effectively

Reviewer A is very positive about the film and uses a number of techniques to put his views across to the reader:

- He expresses surprise at the fact that some reviewers have been disappointed with the film. This immediately indicates that he does not agree with this view and so establishes his point of view.
- He makes his position seem reasonable by agreeing with the view that special-effects can become tedious.
- He uses a comparison between Lord of the Rings to show how *King Kong* does not fall into this category.
- He use words and phrases such as "Wow!", "Smashing" and "I was in a daze" to show the effect the film had on him.
- He refers to the original version and comments on how the director, Peter Jackson, has brought something new to his version.

Reviewer B adopts a more negative view and expresses this using a number of techniques:

- He makes his view clear at the beginning by stating that he prefers the original version of the film.
- He focuses on how the film fails to make the gorilla appear convincing.

- He uses words and phrases such as "half-baked politically correct gorilla" and "uninteresting ape" to make his view clear.
- He uses a comparison with Spiderman 2 to show how a much more convincing scene can be created.
- He uses the example of King Kong climbing the Empire State Building to show just how this scene is by comparison.

> **KEY POINT**
>
> Look carefully at the writer's view – it may be very balanced but it might present a very one-sided picture.

3.3 Writing your own reviews

LEARNING SUMMARY

After studying this section you should be able to understand:
- **book reviews**
- **reviews of films and plays**

You might be asked to write a review based on any one of a range of things. Here are some of them:

- a film
- a play
- a music CD
- a computer game
- a product of some kind

Let's have a look at ways of approaching some of these.

Reviews of films and plays

In many ways, reviews of films and plays can be similar to book reviews in that part of the review might deal with **character** and **plot**. However, plays and films also have another dimension – that of **visual effect**. In analysing or writing this kind of review you should also take into account the visual effectiveness of the action on the stage or screen.

This is a review of the DVD release of the film *Planet of the Apes*. Read it through carefully.

Note how the writer **structures** the review and **conveys** ideas.

Details about the film including price of DVD

Negative comment in sub heading

Summary of the storyline

Still from film, given amusing caption

THE CAVE
Watered down horror for the under 15s

SPECS

CERTIFICATE: 12
PRICE: £19.99
LENGTH: 93 mins
DIRECTOR: Bruce H...
CAST: Cole Hauser, Piper Perabo, Eddie Cibrian
YEAR MADE: 2005
DISTRIBUTOR: Sony Pictures Home Entertainment
AUDIO / VISUAL: DD5.1 / 2.35:1 anamorphic
NUMBER OF DISCS: 1   DTS: ✔   UMD: ✔

EXTRAS

- 'Into The Cave' featurette (20 mins)
- 'Designing Evolution: Tatopoulous Studios' featurette (11 mins)

RELEASED OUT NOW

THE STORY

A team of scientists discover ancient ruins with an expansive underground cave network. In search of primitive marine life they send down a team of expert cave explorers who soon come face to face with a whole new species – blood thirsty predators hell-bent on hunting down the trapped explorers.

THE DVD

Describing *The Cave* as regurgitated spew of an overused 'horror' premise would be complimentary. Offering nothing original, the ridiculous plot is clearly spawned from the amalgamation of *Pitch Black*, *Predator* and *The Descent*, as the time old 'explore and escape' scenario reaches new depths of absurdity.

After 45 minutes of stage school acting and a vague attempt at establishing a painfully dubious plot, something actually happens. But, to our horror, the first 'killing' scene is so heavily muted it's painfully devoid of the scares

"CARNAGE THAT RARELY EXTENDS BEYOND DISEMBODIED LIMBS AND FLASHES OF BLOOD"

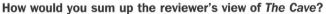

"Anyone who says The Descent was better gets twatted!"

that you associate with a horror movie. Unfortunately the film decides to teeter along in the same muted vein until its abysmal conclusion.

Labelled under the 'teen horror' umbrella, it's not surprising that this 12-certificate features carnage that rarely extends beyond disembodied limbs and flashes of blood. Attempting to crack the under-15 niche, the producers have failed to realise that modern day teenyboppers demand a lot more. Heed our warning and avoid it at all costs.

The extras on this DVD, like the DVD itself, are predictable. The first is a by-

the-numbers making-of that details how the underwater scenes were filmed. This goes some way to explaining how the budget was probably spent, with trips to tropical and frozen locations across the world. The second takes a look at how the 'predator' was made, though by this time we doubt you'll care.

NAT JOHNSON

VERDICT

A dire attempt. This film offers nothing original and will rob you of 93 precious minutes of your life.

FILM ★   EXTRAS ★★

Extra features included in DVD outlined

Sensationalised quote from review

Lists some specific criticisms of the film

Comments on extra features

Verdict on film and star rating

PROGRESS CHECK

How would you sum up the reviewer's view of *The Cave*?
The reviewer is clearly not impressed by it. A point that is made completely clear in the closing comment – "This film offers nothing original and will rob you of 93 precious minutes of your life".

Before we have a more detailed look at how the review has been written, let's begin by thinking about **audience** and **purpose**.

Audience and purpose

The purpose of this piece is to review the DVD release of the film *The Cave*. As such, it combines a film review with a review of the extra features that are available on the DVD recording.

The audience could be a general reader interested in the film but it is likely that this is aimed mainly at a more specialist readership.

PROGRESS CHECK

What evidence can you find that this review might be aimed at a more specialist readership?

Here are some ideas:

- The review is from DVD NEXT, which is a magazine specialising in films and DVDs.
- The review makes reference to other films such as *Pitch Black* and *Predator* which assumes some knowledge of horror films.
- The review assumes a knowledge of the horror film genre e.g. scenes that you associate with a horror movie.
- The use of vocabulary, with words such as 'regurgitated' and 'amalgamation', suggests a relatively well-educated audience.

Structure

The DVD review itself follows a clear structure:

Paragraph 1:   Gives a summary of the plot of the film, which makes it sound exciting.

Paragraph 2:   Makes the reviewer's view clear that this is not a good film. It compares the film unfavourably with some other, better films in the horror genre.

Paragraph 3:   Criticises the acting and the lack of impact of the 'horror' scenes.

Paragraph 4:   Highlights the fact that the film tries to appeal to the under-15 market but fails to realise the demands of the modern teenager. It warns the reader off the film.

Paragraph 5:   The final paragraph deals with the predictable 'extras' the DVD offers.

Paragraph 6:   Makes it clear that the reviewer feels that this is a very poor film and ends with a very damning comment.

Style and techniques

- the use of the sub-heading to signal the standpoint of the reviewer
- the comparison of the film with better examples of the horror genre
- the use of humour by the use of phrases such as: '*teeter along*', '*modern day teenyboppers*', '*...we doubt you'll care*'.
- the placing of the film in the 'horror' genre.
- the use of the cutting final comment
- the use of stills from the film, one with a humorous and cutting caption

When analysing or writing a review, make sure you focus on some examples of specific details.

PROGRESS CHECK

Think about how effective you find this review and why. Would it help you in deciding whether or not to buy the DVD?

3.4 Commenting on texts and ideas

LEARNING SUMMARY

After studying this section you should be able to understand:

- *what 'writing to comment' means*
- *examples of writing to comment*

Writing to comment

As part of your GCSE course 'writing to comment' can take two basic forms:

- You might be asked to comment on a particular idea.
- You might be asked to comment on how a writer uses language to create their effects or the particular methods they use to present their ideas, views etc.

In order to comment effectively you need to:

- have ideas on the issue you are asked to comment on
- be aware of how ideas are communicated or how language is used to create particular effects

> **Make sure you fully understand the views being expressed by the writer.**

Newspapers frequently comment on issues. For example, in the extract from an article on page 50, the journalist comments on plans to detain young offenders.

PROGRESS CHECK

Read the extract through carefully. What view does this comment express?

The comment reveals that, although the journalist agrees in principle with the idea that young offenders should not be free to roam the streets, at present we do not have the facilities to house all these young offenders.

What techniques does the writer use to make her comment more effective?

Here are some ideas:

- The writer agrees with the logic that young offenders should not simply be released to offend again.
- Then she points out some shortcomings in this 'logic', such as there are no facilities to keep these offenders.
- She uses supporting evidence from the probation officers' union.
- She uses statistical evidence to support comment.
- She uses rhetorical question to suggest alternatives.

THE INDEPENDENT
Wednesday 17 April 2002

EDITORIAL & COMMENT

Confine these youths in school, not in prison

DEBORAH ORR

The logic is simple, and states that if more known criminals are put in jail, then there are fewer on the streets to threaten the public. For those who have been the victims of juvenile criminals in their communities, and who have watched those young criminals being bailed to commit their crimes again and again, this will surely prove to be a popular solution.

But the sad fact is that it can only ever be a short-term solution. Children jailed for minor crimes will have to come out of custody again, and sooner rather than later. What happens then? Anyone who insists on believing that a spell under lock and key alone will act as a deterrent to these children, or others, is simply in total denial of reality. The opposite is true – young people exposed to custodial sentences in this country generally emerge as more sophisticated and more brutal criminals.

I don't, as it happens, believe that young criminals should be allowed to roam the streets, free, in the words of the Metropolitan Police Commissioner Sir John Stevens, to go "strutting across the estates". But I still think that this decision is at best an irrelevance and at worst an act of gross cynicism.

It is common knowledge that there is actually nowhere to put these young offenders. Harry Fletcher, general secretary of Napo, the probation officers' union, summed up the problem best. He pointed out that there were six empty spaces in secure accommodation across England and Wales, and 30 prolific young offenders eligible as of June for the new secure remand appearing in the courts each day.

It doesn't take a rocket scientist to work out that this new initiative will have dealt with as many potential recruits as it possibly can, within hours of it coming into effect. What is the point of changing laws and altering procedures without initiating new infrastructures in order to deal with them?

For those somehow able to discount the fact that street crime has risen over the past five years against a sentencing culture which has seen the number of those in custody rising by 20,000 to capacity, the solution is to build more prisons. For those who wish to prevent young people from becoming embroiled in crime in the first place, the answer is to build more schools. The two approaches have for so long been on opposite shores of the political seascape, that compromise is seen as impossible.

But maybe it is not. At present, we have the worst of both worlds. While it might be difficult to get low-level child offenders into custody, once they are in educational provision is appalling. Child prisoners have a right to far less education than is expected of schoolchildren, and even that provision is more often than not unmet. More than 50 per cent of young offenders have a reading age of less than 11, and whether inside the prison system, or outside it, special needs programmes of the type they require are difficult to come by.

Why not then, instead of placing young criminals, or even young repeat suspects, in secure council accommodation, place them in secure boarding schools from which they can return at weekends, tagged if necessary? This may not be the most liberal of ideas, but in a polarised debate, such institutions may break the impasse between locking 'em up, and rehabilitation. Any suggestion that difficult pupils of any kind should be placed in schools that cater to their needs exclusively, are subject to cries from the left of "sin bin". The spectre of Borstal still looms large, but there is every reason for these new institutions to learn from past mistakes.

Troubled and troubling children will first and foremost be under close scrutiny, in an environment where doing harm to others or themselves is less likely, and where routine and stability is guaranteed. At the same time they will be getting a full education from professionals trained to deal with their exacting demands.

KEY POINT Be aware of the views expressed through comments and the techniques that writers use to present them.

Sample GCSE questions

Write a review of a book that you have read recently.

Book Review: Of Mice and Men

John Steinbeck's novel `Of Mice and Men' is set in America during the Depression and tells a moving story of two itinerant workers, George and Lennie. The novel opens as the two men are making their way across country to a ranch where they gain employment and it is in this opening scene where we learn a great deal about their relationship.

The two men are portrayed as being very different. George is described as being "small and quick" whereas Lennie, who has the mentality of a small child, is "huge" and "bear"-like. However, it soon becomes clear that, despite the stark contrast of their physical appearances and mental capacities, they share a deep and well-established friendship. George is seen to act as a kind of `parent' figure to Lennie who, because of his actions whilst in their previous place of employment, is the cause of them having to `move on'.

In addition to them sharing a deep friendship, they also share a dream - one of owning their own farm. We learn of the dream early on in the novel where we see George reassuring Lennie by painting a wonderful picture of how, one day, they will have the security of owning and working on their own farm and being able to settle down and "live off the fatta the lan'". Lennie is seen to draw a great deal of comfort from being told what could be seen as a `bedtime' story, especially as it is promised that he will "tend the rabbits".

`Dreams' is just one of the themes that Steinbeck explores in `Of Mice and Men' and they seem to be born out of loneliness, another major theme of the novel. Although the story is mainly set on the ranch, Steinbeck introduces a variety of characters through which he explores the effects of loneliness and isolation. For example, Crooks is a man hired to look after the horses on the ranch. Not only is he seen to be socially isolated through a physical disability but he bears the added burden of being discriminated against because he is black. Crooks lives and works separately from the rest of the men, which highlights the sense of his isolation, and is seen to have developed very little self-worth: "Crooks had reduced himself to nothing".

Other characters are seen to live a lonely existence too. For example, Candy, an old ranch hand, has only his dog for companionship and the only woman on the farm also suffers in her loneliness due to her unhappy marriage to the ranch owner's son, Curley. The fact that Steinbeck doesn't give her a name emphasises her apparent `insignificance' and the flirtatious behaviour she demonstrates seems to be how her loneliness manifests itself. However, even she has a dream.

Steinbeck's success in portraying believable characters, along with his ability to use language effectively to describe both characters and setting, make this novel extremely entertaining and, although the sense of foreboding which can be detected throughout the novel makes the ending somewhat expected, it doesn't affect the level of suspension that Steinbeck achieves.

Good opening – brief outline of plot sets the story in context.

Clear initial impression of characters supported by references to the text.

Moves on to mention a key theme of the novel. Again the comments are firmly rooted in the text.

Discusses other themes and how they relate to the other characters and the setting of the story.

Discusses other characters.

Gives a judgement on the novel and the effectiveness of the ending.

Exam practice questions

Look carefully at this review of the competition game *Who Wants to be a Millionaire?*

Analyse the techniques used to present this review and comment on its effectiveness.

REVIEW
WHO WANTS TO BE A MILLIONAIRE? 2ND EDITION

Tarrant's gormless but intense stare almost wills you into plumping for the wrong answer.

Which part of the atmosphere absorbs ultraviolet radiation?

A: Ozone seam   B: Ozone layer
C: Ozone strip   D: Ozone deck

WHO WANTS TO BE A MILLIONAIRE? 2ND EDITION
Are you happy to go orange? Frankly, no.

The virtual *WWTBAM? 2nd Edition* studio tries to emulate the atmosphere of the TV show – with mixed results.

WHO WANTS TO SAVE £35?
Play *WWTBAM* online at www.itv.co.uk for free.

The ultimate WWTBAM con is that you can play what is essentially the same game online at ITV's Web site for free, as advertised by Chris Tarrant at the end of each TV episode. Sure, you don't get Tarrant's voice reading the questions, or his deformed digitised mug staring at you while you answer, but some would put that down as an advantage. And because you don't have to wait for the game to load every little piece of Tarrant's speech, if you've got a decent Net connection, the free online game actually moves a lot quicker than the PS2 version.

Publisher: Eidos
Developer: Revolution
Players: 1-4
Price: £34.99
Out: Now
Website: www.eidosinteractive.co.uk/games/info.html?gmid=122

Back story
Like, duh! Based on one of the most successful TV quiz show concepts of all time, *WWTBAM? 2nd Edition* is the new-and-improved update of the PSone game that appeared last Christmas. First time around, *WWTBAM* was the fastest game ever to sell a million copies in the UK

Unless you've spent the last few years living in a cave, on Mars, with a sack on your head and a vehement belief that the slightest exposure to Chris Tarrant will result in universal apocalypse, you'll know what's going on here. Answer 15 questions in a row correctly and you win a million quid. It's just like the TV show.

Except, of course, that you don't win a million quid. Nor is your nervous spouse squirming behind you in the audience as you throw away seven grand by thinking that the capital of Australia is Sydney. Nor do you get to phone a friend. Instead you hear a pre-recorded message from someone pretending to be Bert from Barrow-In-Furness, who isn't your friend at all.

Tarrant's here this time, though. As reported last issue, the great smirking one rattled off a thousand questions and answers, plus a few trademark squeaks and smarms, in order to have his words synched to the lip movement of an 'accurate model' of his smug face. All very nice in theory, but actually the digital Tarrant is a monstrosity, more akin to something out of *Silent Hill 2* than a genial quiz show host. The lip-synching is poor, making the zombie-Tarrant look like he's chewing his own tongue. Even scarier is when you dither over an answer and his face starts twitching dementedly. It's meant to add to the game's authenticity, but having a disfigured Tarrant stare you out is rather off-putting when you're trying to remember who wrote *Moby Dick*.

Otherwise, the game functions much as you'd expect. You can opt for the 'fastest finger' qualifier or just dive right into main event, playing by yourself or taking turns with up to three other people – if you can really be bothered to wait around while your aunties all crack the same joke about that being their final answer before you get another go.

When the first *WWTBAM* game appeared, there were many complaints along the lines of "Well, if you can't really win a million pounds, what's the point?" Of course, you can hardly have expected Eidos to start coughing up the green – the company is trying to make money, not give it away – but the format of the TV show does rely on people gambling a real stake as part of its tension and appeal. With only glory on offer, you're much more likely to take a risk on a tricky question, making the whole thing a little facile. Worse still, *OPS2* found itself reaching the million question a tad too easily, and thus it soon becomes a chore having to plough through the idiot-proof teasers early on. This is tedious stuff and yes, that is our bloody final answer ☐ **Sam Richards**

15 questions, three lifelines, infinite smarm.

Peter Ebdon and Ronnie O'Sullivan are known for which sport?
A: Squash   B: Darts
C: Table tennis   D: Snooker

And the campaign to bring back *Bob's Full House* started here.

WHO WANTS TO BE A MILLIONAIRE? 2ND EDITION

Why we'd buy it:	Why we'd leave it:	
- Even quiz freaks need their fix	- Tarrant looks hideous	Buy the board game, play online or attend your local pub quiz to avoid supporting this rush-developed cash cow.
- You can't expect the whole family to flock round *Devil May Cry* on Boxing Day	- Answering easy early questions annoyingly repetitive	
	- Quiz book or board game would be better	

Graphics	The digital Tarrant is plain freaky	03
Sound	As much Tarrant as you can take	07
Gameplay	Slow-paced and simple trivia quiz	04
Life span	Depends on your patience levels	04

04

PlayStation 2 VERDICT

Writing to inform, explain, describe

The following topics are included in this chapter:

- Writing to inform
- Writing to explain
- Writing to describe

4.1 Writing to inform

LEARNING SUMMARY

After studying this section you should be able to understand:

- **the purpose of writing to inform**
- **how to consider your audience**
- **how to write an informative response**
- **how to structure your response clearly and logically**

The purpose of writing to inform

When you are writing to inform, your main **purpose** is to **convey** to your reader certain information as **clearly** and **effectively** as possible. Informative writing, though, can come in many different forms.

Look at these two examples, which tell the reader about the Welsh mountain, Snowdon.

> **Snowdon** (Y Widdfa in Welsh). The highest mountain peak in England and Wales (1085m/3560ft), in the Northwest corner of Wales, in Gwynedd. Its top can be reached in one hour from Llanberis on the country's only narrow-gauge rack and pinion railway, opened in 1896 and still using steam engines. The mountain's Welsh name, meaning 'great tomb', derives from the legend that a giant killed by King Arthur is buried at its summit.

> ### MOUNTAIN RAILWAY, SNOWDON
> Majestic Snowdon dominates the glorious, ancient landscape of North Wales. At 3,560ft (1085m) it is a true mountain and a place of legend – said to be the burial place of the giant ogre Rhita, vanquished by King Arthur. Some believe that Arthur's knights still sleep beneath. Since 1896, the Snowdon Mountain Railway has been making it easy to claim this mountain peak as one of your lifetime achievements. In a tremendously ambitious feat of engineering, and uniquely in Britain, a rack and pinion railway was built which rises to within 66ft of the summit of the highest mountain in England and Wales.

What do these two informative pieces of writing have in common?

You might have noted that they both:

- use **clear** and **straightforward** language
- base the ideas on facts
- cover the same points
- get straight to the point
- **structure** the ideas **logically**

Although they have much in common in terms of their content, they do differ in the way they present their information. What differences do you note?

The first piece is much plainer in style and simply presents the information in a factual way. The second one, however, uses a much more colourful description in order to put the information across to the reader. For example, instead of the plain '*The highest mountain peak in England and Wales*' we have '*Magnificent Snowdon dominates the glorious, ancient landscape of north Wales*'. The '*narrow-gauge rack and pinion railway, opened in 1896 and still using steam engines*' becomes '*…a tremendously ambitious feat of engineering*', which is described as unique in Britain.

Both these pieces set out to give the reader information about Snowdon but why do they present it in such different ways? To find the answer to that question we need to think again about those key elements, **audience** and **purpose**. The difference between the two becomes clear when you know that the first one is taken from an encylopedia, which sets out to present the **plain facts** as **clearly** as possible. The second is taken from an information leaflet on the Snowdon Mountain Railway. Although these two share the common purpose of informing their readers about Snowdon, the leaflet also has the added purpose of attracting potential visitors to the railway. The language that is used to present the information, therefore, is designed to emphasise the dramatic, romantic and unique nature of the place.

> Note that although both these pieces of informative writing contain mostly facts, some types of informative writing contain not just facts but opinions too.

Information can be presented to the reader in many forms including:

- advertisements
- articles
- guide books
- leaflets
- reports
- reference books
- web pages

Read the following example carefully. It is a pamphlet about the Cabinet War Rooms in London.

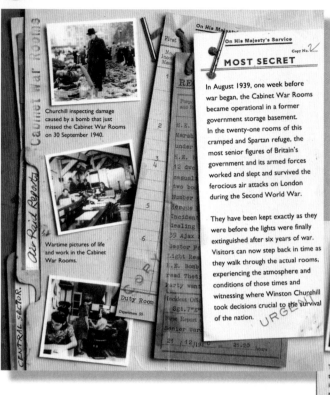

Churchill inspecting damage caused by a bomb that just missed the Cabinet War Rooms on 30 September 1940.

Wartime pictures of life and work in the Cabinet War Rooms.

MOST SECRET

In August 1939, one week before war began, the Cabinet War Rooms became operational in a former government storage basement. In the twenty-one rooms of this cramped and Spartan refuge, the most senior figures of Britain's government and its armed forces worked and slept and survived the ferocious air attacks on London during the Second World War.

They have been kept exactly as they were before the lights were finally extinguished after six years of war. Visitors can now step back in time as they walk through the actual rooms, experiencing the atmosphere and conditions of those times and witnessing where Winston Churchill took decisions crucial to the survival of the nation.

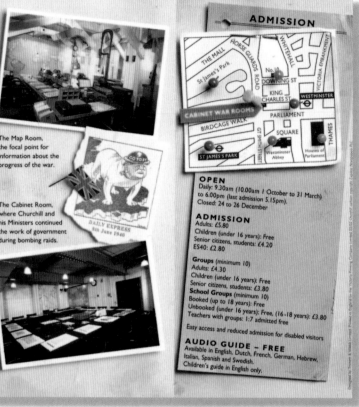

The Map Room, the focal point for information about the progress of the war.

The Cabinet Room, where Churchill and his Ministers continued the work of government during bombing raids.

ADMISSION

OPEN
Daily: 9.30am (10.00am 1 October to 31 March) to 6.00pm (last admission 5.15pm). Closed: 24 to 26 December

ADMISSION
Adults: £5.80
Children (under 16 years): Free
Senior citizens, students: £4.20
ES40: £2.80

Groups (minimum 10)
Adults: £4.30
Children (under 16 years): Free
Senior citizens, students: £3.80
School Groups (minimum 10)
Booked (up to 18 years): Free
Unbooked (under 16 years): Free, (16-18 years): £3.80
Teachers with groups: 1:7 admitted free

Easy access and reduced admission for disabled visitors

AUDIO GUIDE – FREE
Available in English, Dutch, French, German, Hebrew, Italian, Spanish and Swedish. Children's guide in English only.

What kind of information does this leaflet contain?

Here are some ideas:

- The title and sub-heading 'The nerve centre of Britain's war effort' tell the reader what the Cabinet War Rooms are.
- The text informs the reader about the rooms, when they became operational etc.
- The second part of the text tells the reader what the visitor will experience in going to see them.
- The third block of text informs the reader of new developments that are planned for the future.
- The photographs give the reader visual information about wartime life and the Cabinet Rooms as they look now.
- The captions give further information about the photographs.
- The map gives information about the location of the rooms.
- Underneath this are details of the opening times and admission prices.
- Other information is included, such as details of 'corporate hospitality' facilities, education services provided and other, related museum sites.

Writing your informative response

If you are asked to write to inform, make sure you include all the information needed by your reader.

Clear planning is essential when writing informatively. If you are answering a question that requires you to write informatively in an exam, it is very important that you plan your ideas out carefully before starting to write.

Here's one way of approaching this:

Examiner's tips	
Identify your audience.	Read the question carefully. The exact wording of the question is very important in helping you establish the nature of your audience.
List the key points you want to tell your reader.	Careful identification of the essential information is important.
Put them in the order you are going to deal with them.	Structure is always important. Your information should be presented logically and developed in an ordered way.
Decide on the level of detail.	Again this will be closely linked to your purpose.
Plan how you are going to present your information to make it relevant to your audience.	Planning is very important to make sure you don't leave anything out.
Make sure your information can be easily understood.	Use clear language and present ideas in a straightforward way.

4.2 *Writing to explain*

LEARNING SUMMARY

After studying this section you should be able to understand:
* *the purpose of writing to explain*
* *how to write appropriately for your audience*
* *writing your explanation*

The purpose of writing to explain

When you are writing to explain, your main purpose is to make something clear to your reader and to convey this information as effectively as possible. As with writing to inform, writing that explains can take many different forms and in many cases there is an overlap between writing to inform and writing to explain. An explanation often addresses the questions: **what? how? why?** and provides the answers to your reader.

However, the ways in which explanations do this can vary greatly depending on the purpose of the explanation.

Look at this example from an instruction booklet on how to use a mobile phone.

Selecting Functions and Options

To view the various functions/options available and select the one required, proceed as follow.

1. Press the appropriate soft key.

2. **To...**	**Then press the...**
Select the:	**Select** soft key or ⟩ key.
● Function displayed	
or	
● Option highlighted	
View the next function or highlight the next option in a list	⌣ key or ▼ key on the left side of the phone.
Move back to the previous function or option in a list	⌢ key or ▲ key left side of the phone.
Move back up one level in the structure	⟨ key, ⟲ soft key or **C** key.
Exit the structure without changing the settings	☎/⏻ key.

In some functions, you may be asked for a password or PIN. Enter the required code and press the OK soft key.

Note: When you access a list of options, your phone highlights the current option. if, however, there are only two options, such as On/Off or Enable/Disable, your phone highlights the option that is currently not active, so that you can select it directly.

Notice that this explains:

- **what** functions the phone offers
- **why** the phone displays certain signs
- **how** to view the various options and select them

PROGRESS CHECK

What do you notice about the way this explanation is presented?

It is:

- clearly and logically structured
- concise
- presented visually in a form that makes it easy to understand

This is one form of explanation text but there are many other ways that text can be presented in order to explain. The way in which a text explains is determined by the other purposes it serves (apart from that of 'explaining' something) and the audience that it is written for. Even texts that explain the same thing can be written in very different ways.

For example, recipes are an example of texts that 'explain'. They explain how to make a particular dish. The following recipe and the one on page 60 both explain how to make a chocolate dessert but there are some major differences in how the recipes are presented.

Quick Chocolate Cake

Metric/Imperial
2 eggs, beaten
2 tablespoons caster sugar
225g/8oz butter or margarine,
  melted
225g/8oz plain chocolate,
  melted
225g/8oz digestive biscuits,
  broken into small pieces

Lightly beat the eggs with the sugar. Gradually beat in the melted butter or margarine, then mix in the chocolate. Fold in the biscuits.
Spoon into a greased 15cm/6 inch loose-bottomed cake pan and spread out evenly. Chill overnight.
The next day, remove from the pan and serve with whipped or fresh cream.
Serves 6

Although the basic task for each is the same, the way each recipe explains how to make the dessert is very different.

PROGRESS CHECK

What features do you think they have in common?

- They both explain the process of making the dessert.
- Both contain details of ingredients.
- Both contain details of preparation, cooking/chilling times etc.

What are the main differences between the two explanations?

The recipe above provides a **straightforward explanation** of how to make the cake. It gives a list of ingredients with weights/quantities, together with a simple explanation of exactly what to do.

The recipe on page 60 gives this **information** too, explaining the ingredients, quantities and what to do. However, this recipe also contains much more than a simple explanation of how to make the 'pud'. Here are some key differences:

- The recipe is provided by a well-known TV chef and the accompanying explanation gives a sense of the chef speaking **directly** to the reader.
- The tips and 'sauce secrets' again give a sense of the **personal voice** as well as adding further detail on what to do.
- The stage by stage **photographs** give **visual details** to accompany the explanations.
- The headings and **sub-headings** make clear what type of dish the recipe is for. They also show that it is a special Gary Rhodes recipe. This is emphasised further by the inset photograph of Gary Rhodes.

GARY RHODES'

Quick steamed
Chocolate pud
with a warm chocolate syrup sauce

Gary's simple steamed chocolate pudding for four people is microwaved and ready in less than 30 minutes. Accompany with a clever five-minute sauce **Photographs ROGER STOWELL**

"I know it normally takes 1½-2 hours to steam a good rich, softly textured sponge, but this is super quick because you microwave it. There's no steam, but the texture is almost identical.

"The chocolate sauce is made with golden syrup – this makes the flavour richer, and it also gives the sauce a lovely rich, glossy shine. Serve with a dollop of extra thick cream or a spoonful of pouring cream – either will help balance the very rich chocolate flavours in the sponge and sauce."

BUMP UP THE CHOCOLATE
Use a quality dark chocolate containing 50-65 per cent cocoa solids for a superior flavour. I've given a range of amounts for the chocolate purely to suit your taste – 50g/2oz will make a good chocolatey pudding, but hardcore chocoholics can use anything up to 100g/4oz chocolate.

QUICK STEAMED CHOCOLATE PUD WITH A WARM CHOCOLATE SYRUP SAUCE
Serves 4
100g/4oz softened butter, plus extra for greasing
50-100g/2-4oz good quality plain chocolate (see tip)
85g/3oz self-raising flour
25g/1oz cocoa powder
100g/4oz caster sugar
2 medium eggs
1-2 tbsp milk (optional)
chocolate curls and icing sugar, to decorate (see tip)
extra thick or pouring cream, to serve
FOR THE CHOCOLATE SYRUP SAUCE
175g/6oz good quality plain chocolate, chopped
150ml/¼ pint milk
3 tbsp double cream
2-3 tbsp golden syrup, according to taste
25g/1oz butter

1 Prepare the ingredients Lightly grease a 850ml-1.2 litre/1½-2 pint microwaveable pudding basin. Grate the chocolate (**picture 1**).
2 Make the sponge Whizz the butter,

EASY CHOCOLATE CURLS
Spread melted chocolate on a cold, smooth, flat surface to a 5mm-1cm/¼-½in thickness. Leave until firm but not solid. Hold a large straight knife at a 45 degree angle and scrape it across the surface.

SAUCE SECRET
A chocolate sauce made with solid chocolate rather than cocoa powder must not be overheated. If the sauce boils, the solids separate, leaving a grainy texture.

flour, cocoa, sugar and eggs in a food processor until smooth (**picture 2**). The mixture should have a soft dropping consistency (**picture 3**) – if not, add milk until it does. Transfer to a bowl and stir in the grated chocolate.
3 Cook the pudding Spoon the mixture into the pudding basin, smooth the top with the back of a spoon and cover with plastic film (**picture 4**). At this stage the pudding can be chilled for up to 2 hours until ready to cook. Before microwaving, pierce the film with a knife. For a 500W microwave, cook on High for 4½-5 minutes until a skewer pushed into the centre comes out clean. (For every 100W above this, decrease cooking by 15 seconds.) Rest for 1-2 minutes before turning out.
4 Make the sauce Tip all the ingredients into a microwaveable bowl and cook on High for about 3 minutes until the chocolate and butter have just melted – do not allow them to boil (see tip). Whisk the sauce to a smooth, shiny consistency (**picture 5**). To serve, pour the hot sauce over the pudding, decorate the top with the chocolate curls and lightly dust with icing sugar, if liked. Serve with cream.

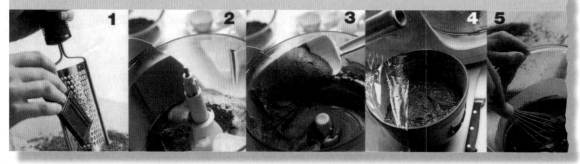

Writing your explanation

Here are some points to bear in mind when writing to explain:

- Make sure you are aware of what the task involves.
- Be clear in your mind what the **purpose** and the **audience** of this writing are.
- Underline or highlight the key words or phrases.
- Write down the ideas you are going to use.
- Put them in the order you are going to deal with them in your answer.
- Make sure that you explain your points clearly.

Read the question carefully and make sure your writing does what the task asks you to do.

4.3 *Writing to describe*

After studying this section you should be able to understand:

- **the purpose of writing to describe**
- **how writers make their descriptions vivid and effective**
- **how to plan your own descriptive writing**

The purpose of writing to describe

When you are writing to describe, your main aim is to create a **picture** with words so that your reader can imagine **vividly** the scene, person, situation etc. that you are describing. This means that the words you choose when you write a description are very important and you need to think about them and select them very carefully. However, this does not mean that you should try to cram as many impressive sounding words into your writing as possible. It is just as easy to overdo the description as it is to underdo it.

For example, look at this student's description of a sunset:

Evening was approaching as the fiery, golden, flaming orb slowly, ever so slowly, began to lose the intensity of its daytime heat when it seared the heavens with its remorseless, blistering rays. Millimetre by millimetre the blazing disk, now reddened to the colour of a ripe tomato, slipped ever closer to the horizon, darting its dying rays over a land soon to be enclosed in darkness.

How effectively do you think the student has described the scene?
Another student took a more straightforward approach:

The heat of the day had gone and the air held a coolness that signalled the approaching night. The sun, which had burnt brightly all day in a clear sky, had now lost some of its intensity and had turned a deeper orange as it moved lower and lower in the sky. As it began to slip below the horizon it bathed the whole valley in a mellow, golden glow, which quickly faded giving way to darkness and the approaching night.

How does this compare with the previous student's description?

The first description seems a little 'over the top' and uses some overly descriptive words and phrases. The second one is more restrained and because of that is the more effective of the two.

Effective description involves carefully selecting the right words but make sure you don't over describe as this can start to be over-elaborate and wordy.

How descriptions can be made vivid and effective

In making your writing vivid, you can draw on a number of sources. You could draw ideas from:

- people you have met
- situations you have encountered
- experiences you have had
- sensations you have experienced through your senses (sight, touch, taste, smell and hearing)

You can also use various techniques to make your writing more vivid and effective. You can use:

- imagery, such as similes and metaphors, to help your readers recreate the scene or experience in their imaginations
- alliteration, onomatopoeia and assonance to give particular sound 'effects' to your writing
- various sentence structures and rhythm patterns to build up the desired effect and create a sense of a particular mood or feeling

Here is an example of a writer creating a description.

In this extract Dickens describes the town of Coketown.

It was a town of red brick, or of brick that would have been red if the smoke and ashes had allowed it; but, as matters stood it was a town of unnatural red and black like the painted face of a savage. It was a town of machinery and tall chimneys, out of which interminable serpents of smoke trailed themselves for ever and ever, and never got uncoiled. It had a black canal in it, and a river that ran purple with ill-smelling dye, and vast piles of buildings full of windows where there was a rattling and a trembling all day long, and where the piston of the steam-engine worked monotonously up and down, like the head of an elephant in a state of melancholy madness. It contained several large streets all very like one another, and many small streets still more like one another, inhabited by people equally like one another, who all went in and out at the same hours, with the same sound upon the pavements, to do the same work, and to whom every day was the same as yesterday and tomorrow, and every year the counterpart of the last and the next.

From *Hard Times* by Charles Dickens

How does Dickens make his description effective here?

- He uses vocabulary, which creates a sense of colour especially of 'red' and 'black' that he uses to emphasise the 'unnatural' feel of the place.
- He uses metaphors, such as '*...tall chimneys, out of which interminable serpents of smoke trailed themselves*'.
- He uses similes, such as the one he uses to describe the working of the steam engine which '*...worked monotonously up and down, like the head of an elephant in a state of melancholy madness*'. Again, this is an unnatural image that emphasises the mechanical, monotonous, industrial nature of the place.
- He uses repetition to give a sense of the streets that all look '*...very like one another and many small streets still more like one another, inhabited by people equally like one another*'.
- He also uses language that appeals to the senses – '*...evil smelling dye*', '*...there was a rattling and a trembling all day long*'.

> **KEY POINT** Writers use a range of techniques to make their descriptions more effective. You can use them too in your own writing.

Sample GCSE questions

Write a leaflet designed to provide the reader with information about a tourist attraction of your choice.

In designing your leaflet you should think about:

- the title and headings
- the information it should contain
- the kind of language you should use
- the layout
- any other ideas you think important

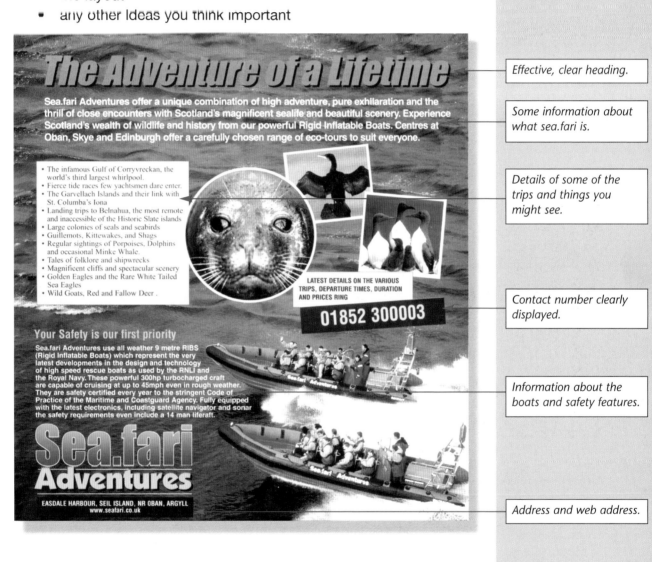

Effective, clear heading.

Some information about what sea.fari is.

Details of some of the trips and things you might see.

Contact number clearly displayed.

Information about the boats and safety features.

Address and web address.

Exam practice questions

Describe a particular memory that is special to you.

....

....

....

....

....

....

....

....

....

....

....

....

....

....

....

....

....

....

5 Media and the moving image

The following topics are included in this chapter:

- **Examining newspapers**
- **Looking at advertising**
- **Film and television**

5.1 Examining newspapers

LEARNING SUMMARY

After studying this section you should be able to understand:

- **how to look at a newspaper report**
- **the difference between fact and opinion**
- **how to compare newspaper reports**
- **how newspapers present issues**

Looking at a newspaper report

The main function of a newspaper is to **report** news of all kinds to the reader. This covers a very wide area and can range from very serious issues to trivial ones. Think about all the different kinds of news and make a list of them. Your list might include some of the following:

- news of world events
- political news (world, Britain and local)
- sports news
- entertainment news (film, TV, theatre etc.)
- minor news items
- gossip

In addition to presenting news, newspapers often do something else too – they:

- comment on events
- make judgements on them
- give their opinions

Look at the article on page 66 and think about the impact that it has on you, the reader.

Back home, the probe that could unlock secrets of solar system

By Andrew Gumbel
in Los Angeles

A space capsule from the *Stardust* mission, carrying dust and comet fragments that scientists hope will unlock some of the most ancient secrets of the solar system, has landed safely in the Utah desert – the culmination of a hazardous and potentially groundbreaking seven-year mission.

Nasa scientists and researchers at the Johnson Space Center in Houston cheered as the capsule parachuted to earth on the arid salt flats west of Salt Lake City. A helicopter recovery team located the capsule shortly after its landing early yesterday morning and ferried it to a nearby military air base, where it will stay until its transfer to Nasa headquarters tomorrow.

"It's an absolutely fantastic end to the mission," Nasa scientist Carlton Allen told reporters.

Stardust was launched on its interstellar mineral collection expedition in February 1999. Five years later, it collected an estimated million or so fragments, some of them thinner than a human hair, from a comet called Wild 2 that was passing near Jupiter. The fragments, some of them from the comet, others possibly from outside the solar system, were collected in a large, tennis-racket shaped device smeared with a light, porous material called aerogel.

Scientists are excited because they believe the comet fragments may be older than the solar system and thus capable of offering vital new clues on the formation of the sun and planets around us. If, as expected, the mission collected interstellar dust carried in the comet's wake, researchers may also have their first opportunity to examine unaltered pieces of primordial matter from outside the solar system.

"The samples we collected are the same particles that went into the formation of the comet four and a half billion years ago," the Nasa mission's principal investigator, astronomy professor Donald Brownlee, told *National Geographic* magazine. That makes Wild 2 almost exactly the same age as the solar system.

Since comets are regarded as the building blocks of planets and suns, the residues collected from Wild 2 may be uniquely able to tell a very ancient story. Professor Brownlee likened the haul to the discovery of an ancient book we are still able to read and understand.

Wild 2 offered a unique set of circumstances – a comet close enough to earth to be reachable, and one travelling fast enough to prevent the destruction or alteration of its particles by the heat of the sun. Wild 2 entered the sun's orbit in 1974 and was then tugged in by Jupiter's gravitational pull until it came almost as close as Mars.

Stardust made its fragment collection in January 2004. The dust and other particles hit the aerogel at about six times the speed of a bullet.

Bringing the cache safely back to earth was far from a failsafe proposition. *Stardust*'s sister spacecraft *Genesis* sent a capsule back in September 2004, but the parachutes failed to open as it hurtled towards the Utah desert and its harvest of solar wind particles was exposed to the elements and compromised.

Until yesterday, no mineral retrieval operation had successfully returned to earth since the unmanned Soviet Luna 24 mission in 1976, which brought back moon rocks and soil. *Stardust* itself travelled three billion miles and circumnavigated the sun three times. Two years ago, it beamed back 72 black-and-white photographs of the surface of Wild 2, showing broad mesas, craters, pinnacles and canyons.

Even after the successful return of the capsule, the mothership remains in orbit and is on standby for further missions to other comets or asteroids.

Journey through space

During the past seven years, Stardust has travelled three billion miles, orbiting the sun three times

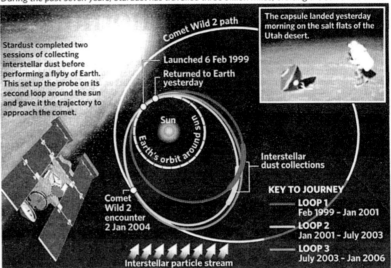

Stardust completed two sessions of collecting interstellar dust before performing a flyby of Earth. This set up the probe on its second loop around the sun and gave it the trajectory to approach the comet.

Comet Wild 2 path

Launched 6 Feb 1999
Returned to Earth yesterday

The capsule landed yesterday morning on the salt flats of the Utah desert.

Sun

Earth's orbit around sun

Comet Wild 2 encounter 2 Jan 2004

Interstellar dust collections

Interstellar particle stream

KEY TO JOURNEY
LOOP 1 Feb 1999 – Jan 2001
LOOP 2 Jan 2001 – July 2003
LOOP 3 July 2003 – Jan 2006

The sample return capsule was retrieved in the Utah desert EPS

When analysing the effect of a newspaper article, there are a number of features to take into account, all of which add something to the effect of the piece.

Here are some ideas:

- The headline – this is the first thing you notice and read when looking at an article.
- The photographs or illustrations (if used) – again, the reader's eye is drawn to these, often before reading the content.
- Captions that go with photographs and illustrations.
- The content of the article – this is very important because it contains the main body of information to be communicated to the reader.

KEY POINT   **All these elements combine to create the effect of the article.**

Look carefully at the article 'Back home, the probe that could unlock secrets of the solar system'.

1. How effective is the headline?
2. What kind of information is presented in the story?
3. What do the pictures and captions add to the overall effect of the article?
4. Why do you think the writer includes the diagram of the 'Journey through space'?

1. The leading words of the headline, '*Back home*', immediately tells the reader the probe has returned and the phrase '*could unlock secrets of the solar system*' gives the impression that the mission has been successful and the probe has returned with something exciting.
2. The information in the article is mainly factual, explaining what the probe has done, the material it has collected and its return to Earth. There is some description of the feelings of the scientists, '*scientists are excited*' and one scientist expressed an opinion, '*It's an absolutely fantastic end to the mission.*'
3. The smaller of the photographs shows the probe safely landed in the Utah desert and enables the reader to visualise the craft. The larger photograph shows the scientists retrieving the probe. The captions simply describe in a straightforward way what the photos depict.
4. The large diagram graphically illustrates the orbits of the sun made by the probe over the last seven years. The words '*interstellar*', '*particle stream*' and '*trajectory*' emphasise the scientific content of the article.

Comparing newspaper reports

The effect that a story has on the reader depends very much on the way the story is written and presented. Sometimes newspapers treat the same story in quite different ways to create different effects.

Writers can influence the effects their stories create in various ways. Here are some of the main ones:

- by the language they use to tell the story
- the particular ideas they choose to include
- the way they present the facts
- the use of opinion and comments
- the tone they create in their writing
- the way they use photographs and illustrations
- the headlines and sub-headings they use

These two reports give details of a survey of garden birds carried out by the Royal Society for the Protection of Birds. The first is from the *Daily Express*; the second is from *The Independent*.

DAILY EXPRESS   Thursday April 25 2002

Golly! Polly to top the bill in gardens

BOLSHIE BIRD: The ring-necked parakeet, left. The bird from India escaped into the wild in Britain in the 1960s

Top 10 garden birds
- Starling
- House sparrow
- Blue tit
- Blackbird
- Chaffinch
- Greenfinch
- Collared dove
- Great tit
- Wood pigeon
- Robin

By **John Ingham**
Environment Editor

A NOISY, bolshie bright green parakeet is destined to be Britain's bird of the 21st century, experts predicted yesterday.

The ring-necked parakeet, a member of the parrot family that is found across northern India, escaped into the wild in Britain in the 1960s. Its stronghold is in southern England, where about 4,000 live.

But the 24th Big Garden Birdwatch – the largest ever British wildlife survey – found that the parakeet, which has a red bill and long pointed tail, is spreading.

The Royal Society for the Protections of Birds claimed it is set to emulate the population boom enjoyed by the collared dove in the 20th century. In 50 years, the dove spread from Turkey right across Europe to most corners of the UK.

An RSPB spokesman said: "Ring-necked parakeets will eventually get into the top 10 of garden birds, probably in the next 20 years.

"They are already expanding very quickly. They will be the collared dove of the 21st century.

"But they may pose problems because they are fruit eaters and are big, bolshie, colourful characters. They nest in holes in trees and have already taken over woodpecker nests."

More than 250,000 birdwatchers – five times more than expected – spent an hour during the last weekend of January recording the highest number of species seen in their garden or local park. The watchers included 41,000 children.

Starlings took top spot in the battle of the back garden birds, with house sparrows finishing runners-up and blue tits in third place as the most common visitors to gardens throughout the country.

Next came blackbirds, chaffinches, greenfinches, collared doves, great tits, wood pigeons and robins.

But the figures reveal a rapidly changing picture. The average numbers of starlings in each garden dropped from 15 in 1979 to 4.5 in 2002 and house sparrow numbers fell from 10 per cent to four per cent, mirroring their decline since 1970.

When the survey was launched in 1979, the collared dove and wood pigeon did not come even close to being the most popular birds.

Losers since that first survey include the song thrush, which came seventh then, and the dunnock, which was tenth. This year they did not figure.

Song thrush numbers have plunged by 59 per cent while dunnocks have dropped by 44 per cent.

The success of the survey astonished the RSPB. Officials had hoped to double the previous record of 52,000 participants but numbers soared fivefold despite cold weather. Last night Big Garden Birdwatch co-ordinator Richard Bashford said: "We are delighted that so many people across the UK took part in the survey.

"More than a quarter of a million people took part – around four times as many as will be at the Millennium Stadium in Cardiff to watch this year's FA Cup Final between Arsenal and Chelsea.

"It's a fantastic response and demonstrates just how much interest people have in the birds around them."

THE INDEPENDENT
Thursday April 25 2002

Birdwatchers confirm plight of starlings and sparrows

BY BRIAN UNWIN

MORE THAN 250,000 people – twice the expected number – participated in the biggest mass birdwatch in the gardens, parks and schoolgrounds of Britain at the end of January.

But the results of the Big Garden Birdwatch provided a depressing reminder of the continuing decline of Britain's most common birds, the starling and the house sparrow.

Although more of these species were spotted – 700,000 and 673,000 respectively – well ahead of the blue tit in the No 3 spot on 455,000, the survey shows starling numbers have dropped by 70 per cent and house sparrows by 57 per cent since 1979. Both are candidates for the official red list of species of conservation concern. Garden Birdwatch, organised annually for the past 23 years by the Royal Society for the Protection of Birds, has monitored their decline.

The figures tally with the evidence produced by *The Independent*'s two-year campaign to find a cause for the sparrow slump, particularly in urban centres, their former strongholds. In a classic example, in Kensington Gardens, London, only 12 were counted in the summer of 2000, compared with 2,603 in 1925.

Also in the summer of 2000, checks in the centre of Sunderland found only eight sparrows – yet in the RSPB survey 56 were counted in one garden just five miles away at the village of Whitburn, highlighting the stark contrast between city centres and semi-rural areas on their outskirts. Richard Bashford, the survey co-ordinator, said such results confirmed the disappearance of sparrows from population centres.

Despite the bad news, he was delighted with the response of the public. "More than a quarter of a million people was far beyond what we hoped to achieve – it was a fantastic response, demonstrating the extent of public interest in birds. Also with over 4 million birds counted nationally, it shows how important gardens are to wildlife – add them all together and we have a quite considerable nature reserve."

Unlike sparrows and starlings, some species are increasing in numbers. The garden populations of collared doves – which only colonised Britain in the 1950s – were the

A blue tit (top) and a blackbird

MOST COMMON GARDEN BIRDS

1) Starling: More than 700,000 counted but the starling population is down by 70 per cent since 1979.

2) House sparrow: 673,000. Numbers have fallen almost as sharply as starling (57 per cent).

3) Blue tit: 455,000. Found to be in particular decline in Scotland and Northern Ireland.

4) Blackbird: Spotted the length and breadth of the United Kingdom. 411,000 recorded.

5) Chaffinch: Commonest garden bird in Scotland, seen relatively infrequently in England. Total sightings 369,000.

seventh most commonly seen species and the woodpigeon ninth. Populations have increased by 500 per cent since the survey began. Milder winters are given as the reason for the 150 per cent increase in the numbers of wrens since 1979.

Blackbirds were found to be the most widespread UK garden birds, cropping up in 89 per cent of all gardens, and other similar areas, covered by the survey. However, the distribution maps showed lower numbers in more westerly and southerly parts of the country – probably a reflection of greater breeding success in eastern regions.

Look carefully at each report and think about the things they have in common. Here are some ideas:

When analysing newspaper articles and reports, be specific, give examples and comment on them. Remember to look at all the features, not just the text.

Things in common

- They are based on the same survey and information.
- They report the same results and facts and figures.
- They both report a decline in numbers of some common species.

However, although they both draw on the same information, there are some significant differences in how it is presented.

Differences

Daily Express	The Independent
THE HEADLINE	
• The headline creates a light-hearted tone and gives the impression (misleadingly in some respects) that the article will be amusing.	• The headline creates a serious tone, speaking of the '*plight*' of starlings and sparrows.
THE CONTENT	
• The article features the spread of the ring-necked parakeet. Almost half of the article is given over to describing the bird, its habits, characteristics etc. and the prediction that they will become common in the next 20 years. • The results of the survey are then described and the drop in the number of birds observed noted and put in the context of a general decline. • The success of the survey in terms of the number of people taking part is noted and a comparison drawn between these numbers and those who will watch the FA Cup Final.	• The content focuses on the serious issues of the '*depressing*' picture the survey presents of the continued decline of Britain's most common birds. • It regards the results as '*bad news*' and uses specific examples to back up the idea of a decline in bird numbers. • The one encouraging thing was the number of people who took part.
THE LIST	
• Title "*Top 10 garden birds*" keeps the lighter tone. • Ten birds are listed – no further details given. The list has a picture of a starling with it.	• Clearly entitled '*Most Common Garden Birds*'. • The first five are listed together with specific details.
THE PHOTOGPAPHS	
• The photograph shows the head of the ring-necked parakeet. Readers will probably not be familiar with this species so it gives them some idea what it looks like but doesn't focus on the key point of the report – the declining population of **native** garden birds.	• The photographs show two of the five most common garden birds. This helps the reader visualise exactly which birds they are talking about (if they don't know already).

KEY POINT Articles about the same story can be very different in terms of the message they put across and the effect they create.

5.2 Looking at advertising

After studying this section you should be able to understand:

- **some of the features of advertisements**
- **product advertisements**
- **charity advertisements**

Some features of advertisements

Advertising is all around us. We encounter it every day and in all kinds of ways. The range of advertising and the techniques it uses are vast, but in the end all advertising has one thing in common – to make us **behave** or **think** in a particular way. Not surprisingly, advertising is big business and a huge amount of money is spent each year in producing advertisements. It has become such a specialised business in modern times that many companies employ agencies to design and advertise their products for them.

Advertising agencies usually do several things to ensure that their advertising works:

- They carry out market research to make sure that their advertising campaign is correctly **targeted** and likely to be successful.
- They assess the strengths and qualities of the product they are advertising and sample **consumer reactions** to it.
- They use their imaginative, artistic and language skills to produce an **appropriate** advert.

All the adverts we will look at in this section are the product of all these processes.

In designing an advert, the advertiser takes a number of factors into account:

- **The appeal** – all adverts are designed to appeal to something within us. For example, wealth or status, comfort, security, fashion sense, leisure pursuit, health fears, conscience etc.
- **The headlines or slogans** – these are the key words that catch the eye and draw attention to the advert. They need to be eye-catching and persuasive.
- **The language of the advert** – some adverts rely entirely on photographs or pictures of some kind and contain no words. Some rely entirely on the catchy slogan or headline. Many use text as well in order to create their effects and they use particular techniques to make the language they use as effective as possible.

Here are some features that you will often find in the 'language of advertising':
- Exaggeration – words are often used to claim that the product is the best in some way – the fastest, most comfortable, most advanced etc.
- Imperatives – verbs that issue commands, like 'Buy now!', 'Don't miss this!' etc.
- Claims that cannot be proved, like 'this will save you money', 'the finest that money can buy'.
- Repetition – key words are often repeated to drive the message home.
- Appealing words – such as 'bargain', 'beautiful', 'luxurious' etc.

- Sound appeal – the use of alliteration, assonance or rhyme, e.g. 'silky and super soft'.
- Words that appeal to taste – 'tangy', 'tasty', 'sweet' etc.
- The use of imagery – similes are commonly used, e.g. 'as fresh as morning dew'.
- The use of pseudo-technical or scientific language.
- The use of humour and puns (plays on words) – words with double meanings are often used.

> The effects of an advert are often the result of a combination of a number of factors.

KEY POINT

When analysing advertisements, look for:
- the visual impact
- who the advert is designed to appeal to
- the use of the slogan and pictures
- the language used
- the relationship between these features

Product advertisements

Adverts for a vast range of products appear in newspapers and magazines. Sometimes they can look very simple but often there is more to them than first appears.

When analysing them, you should consider four basic things:

- **Picture/layout** – look carefully at the way the pictures and words are arranged.
- **Slogan** or **catchwords** – these are often in large print and immediately obvious.
- **Blurb** – the more detailed text, describing the product, giving information about it etc. This is often in smaller print.
- **Effect** – the overall effect produced by the advertisement.

Look at the two adverts on pages 73 and 74.

PROGRESS CHECK

Think about the approach each adopts to advertising the product and write down your ideas.

The W800i Walkman Phone
- Picture of phone centre page – eye drawn to it immediately.
- The headline *'Soundtrack to your life'* suggests the idea of personalised music choices, which are important to the individual.
- Underneath this slightly larger lettering we get the model number and trade name, *'Walkman'* and it is clear that this is also a phone.
- The earphone wires are arranged to create the impression of a lively figure full of movement.
- The text at the bottom of the page gives some important information such as how many tracks it will hold, the ease with which you can transfer music from CDs or computer.
- The phrase *'crystal clear stereo headset'* emphasises the sound quality.
- Attention is drawn to the *'2.0 Megapixel camera with auto focus'*.
- The phrases *'breathtaking shots'* and *'prized music collection'* make what the phone has to offer sound really special.

The Soundtrack to your Life
THE W800i WALKMAN™ PHONE

The WALKMAN™ logo and symbol are registered trademarks of Sony Corporation. WALKMAN™ is a registered trademark of Sony Corporation. Headset image is not representative of the HPM-70.

Carry up to 125 of your favourite tracks on your mobile with the new Sony Ericsson W800i WALKMAN™ Phone. Simply transfer songs from your computer or CDs and enjoy your music through the crystal clear stereo headset. The W800i also has a 2.0 Megapixel camera with auto focus. So you can take breathtaking shots and store them alongside your prized music collection.

Sony Ericsson

www.SonyEricsson.com/W800i

certain
    people
        have
          it.

unique
1-Bit
technology
    from Sharp

As if by a sixth sense, some people just seem to know exactly where the future's heading. Which explains why they're always the first to experience new ideas, like our unique 1-Bit audio technology. This lets you hear what was impossible, until now. Bringing together all the warmth of analogue and clarity of a digital recording it recreates more than just the music, it recreates the original performance space itself. 1-Bit CD/MD systems from Sharp. **1** BIT TECHNOLOGY   The future of audio, for certain.   **SHARP**

Sharp 1-Bit Technology

PROGRESS
CHECK

- The catchwords '*certain people have it*' suggests that the product is for 'special' people – if you buy it, you will become part of an exclusive elite.
- The word '*unique*' gives the impression that no other system is like this one.
- 1-bit technology is the use of a kind of scientific jargon – we probably don't know what it means but it sounds impressive.
- The photograph, which forms the background to the whole advertisement, shows the sound system in a kind of hi-tech modern environment. The smartly dressed man with dark glasses representing the elite '*certain people*', creating the impression that 'special' people have this equipment.
- The text focuses on '*some people*' – the ones who have the vision to appreciate the new technology. It suggests that if you buy the product you will become one of the first to experience new ideas.
- The second part of the text describes what marks Sharp's sound systems out as special – they let '*...you hear what was impossible, until now*'.
- The large type name in contrasting red at the bottom of the advert leaves you with the name of the manufacturer – SHARP.
- The advert uses little text but appeals very strongly to the image of the potential buyer being young, discriminating and having very good taste.

Charity advertising

Not all advertisements are designed to sell products. Advertising is also often used by charities or other groups or organisations who believe in a specific cause. Very often the purpose of these advertisements is to persuade you to join a particular organisation or to donate your time and/or money to help support it.

Look at these two advertisements.

SHE HAS NOWHERE LEFT TO TURN.

PLEASE DON'T TURN THE PAGE

PHOTO: MARK MCNULTY

You could be Tsering's last hope. She has little or no food to eat, and lives in a tiny, insanitary mud shack. Without help soon she could die.

Yet by sponsoring an elderly person like Tsering for just £3 a week, you could provide the food, clothing and medicines they need to survive.

In return, you'll receive regular reports on your adopted grandparent. For more details, please complete the form below.

Yes, I'm interested in helping an elderly person overseas. Please send me details.

Mr / Mrs / Miss / Ms

Address

Postcode   Tel.No.

98 22 - APX BD01

Help the Aged

Adopt a Granny
Registered Charity No. 272786

www.dianfossey.org

Adopt a *Gorilla*

...for your valentine

£24

Amy is a six year old mountain gorilla. One of only 650 left in the world. For just £24* a year you can adopt her and help the Dian Fossey Gorilla Fund protect all the endangered mountain gorillas from extinction. In return we'll send you a beautifully illustrated T-shirt, a photograph of Amy and your own adoption certificate.

Adoptions make a perfect gift

Call today to order your Amy adoption gift pack

Yes, I want to adopt Amy

☐ for myself   ☐ as a gift for the person named at B. below

A. My name is (Mr/Mrs/Ms) _____

Address _____

_____ Postcode _____

Tel/day _____ Tel/evening _____

B. Their name is (Mr/Mrs/Ms) _____

Address _____

_____ Postcode _____

Tel/day _____ Tel/evening _____

Age of adopter if under 16 _____

Please send T-shirt size: S ☐ M ☐ L ☐ XL ☐

I enclose a cheque/PO for *£24 ☐
made payable to The Dian Fossey Gorilla Fund
OR Please debit my

Visa ☐   Access ☐   Switch ☐   Amex ☐

Expires _____ / _____   Switch issue number _____

Signed _____   Date _____

*£4.95 pays for the gift pack and contributions beyond this are a donation to the fund. The pack is available without the donation.

Thank you

The Dian Fossey
Gorilla Fund
Reg Charity No. 801160

What do these two advertisements have in common?

They both use a technique that is commonly used in this type of advertising – that of **adopting** or **sponsoring** somebody or something.

This type of advertisement often offers you something in return for your sponsorship. Usually this is in the form of information on your 'adoptee', and perhaps a photograph, reports and news about them as time goes by.

Now look at this advertisement and think about the techniques it uses to achieve its effects.

Here are some ideas:

- It uses little **text** but has a strong **visual** effect.
- **Visual impact** – the cardboard box on a newspaper strewn on the office floor, and the tatty office chair create an image of the cardboard boxes that the homeless sometimes sleep in and the tatty environment of 'perhaps' a derelict office in which they might sleep. Notice how colour is used to contrast the grey cardboard box against the subdued blue background.
- **Main text** – the large print '*75%*' catches the eye and leads us to read the remainder, which refers to the number of '*Big Issue in the North*' vendors who have slept rough in the last 12 months.
- **Impact** – this high figure has a shock effect that so many have nowhere to sleep. This is followed by information on how many people the Big Issue in the North Trust helps to find temporary accommodation.
- **Remaining text** – the remaining text reinforces the good work that the Trust does and ends by appealing for support.

> **KEY POINT**
>
> **Charity advertisements work in the same way as other adverts but their purpose and some of their techniques are slightly different. On the whole, though, they use the same techniques as other kinds of advertisements.**

5.3 *Film and television*

LEARNING SUMMARY

After studying this section you should be able to understand:
- *the purpose of film and television previews and reviews*
- *interviews with stars*
- *the moving image*

Previews and reviews

Film and television previews and reviews appear every day in a whole range of publications, from newspapers to specialist film and television magazines. Although previews and reviews are often similar in style and content, they do have different purposes.

The preview

A preview of a film or television programme is written to be read before a film is released or before a television programme is screened. It serves several functions including:

- giving the reader an idea of **what** the film or programme is about but **without** revealing so much as to spoil the later enjoyment of it
- giving an idea of **who** is in it
- giving some **background** about the actors, production etc.
- telling the reader **when** it will be released, screened etc.

The review

This is a report on a film or programme that has already been screened. It also has several functions, including:
- giving an **outline** of what the film or programme is about for those who haven't seen it
- giving **information** on who is in it
- giving views on the **strengths and weaknesses** of aspects of the film or programme, e.g. the acting, the plot, the setting etc.
- commenting on the **overall success** of the film or programme

Here is an example of a preview that was published nine months before the release of the film.

FORTHCOMING SEQUELS

THE LORD OF THE RINGS: THE TWO TOWERS

Peter Jackson's fantasy epic moves into second gear!

Frodo (Elijah Wood), catching that troublesome ring

YOU COULD almost hear the sigh from half way around the world, a huge sense of relief that **The Fellowship of the Ring** turned out so well. Because the three **Lord of the Rings** movies were made as one production, the treatment of all three will be more or less the same. If Peter Jackson had got it wrong, we (and he) could have been in for a painful couple of years. But he got it more than right, and we can be pretty sure that **The Two Towers** and **The Return of the King** will be of similarly high quality.

To an extent, we also know what to expect. Now that we've seen how **Fellowship** was tackled, what we'll get from **The Two Towers** will be a similar version of that book. As a book of **The Two Towers** poses a different set of problems than **Fellowship**. It is by far the least eventful as the plotlines are already up and running as it opens and they aren't wrapped up at the end. Instead, we flit between the two groups of characters as they progress through a sequence of ordeals and tribulations.

While doing the promotional rounds for **Fellowship**, Peter Jackson gave some indications as to how he and his scripting team (Frances Walsh, Philippa Boyens and Stephen Sinclair) have tackled it. One of the problems they have faced with all three films is that the female roles are quite weak. **The Two Towers** is the most problematical chapter on this count. Accordingly, Liv Tyler will feature again as Arwen, despite the fact that the character does not appear in the book. For similar reasons, and to provide more variety in the material, the romance between Faramir and Eowyn will be expanded.

"It's a 50-year-old book," says Jackson. "We can't change the title. Tolkien fans would crucify us!"

The title will not change despite the extra dimension that it has gained since September 11. "It's a 50-year-old book," Jackson told the *Chicago Sun-Times*. "We can't change the title. Tolkien fans would crucify us."

Thus far, the fact that Tolkien fans *haven't* crucified the production team is remarkable. It's a well-worn cliché that big-screen adaptations can never quite live up to the books on which they are based, and the bigger the cult following a book has, the tougher the fans are to please. It's hard to find anybody, however, who doesn't agree that **Fellowship** was a damn fine piece of work. This generous reception will hopefully continue for the rest of the trilogy.

Rings fans should be getting their first look at **The Two Towers** right about now, as a preview was put together and attached to the final reel of **Fellowship** at the end of March. This will give audiences an excuse to hand over yet more cash to see **Fellowship** in the last few weeks of its theatrical run, adding to the already vast amount of money it has taken at the box-office.

Because **Fellowship** has already recouped the production costs of the trilogy on its own, this also means that the pressure is off for **The Two Towers**: any more cash that **Lord of the Rings** makes is pure profit. The trilogy can only get bigger from here. *ER*

SEQUEL TO The Lord of the Rings: The Fellowship of the Ring (2001) **STARS** Elijah Wood, Ian McKellen, Sean Astin, Viggo Mortensen, Liv Tyler, Orlando Bloom, Billy Boyd **DIRECTOR** Peter Jackson **OPENING DATE** December 13 TBC

64 FILM REVIEW SPECIAL #39

PROGRESS CHECK

What features of a preview can you identify here?

Here are some ideas:

- It establishes a link between the new film and the first film.
- It highlights some differences between them.
- Because it is based on Tolkien's books, we know what it is about.
- Some reference is made to how problems were tackled.
- Details of the opening date are given.

Here is a review of the well-known film, *Harry Potter and the Goblet of Fire*:

HARRY POTTER AND THE GOBLET OF FIRE 12A

The first year of GCSEs for Harry'n'chums. Time to grow up. Again...

OPENS 18 NOVEMBER

Director *Mike Newell*
Starring *Daniel Radcliffe, Emma Watson, Rupert Grint, Michael Gambon*
Screenplay *Steven Kloves*
Distributor *Warner Bros*
Running time *157 mins*

WHAT'S THE STORY?
It's Harry Potter's (Daniel Radcliffe) fourth year at Hogwarts and the shadow of He-Who-Shall-Not-Be-Named looms ever closer. The last thing Harry needs is the international Triwizard Tournament. Or the even scarier prospect of finding a date for the Yule Ball...

Half-smoked Marlboro and Diamond White in hand, Harry turns to Ron and belches, "That Cho Chang is really hot. But she's well out of my league and, like, I've got all that Voldemort stuff to sort out." "Bloody hell, mate. Girls? Eurgh!" slurs Ron. "Oh, honestly," shrieks Hermione. "Men!"

Not really. But our spell-casting sprogs are shooting up so sharpish that Dumbledore's "dark and difficult times lie ahead" portent applies just as much to puberty as it does to the constant threat of the Avada Kedavra curse.

The fourth instalment of JK Rowling's absurdly successful boy-wizard books is the one everyone's been tingly for, with the promise of fantastic set-pieces, intertwining subplots and adolescent blossoming. To the latter's end, Rupert Grint's Ron has – gasp – started swearing, Harry's getting all flushed around Cho (Katie Leung) while Emma Watson's Hermione emotes like the not-a-girl-not-yet-a-woman 15-year-old she is. Never more comfortable than with the "well-mannered frivolity" of the terrific Yule Ball, Mike Newell's *Four Weddings* touch gives Hogwarts' teens an everyday edge – girls grow up faster, boys are crap, teen parties end in tears. "They're scary when they get older!" exclaims Ron after a hormonal Hermione hollering.

But, of course, this is Hogwarts, where there be spells, weirdos (newcomer 'Mad-Eye' Moody, riotously played by Brendan Gleeson) and the parent-consent-form-dodging Triwizard Tournament. Killer dragons and carnivorous mazes form the crux of the 636-page novel and, with much to cram, Newell makes a breakneck start, continuing at a pace that isn't too fussed about holding newcomers' hands. But this rushing pushes the thrillingly realised Quidditch World Cup into a five-minute slot without any actual Quidditch and trims back faves Snape, Malfoy and Sirius Black to cameos.

On top of the virgin-baffling torrent of new characters and replaced characters and major developments whizzing by as bite-sized chunks, Newell is also clearly constrained by the book's flip treatment of key moments. On the page, they seem sharp and shocking, but up on-screen, jarring and underdeveloped.

In other words it's Harry's game – and Radcliffe's stage – to prove he can convey the burden of having the entire magical world perched on his slender shoulders. And up against Ralph Fiennes' terrifying Voldemort (slits for nostrils, rotting body, Nosferatu stoop) Radcliffe's range of corny startles still feels lacking.

Still, like *Star Wars*, the acting quibbles are absorbed into Newell's bigger, crowd-pleasing picture of spell and spectacle. But consider this: next in the series is the 776-page, filler-packed snorefest *The Order Of The Phoenix* – entirely empty of *Goblet*'s set-piece sexiness, meaning Harry's box-office dazzle may yet dim. Dark and difficult times indeed for the franchise, the magical world and tortured teens with little hairs sprouting in odd places.
Jonathan Dean

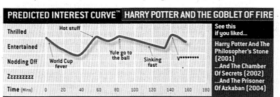

PREDICTED INTEREST CURVE™ HARRY POTTER AND THE GOBLET OF FIRE

See this if you liked...
Harry Potter And The Philosopher's Stone (2001)
...And The Chamber Of Secrets (2002)
...And The Prisoner Of Azkaban (2004)

VERDICT
Newell vividly conjures up a world fraught with real danger. Potter nuts will lap it up, but those just flirting may feel like gatecrashers at the ball.
★★★

Look carefully at the structure and content of this review.

| Brief summary of the story | Comments on the 'teenage' elements of the film and the way that Harry is more grown up | References to the book and the problems of translating this into film | Some comments on the film's weaknesses | An overall comment and judgement on the success of the film |

PROGRESS CHECK

What other features might you comment on in this review?

- The effect of the catch-line 'The first year of GCSEs for Harry'n'chums'.
- The use of humour in the writing.
- The attention to detail in the comments.
- The use of the photographs and visual features.

Interviews

Interviews with the stars of film and television are very popular with the public, whether performed on television chat shows or published in print in magazines, newspapers or on websites. When produced to be read rather than seen and heard, they can be presented in a variety of ways. Two examples are described below.

In the first example, the interview is presented as a kind of transcript where the interviewer's questions are asked and the actor's response given in the words they used. Here, *Emmerdale* star Emma Atkins is interviewed for the *Emmerdale* official website.

itv .com

Home   TV guide   Soaps & Dramas   Gameshows   Entertainment   Lifestyle   Sport

Home
Gossip
Show Updates
Games & Prizes
Video
Chat
History
Shop
Message Boards

Emmerdale
The Official Website

Interview with Emma Atkins – Part One

On Emmerdale and Acting
Was it daunting entering such a well-established soap?

Emma says: It was a bit scary at first and I was still doing a degree at University when I got the audition and I thought I would go for the experience. I didn't think I would get the job. Then I got a recall the same day. Had a really good audition and two weeks later I got the call to say I'd got the job. Everyone is so lovely and nice here that it wasn't daunting for long. We are one big family here.

You have been playing Charity for a while now. Did you think she would become such a central character in the show?

Emma says: I certainly think that she has grown into her own entity now and is one on her own. She is a Dingle and a Tate, she is rough and ready and also has the astute business side to her and she never used to have that. She has always been very street wise and she came in as a prostitute and she is now no longer that. She wheedled her way into Chris Tate's life and is building up Tate enterprises.

Do you think the producers or storyliners had another Kim Tate style character in mind then?

Emma says: Yes probably they have although I would like to think she would be different from Kim Tate, because to just turn Charity into another bitch from hell I think that would be a bit repetitive and not necessarily what the audience wants to see. Although it does work all this conflict and confrontation. Marriage can't be made in heaven forever as it becomes boring in soap land. She has definitely got to continue to be mischievous and devious.

Are there any surprises in store for her in the near future?

Emma says: Definitely, we have just had the immigrant storyline which is coming on to the screen soon. The follow up to that no one knows where it will go. You will have to wait and see. There is always room for things to go wrong with Charity as she always goes headfirst into things. So I hope there will be a lot more trouble on the cards.

What would be your ideal acting role?

Emma says: To play the lead in a gritty drama or a great British film. A kind of Cold Feet drama-based thing perhaps. I want to be able to play lots of different and varied roles. I would like to go back and do a bit of Shakespeare in the theatre. I want to try a bit of everything. I would also love to do a voice over for something like the Simpsons.

Who or what inspired you to act?

Emma says: Nobody really inspired me really. I used to take part in all the classes at school and joined a drama group called The Bottle Shop on Saturday afternoons in Lancaster and it went from there really. And I thought oh I like this. We use to have to improvise and I never knew what that was. Then once I got into it I loved it, it's like make something up then act it out. It was absolutely fantastic and a lot more interesting than writing essays and reading text books. As soon as I experienced what it was like to perform I knew it was my kettle of fish.

Would you like to see more comedy written in to Charity's storylines?

Emma says: I feel there is enough comedy there actually. I feel that they (the storyliners) are writing really well for my character and I'm really pleased that when I pick up the script and I read really in your face, abrupt and abusive line, they are really comical and that's great.

Who would you like to work with if you had the chance?

Emma says: Definitely Julie Walters, Celia Imrie I think is fantastic and she really makes me laugh. There are so many.

On her background
Are you from a large family?

Emma says: Not really, there is my Mum and Dad and my sister who is a year older than I am.

Where did you grow up?

Emma says: I grew up in a village called Silverdale, which is near Kendal. A really beautiful little village close to Carnforth, a steam town where they filmed Brief Encounter years ago.

What did you want to be when you were growing up? Did you always want to act?

Emma says: Yes really just from being a kid and taking part in drama as I mentioned before. I always said if I weren't an actress I would be an artist or a teacher.

What is the best piece of advice anyone has ever given you?

Emma says: My Mum, for just telling me to be myself and be honest and don't be fake basically.

What was your worst job ever?

Emma says: Washing pans in a DHSS centre for two quid an hour. They always had fish for dinner and it stank. And the pans were really deep and you had to get your arms in them to clean them. It was disgusting and it make me chunder the whole time.

What is your most extravagant purchase?

Emma says: My car. It's only a Peugeot but it was still a lot to me.

What is your favourite CD or music artist?

Emma says: Joni Mitchell and Lauren Hill

Who is the most famous person you have ever met?

Emma says: A guy called Chris Moon at a business convention. He was giving a talk and he had been blown up in a landmine in Cambodia. He was like my hero and I was mesmerised by his talk on life and what he did in Cambodia - it was so interesting. I went straight out and bought his book. He does loads of running for charity to raise money for amputees in Cambodia, to get prosthetic limbs made. So I would say he is someone I met who I will never forget and who I look up to.
Also Steven Redgrave who I met at Buckingham Palace about three weeks ago, but Chris Moon definitely.

How did you celebrate your last birthday?

Emma says: I went out for a meal with my Mum and Dad, very simple.

Read the interview carefully and think about the following:

- the format of the interview
- the content of the interview
- the use of images

1 Format

The way the interview is presented gives a strong sense of being 'live', by using the **exact** words spoken. It also gives a sense of the **personality** of Emma Atkins because it is as if we can 'hear' the words spoken.

2 Content

The interviewer focuses on the topics readers might want to know about. The answers are quite full and by the time you reach the end of the interview there is a feeling that you have discovered things about the actress and, in a way, 'come to know her' a little better. This is, of course, exactly what fans would want.

3 The use of images

In this instance, the use of **images** is not directly related to the interview. They are 'stills' taken from episodes of *Emmerdale*. However, they do add **interest** to the interview by reminding you of what Emma Atkins looks like and the role she plays in the show.

Sometimes interviews are printed without any questions or a sense that an actual interview has taken place at all. Instead the edited comments of the star, perhaps focusing on one topic, are put together. This is how the interview with John Gordon Sinclair on page 83 was presented.

The effect of this is to produce a more 'in-depth' view of the actor's views. The interviewer becomes almost redundant in this kind of presentation.

KEY POINT | **Interviews can be presented in a number of ways and each creates a different effect and serves a different purpose. You should be aware of the differences between them.**

Learning curve

Actor John Gordon Sinclair, 40, came to fame over 20 years ago in Gregory's Girl. Better known now for appearing in commercials with Prunella Scales and Jane Horrocks, he tells DEANY JUDD...

What I wish I'd known at 21

The current trend to want to be famous, as characterised by shows such as Pop Idol, is totally beyond me. I think to be recognised for what you do, what you have achieved, is one thing, but to want to be famous for the sake of it I find disturbing. George Harrison had everything that our society deems to be important: fame, celebrity, money. Yet all he wanted was to find a meaning to his life and have his family around him. You have to ask yourself, if someone who has experienced the ultimate dream isn't content, then what exactly is it these people are aspiring to?

Experience has taught me that when it comes to auditions it's important not to let your ego get in the way. Auditioning is like being put on trial for a crime you haven't yet committed, and I used to take rejection personally. Having been on the other side, I now know what directors and producers are looking for is not necessarily whether you are capable of doing the job, but whether the chemistry is right between you and the other actors involved. I am now far more relaxed about the whole process.

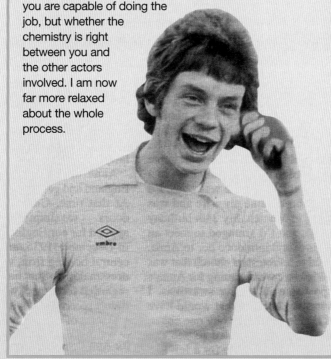

I'm a big believer in learning from others, especially those who have really been up against it and live to tell the tale. Viktor Frankl, the psychiatrist who survived Auschwitz, is one such person. He lost his family, his home, all his money, yet went on to help hundreds of people from all over the world come to terms with their lives. When asked how he managed to cope with what he had to endure, he said it was because he realised that if you were capable of loving someone and can experience the thrill of being in love then you have everything a human being could ever want. Over time, I've realised how true this is.
I have stopped watching the news. I don't want to know any more. In fact, I'd like to live in another country and only learn enough of the language to able to buy food and order a beer. That way, even if the news was on in a café or a bar, I wouldn't know what was being said and could think happy thoughts instead.

Another vital lesson life has taught me: if you have nothing meaningful to say, say nothing.

Happiness really does come from the simple things in life. The French philosopher Montaigne, who could speak five or six languages and was an expert at virtually everything, was sitting on a mountainside when he observed that the goat he was watching eating grass seemed happy and contented, even though it knew nothing. It was probably happier than he was; a man who knew a lot. He concluded that having little or no knowledge would probably make for a more sanguine life. The things that make me happy now are simple things.

John Gordon Sinclair is appearing in a touring production of Tom Stoppard's The Real Thing, *starting May 15, Plymouth Theatre Royal.*

The moving image

Films and television programmes are made up of images that, when seen together, create an impression in the mind of the viewer. Usually dialogue is important too, either through what characters say or commentaries, on documentaries, sports programmes etc.

Here is a series of images from an episode of the soap *Coronation Street*. Fred goes to the house of his wife's ex-husband who he suspects of having an affair with her.

itv .com

Home   TV guide   Soaps & Dramas   Gameshows   Entertainment   Lifestyle   Sport   News & Weather   Kids   Regi

HOME
GOSSIP
EPISODE SUMMARIES
UK Updates
SNEAK PREVIEWS
GAMES & PRIZES
WHO'S WHO
MESSAGE BOARDS
SHOP
HELPLINES
SET VISITS

Meanwhile, on a certain council estate Fred knocks on an all too familiar door.

He immediately confronts Ray Sykes, 'You know who I am.'
'Do I?', says Ray, calmly. 'You should do..', replies Fred, 'You were snooping around my shop earlier. What's going on between you and my wife?'
Ray replies, 'Nothing.' Fred tells him he may be many things but stupid isn't one of them, 'I saw the both of you here last night!' Ray tells him he'd better come inside.

Fred refuses Ray's offer of a drink and demands to know what's going on. 'Hasn't she told you herself?', asks Ray.
'I want to hear it from you!', snarls Fred.
Ray shakes his head, 'You don't get it do you? I'm Ray, Ray Sykes. Her ex. Him she was married to before you came along.'

Fred scowls, 'So what are you doing round here. Trying to get her away from me?'
Ray replies calmly, 'You'll have to ask her.'
Fred roars, 'I don't need to. I can see what's going on. You're having an affair!'

'An affair?', says Ray, 'I'm not the one having an affair. If it's anyone..... it's you!'
Fred is nonplussed but Ray continues, 'And if anyone here is the injured party it's me see......

....We never got a divorce. I'm still married to her!'

Look carefully at the images. Notice the contrast between the facial expressions of Fred and Ray and the way in which the camera moves into close focus so that the viewers can see these clearly. We can see that Ray looks calm and composed, whereas Fred looks angry in Frame 4 and shocked in Frame 6.

Now look at the next series of frames, which show a confrontation between teacher Ken Barlow and one of his students, Aiden.

Ken's in the middle of a lesson regarding retaliation versus being reasonable when the two latecomers finally arrive. He reprimands them but doesn't give them any punishment saying, 'I don't suppose being late for one lesson will do any harm'
'That's very "reasonable" of you sir!', pipes up Aiden loudly, 'Just like the bloke in the book.'
Ken smiles, 'Well, as I said, the ability to be reasonable is the backbone of any civilized society '

'So if I came up and shoved you against the wall you'd react reasonably would you?', sneers the truculent teen.

And before you can say Grange Hill Reject the lad is out of his seat and squaring up to our Ken.
Ken tells him to get back to his seat. 'I find that an unreasonable request!', the lad snarls back.
Ken tells him, 'I don't care what you find it. Now go back to your seat!'
Aiden pushes Ken and sneers, 'When I push you, you're supposed to react reasonably.'
Ken tells him, 'I'm warning you. Go back to your seat....now!'

The lad backs off, telling Ken, 'I'm just trying to get to the truth that's all. You're always telling us we should look for the truth.'

Fortunately the lesson is quickly over but it would appear, as the whey-faced pupil smirks his way out, that Ken is somewhat rattled by the confrontation.

PROGRESS CHECK

What impression do you get of this situation from these frames? How does the camerawork help to create these impressions?

Tension seems to increase quickly from Ken teaching his lesson to the close up confrontation as Aiden moves up to face him, invading his space in a threatening manner.

The camera initially focuses on Ken teaching the class; then it focuses in a little closer to highlight Aiden sitting among the other students. As he moves in to confront Ken, the camera focuses in close so we can see the unpleasant, aggressive look on his face. The camera then switches to Ken again in close focus so we can see that he is both displeased and troubled by Aiden's actions. In the last frame we can see clearly the smug smirk on Aiden's face as he moves away, which suggests that he feels he has come out on top in this encounter.

From looking at these frames you can see that:

- when filming a scene, different camera shots produce different effects
- placing people or objects in a particular place within a film frame is called **framing** and directors use this to produce particular effects
- focusing in close on the faces of the characters can add to the tension of a dramatic movement
- changing from one shot to another is called **cutting** and the director uses this to show the contrast between the expression and reactions of characters

KEY POINT   A combination of factors can create effects used in film and television.

Sample GCSE questions

In the following article the actor Ricky Tomlinson discusses his life. Read it through carefully and then answer the questions that follow.

My best teacher
Ricky Tomlinson

The story so far

1939 Born in Blackpool. Grows up in Liverpool
1955 Leaves school to become a plasterer. Tours pubs as stand-up comedian
1972 A trade union activist in the building industry, he is one of the jailed 'Shrewsbury Two'
1975 Released from jail, turns to banjo-playing in pubs and acting
1982 Lands first major TV role as Bobby Grant in *Brookside*, **which he plays for five years. Followed by various series including** *Cracker*, *The Royle Family* **and** *Clocking Off*
2001 Supports Arthur Scargill against Labour MP Peter Mandelson in general election. Takes title role in *Mike Bassett: England Manager*, **now on general release**

To do anything and get anywhere you've got to be a daydreamer. A long time ago I used to daydream about being a real actor and now it's come true, so I've been lucky.

Several teachers at school in Liverpool had a special influence on me. I went to Hayworth Street school, where there was an English and arts teacher called Mr Jackson — "Jacko". He was quite severe, but if he went out of the room for a minute he'd turn to me to keep the class occupied. I was only 12 but he'd say: "Tommo, get up there and tell the class a story." And I did. And it was like nothing; it was easy.

Then, at Venice Street, there was an English teacher called Mr Vurnette. He ran a theatre called the Birkenhead Bright Lights. He took us all down there once a year and I remember looking at the stage and thinking, "Wow! That's great. I love that". So from an early age acting was calling me.

I moved schools again when I passed the 13-plus, which was for those of us they thought should've passed the 11-plus but hadn't. So I ended up going to Walton technical college, and I stayed there until I was 16.

Elwyn Jones was another English teacher who encouraged me to write. Unknown to him I was a closet writer. I was always the leader of the gang as a schoolboy, so I guess it was these teachers who harnessed my enthusiasm and stopped me going off the rails.

The biggest influence on my life, without a shadow of a doubt, was my mother, Peggy. At the age of 86 she's still a great driving force and she's brilliant. I was a working-class kid with three brothers living not far from the docks in Liverpool. I was a bit of a rough diamond, but she was a great steadying influence. She bought me my first banjo when I was 17, so I learned to entertain. I started doing the pubs and clubs and began to see myself as a performer, even though I got into the construction industry.

So I learned a lot at school and at home, and I was able to take this on and use it positively when I spent two years in prison for industrial action. [In 1972, Tomlinson was sentenced to two years for conspiracy after being involved in a demonstration that turned violent during the national building workers' strike.] I was a pretty awful prisoner, wouldn't wear clothes, went to the toilet on the floor, the lot. I was on hunger strike for 22 days.

I was in solitary confinement most of the time and had all the time in the world on my bloody hands. It was then that I discovered Radio 4, the classics, opera — stuff like that — and I started to write again by keeping a prison diary.

I'd been screaming inside to be a writer, but I never had time because I was always on building sites till eight in the evening and then going straight on to work in the social clubs. But in prison I suddenly had time to write poetry and read books, like *The Ragged Trousered Philanthropists*. I also found that music could reduce me to tears.

The higher I have gone up the ladder, the more chance I've had to read beautiful books and hear beautiful music. I know working-class kids don't have that chance, and it makes me angry and bitter. I never agreed with the 11-plus because children develop at different stages.

I'm probably learning more now at 62 than ever before. I would like to think there are still a few things I haven't done that I will get round to doing in the short time I have left. I'm still dreaming.

Actor Ricky Tomlinson was talking to **John Guy**

TES FRIDAY OCTOBER 12 2001

Sample GCSE questions

1. What is the main purpose of this article and what kind of audience do you think it is aimed at?

It seems that the key purpose of the article is for Ricky Tomlinson to tell the reader about his life. As the title suggests, he focuses particularly on his school days and discusses particular teachers who had an influence on his life. However, he does tell the reader something about his life beyond school too. The audience that this is written for could be quite wide. He is a well-known actor and therefore his comments and details about his life could interest a wide range of people, as people are always interested in reading about the lives of the famous.

> *Clear idea about purpose.*

> *Relevant deductions about the possible audience appeal.*

2. Analyse the ways in which the information is conveyed to the reader in this article. You might comment on:
   - the structure
   - the use of language
   - any other ideas you think important

The article is structured in a clear and logical way, which helps you to follow it. Ricky Tomlinson begins by talking about his schooldays and recalls teachers who had some kind of effect on him. He also talks about other influences on his life, particularly his mother. He then goes on to talk about what happened after school and the time he spent in prison. This gave him the opportunity to read and study and educate himself further. He finishes his piece by mentioning how he feels about life now.

> *Shows an awareness of structure and how the writer develops his ideas.*

The piece is written in the first person and so the reader gets a strong impression that this is the voice of Ricky Tomlinson talking to them directly. He uses straightforward language with the occasional mild swearword, "bloody", which emphasises the impression that this is his genuine voice. He also uses quotations, either from the people he mentions or himself in a different period of his life. The photograph and the headline catch the eye and the smaller heading gives an insight into what the article will be about. The boxed "The Story So Far" is useful as it gives a clear easily-read overview of his life and contains some interesting details that people might not know.

> *Awareness of the writer's voice and the effect that this has on the piece.*

> *Relevant points but could be developed a little more.*

> *Another relevant point could be supported with an example from the text.*

Exam practice questions

The following advert is to appeal to the reader to make a donation to the charity. Look at it carefully and analyse the techniques that it uses in order to achieve its effects.

You might consider:
- the use of headlines
- the use of illustrations
- the photographs
- the language used
- any other ideas you think important

You don't have to go to sea to need the lifeboat crews

It's not just sailors that need the Royal National Lifeboat Institution. It's all too easy to get into danger, even on dry land. Even on a seemingly fine day, conditions can rapidly take a turn for the worse. It just takes a freak wave or the tide to come in quickly to get a passer-by in trouble. But if the unthinkable does happen, you know that you or a loved one can rely on the RNLI's volunteer lifeboat crews to come to your rescue, just like 6,635 people did last year.

Among them were four children and their parents who were walking along the beach. The wind was very strong when Little and Broad Haven's lifeboat headed out to help the family, stranded by the rising tide at the foot of cliffs more than 200ft high. Contending with huge waves which very nearly capsized their boat, the crew brought all of them safely back to dry land.

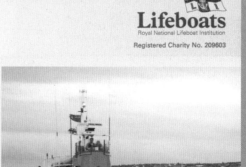

You never know when you or a loved one might need us

You know you can always rely on our volunteer lifeboat crews. Just £5 a month from you will help ensure the crews are always there, for your children and your children's children. It's reassuring to know that virtually all of your gift – 80% – will go directly towards saving lives at sea, leaving just 20% for vital fundraising and administration.

How the RNLI saves lives without even going to sea

The RNLI aims to make people aware of the hidden dangers of the sea by carrying out preventative and educational work – including visiting schools and talking to children. The Sea Safety campaign talks to sea and beach users and the SEA Check service gives free checks on boats to ensure that they have the right safety equipment. All this, plus groundbreaking work in lifeboat design and innovation, shows you the many ways in which the RNLI is saving lives.

You never know, one day you or a loved one might be very glad to see us

What can your £5 a month do?

The Royal National Lifeboat Institution depends entirely on voluntary donations to raise the £240,000 a day needed to stay afloat. There are 224 lifeboat stations around the coasts of the United Kingdom and Republic of Ireland. Over a year, your £5 a month could pay for a lifeboat to be at sea for over an hour. A vital hour which could save lives.

6 Non-fiction texts

The following topics are included in this chapter:

- **Approaching non-fiction texts**
- **Magazine articles**
- **Biographies and autobiographies**
- **Travel writing**
- **Documentary writing**
- **Literary non-fiction**

6.1 Approaching non-fiction texts

LEARNING SUMMARY

After studying this section you should be able to understand:

- **what non-fiction texts are**
- **the kinds of things you might be asked about them**
- **how to approach them**

The term 'non-fiction texts' is a very broad one, covering a wide range of very different kinds of writing, including:

- newspaper articles
- magazine articles
- information leaflets
- advertisements
- diary entries
- biographies and autobiographies
- letters
- travel writing

You will note that we covered some of these kinds of writing in the previous chapter, as they can come under the heading 'media texts' as well as 'non-fiction'.

Whatever the sources, all non-fiction texts have one or more of the following purposes:

- to inform
- to persuade
- to describe
- to advise
- to argue

In order to develop your understanding of non-fiction texts, read as widely and as frequently as possible.

In reading and writing about non-fiction texts, you need to be able to do a number of things:

- **understand** what the text is saying
- **distinguish** between **fact** and **opinion**
- follow an argument
- **select** material from the text to **suit** your task
- be **aware** of how the material is **presented**
- **understand** the effects created by the **ways** in which the material is written or presented

Whether you are writing about non-fiction texts as part of your exam or for coursework, you will understand the text more effectively if you approach it in a **systematic** manner.

Here is one way you could do this:

> Read the question or task carefully.

> Underline any key words or important words.

> Read the text through to get a general idea of what it is about – don't worry if you don't understand everything on the first read.

> Read the text again, this time looking for information that you will need to answer your question or complete your task.

6.2 Magazine articles

LEARNING SUMMARY

After studying this section you should be able to understand:

- *how to follow an argument*
- *how to distinguish between fact and opinion*
- *how illustrations and layout can contribute to the effect of an article*
- *the language techniques used to shape reader response*

Read the article on page 91 from the magazine *Wingbeat*, which is aimed at teenagers.

Following the argument

Having read the article, the first stage is to identify the main point of the argument. This seems very clear here.

Argument: The killing of birds in France is illegal and should be stopped.

Now let's look carefully at how the writer develops that argument.

Paragraph 1: Outlines the range of methods used to kill the birds and points out that it is illegal.

Hunters take aim for migrant massacre

French hunters embark on an orgy of bird killing this month, set to last until the end of next February.

They'll be shooting, netting, trapping in cages, snaring with nooses, or coating branches with glue to bring down unsuspecting victims. It's tough on the blackbirds, song thrushes, skylarks, lapwings, curlews, whimbrels, and others. It's also illegal.

Under pressure from the powerful hunting lobby, the French parliament has passed a law that extends the hunting season into the period when many birds are migrating or preparing to breed. It breaks European regulations set up to protect wild birds. Other countries abide by these regulations, which close the hunting season in January, before migration and breeding starts. Yet France seems happy to stick two fingers up at bird conservation.

In the interests of fair play (yeah, yeah), we did ask our French colleagues to find someone who could give us their views in favour of hunting for *Wingbeat*, but they couldn't find a single soul. However, here's what one of the anti-hunters has to say:

'Aside from rat control and evening mosquito-swatting sessions, I thought that Man no longer needed to prove his superiority over his environment. 'Instead hunters continue to shatter the peace and quiet of their neighbours by shooting lead into the air from behind every bush. 'We should remember, however, that Man has already accorded himself the right over life or death of numerous species in order to feed himself. Though hunting, a now outdated ancestral method for finding food, may remain a tool for maintaining a balanced ecosystem, I cannot put up with the idea of hunting "for pleasure", "for leisure" or out of "tradition".'

Samuel Facioli, Ancy-sur-Moselle, Lorraine, France (aged 18).

Les big shots

➡ France has the longest hunting season in the EU

➡ France has more hunters (1.5 million) than any other EU country. The UK has 625,000

➡ It's legal under French law to hunt 64 different bird species. No other country has more than 42; the UK has 30

➡ Hunters are lobbying the European Parliament to change its regulations to tie in with French law

➡ In France, 24 migratory bird species which are declining or only found in certain areas, are hunted in February.

➡ Hunting overlaps for up to seven weeks with the time when young birds are dependent on their parents.

Sign the Wingbeat petition — it really will make a difference

Our wildlife pals in France, the *Ligue pour la Protection des Oiseaux*, have organised a Europe-wide petition to support the EU regulations the European Union Birds Directive) and force the French Parliament to change their mind. Please turn to page 10, sign it, ask your friends and family to sign too, then return the petition to us. Every name counts!

WB 6

Paragraph 2: Explains the passing of law by the French parliament to extend the hunting season. It states that this '*law*' breaks European regulations set up to protect wild birds. It states that other countries abide by the European regulations.

Paragraph 3: Introduces a quotation from a French person concerned with bird protection.

Paragraph 4: The argument against the killing of birds is strengthened by a direct quotation that is highly critical of the hunters.

Fact and opinion

In this article you are given quite a lot of facts but there are also some opinions. When reading articles it is important to distinguish between **fact** and **opinion**.

Look at the article again and identify three facts and three opinions.

Here are some possibilities:

FACT	OPINION
The French parliament has passed a law.	It was the result of the powerful influence of the hunting lobby.
It breaks European regulations.	France seems happy to "*stick two fingers up at bird conservation*".
France has the largest hunting season in the EU.	Hunting is "*outdated*".

Illustration and layout

Look again at the article and think about the following features:

- the headlines
- the photographs
- the background

The headline gives an immediate indication of what the article is about: '*Hunters take aim for a migrant massacre*'. The '*Hunters take aim*' creates an image of the hunters actually aiming their guns. The use of the word '*massacre*' is an emotive one and gives a vivid impression of the large scale of the killing. The alliteration used in the phrase, '*migrant massacre*' adds further emphasis to the words.

The photographs are all circled as if the birds are being looked at through a telescopic sight. The central one even has the 'cross-hairs' of the sight marked on it. The other two photographs show birds that have been trapped. This again draws attention and adds emphasis to the cruelty involved. It is striking that the birds that are the victims of the 'hunting' are not the kinds of birds normally associated with hunting, such as ducks, grouse or pheasant. These are small birds, such as the robin or the skylark.

The soft, out-of-focus background picture showing a hunter taking aim adds drama to the piece. This is accentuated by the impression of looking down the barrels of the shotgun. Notice how the very tips of the barrels are in sharp focus, unlike the rest of the picture.

> **KEY POINT**
>
> All these features combine to add effect to the words of the article and so make it have greater impact on the reader.

Language techniques

A number of techniques are used to make the language have more impact on the reader.

Look at all the aspects of an article when you are writing about it.

Vocabulary	Words are used that create a particular image or feeling in the reader, e.g. 'orgy of killing', 'massacre', 'unsuspecting victims', 'stick two fingers up'.
Use of quotation	The extended quotation not only provides a view that supports the anti-hunting stance but is given more significance because it is the view of a French person.
Use of bullet points	Bullet points are used to provide a list of facts, which shows the French position on the hunting of birds in a poor light compared with other European countries.

6.3 Biographies and autobiographies

> **LEARNING SUMMARY**
>
> *After studying this section you should be able to understand:*
> - *the features of biography*
> - *the features of autobiography*

Recognise that biographies and autobiographies, although having a common general function, are different in their approach and style, and the effects that these create.

Biographies are texts that tell us about the lives of other people by writers who have usually studied the **life** of the person they are writing about in some detail. When reading a biography, though, you should always remember that the biography presents that particular **writer's view** of their subject. There may be other views too and a different writer may present a quite different picture.

Autobiographies are written by the subjects themselves. This means that the views we get of a person's life and actions are very much those of that person. Of course, their views too may be **coloured** by the writer wanting to give a particular impression or the fact that they see things in a particular way.

One of the most immediate **differences** between these two forms is that biographies are written in the **third person** while autobiographies are written in the **first person**.

Look at the following extract. It is from a biography of the rock-star, David Bowie.

David Bowie turned fifty on 8th January 1997.

In the weeks before and after, the music and trade press became a giant band playing just one tune, with the heavyweight papers singing along. Bowie was profiled in *The Times*, *The Independent*, the *Daily Mail* and the *Evening Standard*: MTV and VH-1 aired specials; ITV and the BBC weighed in with their own po-faced tributes. To no one's surprise, Bowie himself spent the day recording and rehearsing in New York. He had, he said, 'big work to do'. Bowie was, just as he once predicted, 'refus[ing] to opt out of life' on his half-century. His birthday marked a new high point for our acceptance of the idea that pop stars get older.

The next night, Bowie celebrated quietly with a few friends and 20,000 fans at a sold-out show at Madison Square Garden. Apart from an appearance by Lou Reed, the star-studded event looked like modern rock on parade: Billy Corgan of Smashing Pumpkins, Foo Fighters, Sonic Youth, Frank Black and the Cure's Robert Smith – all were trotted out to sing duets with Bowie on old songs as well as on cuts from his new album, *Earthling*. The two-hour show was as stagey as the Sound + Vision tour, if not quite on the scale of the Glass Spider farce. A forty-by-sixty foot backdrop projected giant black-and-white video images of Bowie dancing with a beautiful blonde; tiny puppets with moving faces scowled and twitched around the set; giant rubber eyeballs rained down from the rafters; unmanned cameras zoomed in and out like baby robots; and even the roadies wore masks. The headliner came on in a lacy frock coat, again with his Ziggy cockade, his heavy mascara and milk-pale face making him look uneasily like Archie Rice of *The Entertainer*.

From *Bowie: Loving the Alien* by Christopher Sandford

Now read this extract from the autobiography of Eric Lomax in which he writes about his years spent as a Japanese prisoner of war and the effect this had on his life.

Work and the strong pull of the currents that run through everyday life – no matter how threatening they can seem to someone whose memories are bad – give the illusion of sweeping us away from the past. Like many men who went through Japanese prisons, I found I could allow my professional life to crowd out my desire to settle those old accounts.

Although I relived the past more often that I wished and had, again like many of my wartime comrades, accumulated a library of books about the campaigns in Malaya, the Burma-Siam Railway and the camps, I still felt a certain reluctance to confront that past directly. In the 1970s, my friend Alex Morton Mackay – by then living in Canada – found my address through an ex-POW organization and wrote me an affecting letter in which he described how I had been an example and an inspiration to him, with my arms in splints and my specs taped together; but if I recognized myself in his description, I knew it was not the whole story. No one is a hero to themselves. I found it difficult to reply to Mac, but we did eventually correspond and one day, after a service of remembrance for those who had died in the Far Eastern war, we finally met again. Fred Smith joined us for lunch in London. It was my only reunion with these two men who had meant so much to me.

But that past was not easily denied. The need to know more about what had happened to us in Siam was not some idle curiosity, and it asserted itself powerfully whenever I had time to think. After my retirement in 1982, I could put off no longer the need to know, the desire became more intense than ever. I wanted to find out what had really happened; why the Japanese had made the search of our hut on that particular day, and if somebody had tipped them off. I wished to establish the exact sequence of events. I also wanted to find out more about the Japanese responsible for the beatings and murders, apart from those already brought to justice, and above all more about the Kempei personnel who had tortured me at Kanburi. I knew nothing about their units, their names or their fate after the war. The prospects of finding the right men, of finding them alive, even of making a start were so remote; but as the events receded the obsession grew. It was like trying to reconstruct a coherent story from evidence reduced to tattered rags, faded documents, bones and rusty rails. And memories, which are even less durable.

From *The Railway Man* by Eric Lomax

Make a note of the differences in style of these two extracts.

Biography

- the biography describes events
- it uses quotations to give a sense of Bowie's personal voice
- it is a more detached account

Autobiography

- has a more personal tone
- explains what is in the writer's head
- it describes his memories and their effects on him

6.4 Travel writing

After studying this section you should be able to understand:

- *some of the features of travel writing*
- *how an example of travel writing achieves its effects*

As the name suggests, travel writing is concerned with **describing experiences** concerned with travel in one form or another. However, there is much more to successful travel writing than simply describing journeys or writing about holidays.

The best travel writing can:

- **convey** the experience of a journey or exploration of a new country etc. in a vivid way
- deal with the **inner feelings** and emotions that the experience promotes
- invite us to look at the world in a **different** way
- allow the reader to **participate** in the journey

The following extract is from Bill Bryson's *Notes from a Small Island* in which he describes his experience on a tour around the British Isles.

I went to Milton Keynes, feeling that I ought to at least have a look at a new town. Milton Keynes takes some getting to from Oxford, which is a little odd because it's only just up the road. I selected it as my destination on the basis of a quick look at a road map, assuming that I would, at worst, have to take a train to Bicester or some such place and then another from there. In fact, I had to go all the way back to London, catch an Underground train to Euston and then finally a train to Milton Keynes – an overall journey of perhaps 120 miles in order to travel between two towns about 30 miles apart.

It was costly and time-consuming and left me feeling a tiny bit fractious, not least because the train from Euston was crowded and I ended up sitting facing a bleating woman and her ten-year-old son, who kept knocking my shins with his dangling legs and irritating me by staring at me with piggy eyes while picking his nose and eating the bogies. He appeared to regard his nose as a kind of mid-faced snack dispenser. I tried to absorb myself in a book, but I found my gaze repeatedly rising against my wishes to find him staring at me with a smug look and a busy finger. It was quite repellent and I was very pleased, when the train finally pulled into Milton Keynes, to get my rucksack down from the overhead rack and drag it across his head as I departed.

I didn't hate Milton Keynes immediately, which I suppose is as much as you could hope for the place. You step out of the station and into a big open square lined on three sides with buildings of reflective glass, and have an instant sense of spaciousness such as you almost never get in English towns. The town itself stood on the slope of a small hill a good half-mile away beyond a network of pedestrian tunnels and over a large open space shared by car parks and those strange new-town trees that never seem to grow. I had the distinct feeling that the next time I passed this expanse of grass and asphalt it would be covered with brick office buildings with coppery windows.

Though I have spent much time wandering through new towns trying to imagine what their creators could possibly have been thinking, I had never been to Milton Keynes. In many ways, it was much superior to any new town I had seen before. The underpasses were faced with polished granite and were largely free of graffiti and the permanent murky puddles that seem to be a design feature of Basingstoke and Bracknell.

The town itself was a strange amalgam of styles. The grassless, shady strips along the centres of the main boulevards gave them a vaguely French air. The landscaped light industrial parks around the fringes looked German. The grid plan and numbered street names recalled America. The buildings were of the featureless sort you find around any international airport. In short, it looked anything but English.

From Notes from a Small Island by Bill Bryson

What kinds of information does Bryson include in his description?

Here are some ideas:

- He explains **where** he is and where he is going to.
- He describes the **route** he needs to take.
- He describes some of the **things that happened** on the journey.
- He describes his **initial impression** of his destination.
- He goes on to give a more **detailed description** of the place.

Bryson gives us a range of information about his journey but he goes further than simply cataloguing where he went and what he saw.

What techniques does he use to make his writing more interesting and effective?

- Much of the effect of his writing comes from the **humour** he creates, such as the description of the boy on the train.
- He reveals his **view** of the place indirectly and with irony – "*I didn't hate Milton Keynes immediately, which I suppose is as much as you could hope for the place*".
- He uses quite detailed descriptions so readers can clearly picture the scene in their minds.
- He **compares** the town with other places he has visited.

 KEY POINT Travel writing consists of more than just a description of a journey or place and often uses a variety of techniques and approaches to convey its information to the reader.

6.5 Documentary writing

 LEARNING SUMMARY *After studying this section you should be able to understand:*

- *the features of documentary writing*

You might be more used to hearing the term 'documentary' in connection with film or television but it is also a genre that has been used for many years in writing. Documentary writing often has a strong social or political purpose and is used to:

- **expose** things that the public should know about
- **educate** people in some way
- bring about **reforms**

Writers **observe** and **present**, through their writing, **aspects** of the world they see around them or report on certain issues or situations.

Read the following extract from *Down and Out in Paris and London*, in which George Orwell describes his experiences of living with the homeless on the streets of Paris and London. Here Orwell describes one of the homeless people he encountered.

Paddy was my mate for about the next fortnight, and, as he was the first tramp I had known at all well, I want to give an account of him. I believe that he was a typical tramp and there are tens of thousands in England like him.

He was a tallish man, aged about thirty-five, with fair hair going grizzled and watery blue eyes. His features were good, but his cheeks had lanked and had that greyish, dirty-in-the-grain look that comes of a bread and margarine diet. He was dressed, rather better than most tramps, in a tweed shooting-jacket and a pair of old evening trousers with the braid still on them. Evidently the braid figured in his mind as a lingering scrap of respectability, and he took care to sew it on again when it came loose. He was careful of his appearance altogether, and carried a razor and bootbrush that he would not sell, though he had sold his 'papers' and even his pocket-knife long since. Nevertheless, one would have known him for a tramp a hundred yards away; there was something in his drifting style of walk, and the way he had of hunching his shoulders forward, essentially abject. Seeing him walk, you felt instinctively that he would sooner take a blow than give one.

He had been brought up in Ireland, served two years in the war, and then worked in a metal polish factory, where he had lost his job two years earlier. He was horribly ashamed of being a tramp, but he had picked up all a tramp's ways. He browsed the pavements unceasingly, never missing a cigarette end, or even an empty cigarette packet, as he used the tissue paper for rolling cigarettes. On our way into Edbury he saw a newspaper parcel on the pavement, pounced on it, and found that it contained two mutton sandwiches, rather frayed at the edges; these he insisted on my sharing. He never passed an automatic machine without giving a tug at the handle, for he said that sometimes they are out of order and will eject pennies if you tug at them. He had no stomach for crime, however. When we were in the outskirts of Romton, Paddy noticed a bottle of milk on a doorstep, evidently left there by mistake. He stopped, eyeing the bottle hungrily.

'Christ!' he said, 'dere's good food goin' to waste. Somebody could knock dat bottle off, eh? Knock it off easy.'

I saw that he was thinking of 'knocking it off' himself. He looked up and down the street; it was a quiet residential street and there was nobody in sight. Paddy's sickly, chap-fallen face yearned over the milk. Then he turned away, saying gloomily:

'Best leave it. It don't do a man no good to steal. T'ank God, I ain't never stolen nothin' yet.'

If was funk, bred of hunger, that kept him virtuous. With only two or three sound meals in his belly, he would have found courage to steal the milk.

From *Down and out in Paris and London* by George Orwell

1. What is significant about Paddy as far as Orwell is concerned?
2. How does Orwell convey an impression of Paddy to the reader?

Here are some ideas:

1. Orwell uses Paddy as a typical example of a tramp and states that at the time there were '*tens of thousands in England like him*'. This means that, although Orwell is interested in Paddy as an individual, he also uses him to symbolise the many thousands of other homeless. By doing this he allows his reader to identify with an individual and therefore understand the plight of the many.

2. He begins by describing his physical appearance to give the reader a visual picture of him. He goes on to describe his background and how he felt about being a tramp. He uses a specific incident (the finding of the newspaper parcel) to give us a deeper insight into Paddy's character and then tells us more about him (that he 'had no stomach for crime'). Orwell also uses direct speech, which he writes in such a way as to capture Paddy's Irish accent, and this also give us a vivid impression of the characters.

Like much documentary writing, Orwell's book deals with a social issue.

> **KEY POINT**
>
> Very often, this kind of writing:
> - adopts the style of reporting on an event, issue or idea
> - uses detailed description to convey ideas
> - focuses on 'human interest' aspects of a story
> - uses specific events or experiences to explore broader issues

6.6 Literary non-fiction

> **LEARNING SUMMARY**
>
> After studying this section you should be able to understand:
> - **what literary non-fiction is**
> - **examples of it**
> - **some of its features**

'Literary non-fiction' is a genre of writing that can encompass a number of the types of writing already discussed and there are no hard and fast boundaries between them. Essentially, 'literary non-fiction' is a term used to describe texts that are written in a style that applies the techniques of 'literary' writing to topics that are non-fiction.

An example of this kind of writing is the book *Fever Pitch* by Nick Hornby. Here is an extract from it. Read it through carefully.

I didn't go to Anfield. The fixture was originally scheduled for earlier in the season, when the result wouldn't have been so crucial, and by the time it was clear that this game would decide the Championship, the tickets had long gone. In the morning I walked down to Highbury to buy a new team shirt, just because I felt I had to do something, and though admittedly wearing a shirt in front of the television set would not, on the face of it, appear to offer the team an awful lot of encouragement, I knew it would make me feel better. Even at noon, some eight hours before the evening kick-off, there were already scores of coaches and cars around the ground, and on the way home I wished everyone I passed good luck; their positiveness ('Three-one', 'Two-nil, no trouble', even a breezy 'Four-one') on this beautiful May morning made me sad for them, as if these chirpy and bravely confident young men and women were off to the Somme to lose their lives, rather than to Anfield to lose, at worst, their faith.

I went to work in the afternoon, and felt sick with nerves despite myself; afterwards I went straight round to an Arsenal-supporting friend's house, just a street away from the North Bank, to watch the game. Everything about the night was memorable, right from the moment when the teams came on to the pitch and the Arsenal players ran over to the Kop and presented individuals in the crowd with bunches of flowers. And as the game progressed, and it became obvious that Arsenal were going to go down fighting, it occurred to me just how well I knew my team, their faces and their mannerisms, and how fond I was of each individual member of it. Merson's gap-toothed smile and tatty soul-boy haircut, Adams's manful and endearing attempts to come to terms with his own inadequacies, Rocastle's pumped-up elegance, Smith's lovable diligence... I could find it in me to forgive them for coming so close and blowing it: they were young, and they'd had a fantastic season and as a supporter you cannot really ask for more than that.

I got excited when we scored right at the beginning of the second half, and I got excited again about ten minutes from time, when Thomas had a clear chance and hit it straight at Grobbelaar, but Liverpool seemed to be growing stronger and to be creating chances at the end, and finally, with the clock in the corner of the TV screen showing that the ninety minutes had passed, I got ready to muster a brave smile for a brave team. 'If Arsenal are to lose the Championship, having had such a lead at one time, it's somewhat poetic justice that they have got a result on the last day, even though they're not to win it,' said the commentator David Pleat as Kevin Richardson received treatment for an injury with the Kop already celebrating. 'They will see that as scant consolation, I should think, David,' replied Brian Moore. Scant consolation indeed, for all of us.

Richardson finally got up, ninety-two minutes gone now, and even managed a penalty-area tackle on John Barnes; then Lukic bowled the ball out to Dixon, Dixon on, inevitably, to Smith, a brilliant Smith flick-on... and suddenly, in the last minute of the last game of the season, Thomas was through, on his own, with a chance to win the Championship for Arsenal. 'It's up for grabs now!' Brian Moore yelled; and even then I found that I was reining myself in, learning from recent lapses in hardened scepticism, thinking, well, at least we came close at the end there, instead of thinking, please Michael, please Michael, please put it in, please God let him score. And then he was turning a somersault, and I was flat out on the floor, and everybody in the living room jumped on top of me. Eighteen years, all forgotten in a second.

From *Fever Pitch* by Nick Hornby

Think about the ways in which this extract combines the features of literary writing with those of non-fiction writing.

Here are some ideas:

- The topic is clearly a **factual** account describing how Hornby felt as the crucial game approached.
- A good deal of factual **information** is included.
- Literary **techniques** are used to make the description more vivid, e.g. '*...made me sad for them, as if these chirpy and bravely confident young men and women were off to the Somme...*'.
- The players are described almost as 'characters', identified by **key features**, e.g. '*Merson's gap-toothed smile*'.
- **Direct speech** is used to convey a sense of the commentary.
- The varied **sentence structure** helps to heighten the sense of excitement and tension.

> When analysing literary non-fiction, approach it as you would a work of literature and look for the writer's use of literary techniques, as well as looking at the non-fiction aspects of the text.

KEY POINT Many of these techniques are exactly the same as those that novelists or short story writers might use to create their effects.

Another example of literary non-fiction is the book *Pole to Pole* by Michael Palin, in which he describes his journey from the North Pole to the South Pole. This is an example of travel writing too. In this passage, he describes his journey across Norway.

The mountains climb quite steeply to 2000 feet and we have to stop a lot in the first hour, partly to free snowmobiles bogged down by their heavy loads, but mainly to photograph the spectacular views out across King's Fiord, fed by three glaciers and rimmed with sweeping mountain peaks. As soon as the motors are turned off and the natural silence restored, the size and scale and majesty of the landscape is indescribable. There are no trees on Spitsbergen, and therefore few birds except around the coast, and with unbroken snow shrouding the valley below us there is an atmosphere of magnificent peacefulness.

Soon we are across the pass and putting the snowmobiles down a snow-slope so steep that we are warned not to use the brake. This is to prevent the trailers from swinging round and pulling the vehicles over – and presumably sending the driver hurtling downhill in a mass of wreckage, though they don't tell you the last bit. We twist and turn through some perilous gullies which Roger refers to with a certain relish as Walls of Death, as in 'Michael, we'd like to do another Wall of Death sequence'. The whole adventure seems to have gone to his head since he chose the codeword 'Raving Queen' for his end of the two-way radio. Fraser, at the other end, is 'Intrepid One', and I suppose it does take away some of the terror to hear, floating across a glacier, the immortal words:

'Raving Queen to Intrepid One, Michael's on the Wall of Death…Now!'

On the other side of the pass another epic wintry panorama is revealed on the shores of Engelsbukta – 'English Bay' – where an English whaling fleet under Henry Hudson took refuge in 1607 while in search of the north-east passage. Much of the bay is still frozen, and we see our first seals – nothing more than tiny black blobs – waiting beside their holes in the ice. A ptarmigan, in its white winter coat, peers curiously down at us from a pinnacle of rock, and a pair of eider ducks turn low over the bay.

We head towards a wide, level glacier passing ice cliffs of palest blue which are millions of years old and still moving. I ask Geir why they should be such a colour. Apparently it is caused by the presence of air inside the ice.

After the roller-coaster conditions on the pass, progress across the glacier is fast and reasonably comfortable. I am riding pillion behind David, and apart from nursing an occasional numbing cold in my thumb and fingers, I have plenty of time to sit back and take in the glories of this wide, unvisited landscape. A pair of Svalbard reindeer, not much bigger than large dogs, wander across a hillside. God knows what they find to eat.

After five hours we grind to a halt, our vehicles stuck in deep fresh-fallen snow at the top of a pass, still barely halfway to the trapper's hut. Bars of chocolate, nips of Scotch and stupendous views keep spirits up as Geir, Heinich and the team make repeated journeys down the valley to bring up machines that couldn't make it to the top. Once all of them are up on the ridge they have to be refuelled, a slow laborious job, as is anything which involves unloading the trailers.

We are rewarded with a long exhilarating run on wide downhill slopes to our first ice-crossing – on the frozen head-waters of the Ehmanfiord. The surface is scratched and rutted, and it's only on the last stretch that the ice is smooth enough to open out, and we ride like invading Mongol hordes toward the tiny, isolated cabin on Kap Wik where, somewhat improbably, we are to spend what remains of the night.

From *Pole to Pole* by Michael Palin

PROGRESS CHECK

What literary techniques do you find in this writing?

- vivid description
- the use of imagery
- the use of direct speech
- the creation of atmosphere
- the creation of tension

Sample GCSE questions

Read the following extract from 'The Perfect Storm'. Here, Reeves, a Canadian observer on a Japanese fishing boat, the Eishin Maru, contacts the US Coastguard as her ship is hit by the storm.

The radio operator had managed to contact the ship's agent by satellite phone, and Reeves is put on the line to explain what kind of damage they've sustained. While she's talking, Coast Guard New York breaks in; they've been listening in on the conversation and want to know if the *Eishin Maru* needs help. Reeves says they've lost most of their electronics and are in serious trouble. New York patches her through to the Coast Guard in Halifax, and while they're discussing how to get people off the boat, the radio operator interrupts her. He's pointing to a sentence in an English phrase book. Reeves leans in close to read it: "We are helpless and drifting. Please render all assistance." (Unknown to Reeves, the steering linkage has just failed, although the radio operator doesn't know how to explain that to her.) It's at this moment that Reeves realizes she's going down at sea.

"We had no steerage and we were right in the eye of the storm", she says. "It was a confused sea, all the waves were coming from different directions. The wind was picking up the tops of the waves and slinging them so far that when the search-and-rescue plane arrived, we couldn't even see it. The whole vessel would get shoved over on its side, so that we were completely upside-down. If you get hit by one wave and then hit by another, you can drive the vessel completely down into the water. And so that second before the vessel starts to come up you're just holding your breath, waiting."

They're dead in the water, taking the huge waves broad-side. According to Reeves, they are doing 360-degree barrel rolls and coming back up. Four boats try to respond to her mayday, but three of them have to stand down because of the weather. They cannot continue without risking their own lives. The ocean-going tug *Triumph C* leaves Sable Island and claws her way southward, and the Coast Guard cutter *Edward Cornwallis* is on her way from Halifax. The crew of the *Eishin Maru*, impassive, are sure they're going to die. Reeves is too busy to think about it; she has to look for the life jackets, work the radio and satellite phone, flip through the Japanese phrase book. Eventually she has a moment to consider her options.

"Either I jump ship, or I go down with the ship. As for the first possibility, I thought about it for a while until I realized that they'd hammered all the hatches down. I thought, 'God, I'll never get off this friggin' boat, it will be my tomb.' So I figured I'd do whatever I had to do at the time, and there was no point in really thinking about it because it was just too frightening. I was just gripped by this feeling that I was going to have to do something very unpleasant. And it wasn't until the moment we lost steerage that I actually thought we were going to die. I mean, I knew there was a real possibility, and I was going to have to face that.

The Perfect Storm

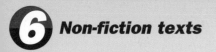

Sample GCSE questions

1. What is the purpose of this extract?

   The main purpose of this extract is to put across to the reader the severity of the storm and the serious position that the people on the boat are in. The writer wants the reader to understand the tension that Reeves felt and get an idea of just how frightening the situation was. The writer also wants to give the reader an idea of the attempts that were being made to rescue the crew.

   Clear focus on purpose of writing and the effects the writer wishes to create.

2. How does the writer use language to achieve his effects here?

   The writer uses a number of techniques to make the description have more impact on the reader. The focus is on the character, Reeves, and the writer uses her experiences to give an account to the reader. We are told what she is doing and what she says to the Coast Guard. The writer uses both reported and direct speech to tell us what she said, and this makes the piece more interesting by giving us the feeling that this is a real person's experiences. Reeves describes the wild state of the sea in direct speech and this again gives a sense of immediacy and the impression that we are getting a first-hand account from someone who was there. The description of boats setting out to rescue them but having to turn back emphasises the desperate nature of the situation. This desperation is echoed by Reeves' words when she finds all the hatches hammered down: "God, I'll never get off this friggin' boat, it will be my tomb." In addition, descriptive phrases, such as "taking huge waves broad-side", "doing 360-degree barrel rolls", and the description of the tug as she "claws her way" through the sea emphasise the severity of the weather conditions.

   A number of techniques identified here, supported well by references and quotations from the text, together with explanations of effects created. Some perceptive points.

Exam practice questions

The following text is a magazine article, which explores New Zealand as a holiday destination and the setting of the film 'Lord of the Rings'.

Read the article through carefully and then answer the questions that follow.

New Zealand
Middle Earth

Sarah Woods, explores the charms of New Zealand's 'Middle Earth' and quickly discovers that it's an enchanting and magical land.

When visionary film director Peter Jackson first revealed his plans to recreate the Lord of the Rings trilogy for the cinema, he was certain that there was only one location that could realistically capture the extraordinary splendour of Tolkien's Middle Earth. With crimson sunsets, steamy rivers, snow-capped mountains, volcanic springs, glaciers and an endless expanse of mysterious dewy rainforests, New Zealand is a treasure-trove landscape. Vast, beautiful and extreme, its kaleidoscopic geography is delicately wrapped by the turquoise ribbon of its coastline, and shrouded in folklore and ancient mythical secrets. "From the Shire to Rivendell, the Misty Mountains to Mordor, it's all here" Jackson enthused.

With the first part of the trilogy – The Fellowship of the Ring – due for release simultaneously across the world on 19 December 2001, Jackson's vision looks set to produce what many predict will be the "epic of our time".

Persuading US film chiefs to entrust him with a NZ$700m budget, native New Zealander Peter Jackson headed straight for his homeland. In an ambitious project, which would see him film all three parts concurrently – an impressive first in the film industry world-wide – Jackson made full use of his extraordinary 100,000 square mile film set and immersed himself in the character of New Zealand's stunning terrain.

The expansive rolling farmlands of the Waikato region provide the film location for the Shire, the agrarian ancestral homeland of the diminutive Hobbit, and where the journey of Middle Earth begins. Centred on the Waikato River, the region is rich in rural country life, with a plenitude of opportunities for horse-riding, walking, trekking and farm-stay holidays.

Despite its vast agricultural planes, Waikato is no soulless barren wilderness. Beneath the rolling green fields to the south are the Waitomo Caves – known as 'the lost world' – a staggering hole of darkness speared by stalactites.

Above the ground, the unusual limestone geology provides good conditions for exploration on foot, with winding scenic pathways and local handicraft stalls in good supply. Fifty miles further north, the riverside university town of Hamilton is home to an impressive collection of Maori treasures. While on the eastern coast, Raglan has an acclaimed surf beach and is a popular family seaside destination. South of Waitomo is the township of Te Kuiti – hailed the "Shearing Capital of the World". To denote this, a giant shearing statue measuring over 20ft towers over the southern end of the town, where the New Zealand Shearing Champion-ships are held each year.

Travelling westward to the foot of the dramatic Kaimai mountain ranges, Kaimai Country comprises three towns – Morrinsville, Matamata and Te Aroha – and is located in the centre of North Island. Matamata, renowned internationally for its horse breeding, provides the setting for Hobbiton – the bucolic community of Hobbits and home to Bilbo Baggins and his 111th birthday celebrations. First constructed in 1998, the film crew left the set empty for over a year ahead of filming, to enable it to weather into character.

In Matamata, equestrian life is evident at every turn. With horse studs, racing stables and training yards in abundance, the open countryside plays host to horse-tracks and riders alike, with stunning vistas across the planes. The nearby sparkling natural mineral springs at Oraka Wapiti Deer Park provide an inviting cool respite from the midday sun. At the base of Mount Te Aroha, visitors come from all across the world to "take the waters" in rejuvenating mineral baths which are fed by thermal springs.

Described by the locals as "nature as it was intended – pure, untouched and energised" the steep bush-clad hills of Kaitoke Regional Park, in the Hutt Valley region south of Wellington, provides the film location for Tolkien's Rivendell – the birthplace of the Fellowship and where the Council of Elrond gathered. With more than 30 per cent of New Zealand's land area safeguarded within national parks, reserves, regional parks and special heritage sites, its ecological preservation is at the forefront of New Zealand's modern-day tourism thrust. Subsequently, at Kaitoke Regional Park, visitors are privy to a primeval world of ancient forests, rare flightless birds, bubbling pools and creatures that have survived from prehistoric times. Flanked by giant ferns, breathtaking views and red beech woodlands, the Hutt Gorge gushes over rocks and ledges, descending into mountain fresh pools of mirror-like translucency. With well-

> "...eastward the sun was rising red out of the mists that lay thick on the world. Touched with gold and red the autumn trees seemed to be sailing rootless in a shadowy sea"
>
> JRR TOLKIEN

4

Exam practice questions

travel

Ian McKellen plays Gandolf in Lord of the Rings

formed tracks, which cut through the bush with ease, Kaitoke Park has a labyrinth of trails, allowing a leisurely-paced stroll or an invigorating hike, with many grassy picnic areas, fishing rivers and tranquil pools for swimming.

Providing the perfect location for Tolkien's Misty Mountains, Queenstown is situated on the shores of beautiful Lake Wakatipu and surrounded by the towering mountains of the snow-rich Southern Alps on New Zealand's South Island. Located 310 metres (1020 feet) above sea level, the region's four distinct seasons provide golden summer days between December-March, baronial autumnal hues from April-May and some of the finest skiing conditions from June-September. The most popular destination for overseas visitors, Queenstown is a 45-minute flight, or 6-hour drive from South Island's international airport in Christchurch.

The Queenstown panorama is a spectacular one. Dominated by the vast peaks of the snowy Alps – termed the "remarkables" by locals – its delicate misty veil shrouds a colourful checkerboard terrain of crystal glacier-gorges, lush pine-tree valleys and multicoloured fauna, zigzagged by swift-flowing rivers. Steeped in tales of a gold rush past, Queenstown also provides the film location for the Mines of Moria, scene of Gandolf's apparent death, with the region remaining at the heart of New Zealand's jade greenstone industry.

With so much to see and do, Queenstown has made sightseeing an enjoyable and effortless business. By sunset cruise, wagon & horse ride, steamship river journey, overnight fjord cruise or gentle cycle ride – Queenstown makes it easy for everyone to enjoy its remarkable vistas.

Glenorchy – hailed the 'Gateway to Southern Wilderness' – is located at the mouth of the Lake Wakatipu, just 40 minutes drive from Queenstown. An ecological reserve and world heritage site, Glenorchy sits on a striking, rugged terrain looped by vast expanses of clear blue water. Paradise, an area of ancient beech forest, which teems with bush canaries, fantails, parakeets, kaka and three species of deer, was chosen as one of the main film locations for Lothlórien – the tree-top elven city of Caras Galadhon – and Amon-Hen – the forested mountainous area close to Mordor.

Tranquil and picturesque, Glenorchy is a popular destination with horse-riders, fly-fisherman, wind-surfers and walkers, with a good winter ski calendar. It also plays host to a legendary horserace on the first Saturday after New Year, which is something of a Glenorchy tradition. Best-explored on foot or by bike, Glenorchy's uncluttered landscape is studded with old miners cottages, wooden fishing huts and traditional kiwi countryside restaurants and lodges.

The journey ends in Wellington on the North Island, home to Peter Jackson's production base

in the midst of unspoilt New Zealand. Much of the filming schedule centred on the rural area that encircles the city of Wellington, its raw natural beauty perfect for the curious twists and tangles of the Lord of the Rings narrative.

Pretty, artisan and convivial, the city is served by Wellington International Airport and provides a picturesque base from which to explore the hidden secrets of the North Island. Unashamedly friendly, with a capacity for fun that is legendary, Wellington's kiwi hospitality permeates through every strata of city life. Harbour-side cafés, wine bars and gastronomic haunts abound and a stroll along the city's tree-lined promenade to the slopes of Mount Victoria or a visit to one of the superb fish restaurant's on the wharves, is a must.

Now immortalized in what is arguably one of the most high-profile screenplays of our time, the unspoilt islands of New Zealand are a film-set dream; with a multi-faceted topography as diverse as Tolkien's story-line itself, mirroring the true magic and drama of this huge rural amphitheatre. Though home to a star-studded cast, it is New Zealand that courts centre stage. "Our own Middle Earth" New Zealanders proudly say, with every night a 'Premier Night' and its landscape in starring role. ■

a) What effect do you think the writer wants to create by linking the description of New Zealand to the film 'Lord of the Rings'?

b) How does the writer use language here to create her effects? You should discuss specific details of the ways in which she uses language in your answer.

7 Reading Shakespeare

The following topics are included in this chapter:

- Types of play
- Plot and structure
- Opening scenes
- Presenting characters
- Shakespeare's language
- Endings

7.1 Types of play

LEARNING SUMMARY

After studying this section you should be able to understand:

- **what the Elizabethan theatre was like**
- **what kinds of plays Shakespeare wrote**
- **the features of each kind of play**

The Elizabethan theatre

> It really is important to try to see the play you are studying performed. It will help enormously with your understanding of it.

Shakespeare's plays, just like any other kind of play, were not written to be read; they were written to be seen on the stage. If you get the chance to see the play you are studying **performed**, this will help you to appreciate it much more than simply reading it. If you cannot see it live on the stage, then at least try to see a video recording of it. This will really bring the action to life and make it mean much more to you. However, it is worth bearing in mind that in Shakespeare's time the theatres were very different from the ones we have today and the way the plays were performed was different too.

Here are some key differences:

- There was no lighting in the theatres and so the plays were performed in daylight. This meant that there were no lighting effects, although sometimes music and songs were used to create a particular atmosphere.
- The actors used few props and costumes.
- There were no female actors and so the female roles were played by boys.
- The theatre was a much rowdier place than it is now. Many of the audience watched the play, standing in a crowd in front of the stage and they often drank beer and ate while watching the play.

If you want to get the flavour of the Elizabethan theatre, visit the Globe Theatre in London, which is a reconstruction of the Globe Theatre of Shakespeare's time.

This is what Shakespeare's Globe would have looked like.

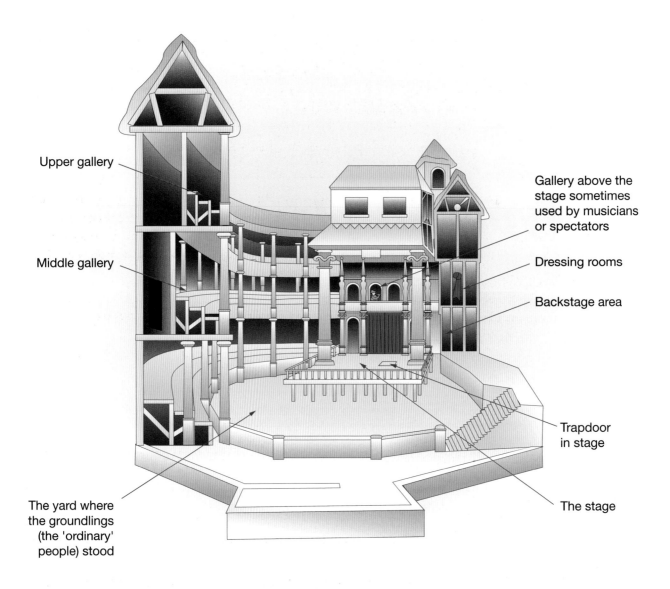

Upper gallery

Middle gallery

Gallery above the stage sometimes used by musicians or spectators

Dressing rooms

Backstage area

Trapdoor in stage

The stage

The yard where the groundlings (the 'ordinary' people) stood

Types of play

Shakespeare wrote nearly 40 plays during his life. These plays can be divided into four types:

- **Tragedies** – these plays focus on a tragic hero (or couple, as in R*omeo and Juliet*) whose downfall is brought about through weakness or misfortune of some kind. This kind of play ends with the death of the central character but also involves the death of a number of other characters.
- **Comedies** – this kind of play involves humour and often confusion, disguise, mistaken identity etc. Unlike our modern idea of comedy, some of Shakespeare's comedies can be quite 'dark' but the main thing is that they end happily and there are no deaths at the end.

- **Histories** – this kind of play is based on historical events and characters, often on kings or important figures from Roman history. These plays often have tragic elements too.
- **Romances** – these are some of Shakespeare's later plays (sometimes called 'Last Plays), and often involve magical worlds and happenings, mysterious events and moral lessons contained within a 'happy' ending.

Here are some of these types of play:

Tragedies	Comedies	Histories	Romances
Hamlet	Twelfth Night	Henry IV (Pt 1)	The Tempest
Macbeth	The Merchant of Venice	Henry IV (Pt 2)	The Winter's Tale
Othello	The Taming of the Shrew	Henry V	
King Lear	Much Ado About Nothing	Richard III	
Romeo and Juliet		Antony and Cleopatra	
		Julius Caesar	

A small number of his plays, however, do not fit easily into these categories. These are plays that fall somewhere between tragedy and comedy and contain dark, unsettling elements but which end 'happily' in so far as no one dies. They are knows as 'Problem Comedies' or 'Dark Comedies'. *Measure for Measure* and *All's Well That Ends Well* are two plays that come into this category.

PROGRESS CHECK

Decide which type of play you are studying and be aware of its particular characteristics.

7.2 Plot and structure

LEARNING SUMMARY

After studying this section you should be able to understand:
- *what is meant by plot and structure*
- *how to approach studying it in your play*

What are plot and structure?

All plays, including those of Shakespeare, have a plot and some kind of structure. Put simply, the **plot** of a play is the 'story' that the play tells and the **structure** is the way that the story is organised and put together.

Plot and structure are important because they make up the whole 'storyline' of the play and so, before you can really begin to study the other aspects of the play, you really need to be familiar with these. You cannot begin to study a play properly until you know what happens in the play.

There are a number of things you can do:

- **Read** the play thoroughly so that you get a basic idea of who the characters are and what is happening.
- **See** the play in performance – on the stage if possible but, if not, then try to get hold of a video of it (a video store or your local school/college library may be able to help).
- **Imagine** how the action might take place as you read the play.
- **Act out** some of the scenes to see how they could be performed.
- **Make notes** on each scene to build up a picture of how the plot develops.

As you are studying the plot of your play, you will begin to notice things about how that plot is put together and develops – these are things to do with structure. Most plays follow a similar basic structure:

An understanding of this general structure can help you to follow the storyline of the play.

1. Introduction to situation

2. Introduction to characters

3. Something occurs that sets off a train of events

4. Chaos or confusion follows

5. Things get worse

6. Reaches a climax. In comedy the confusion is sorted out; in tragedy main characters die

7. A new beginning is signalled

PROGRESS CHECK

Think about the particular play you are studying and make a plan to show how it follows this basic structure.

Here is a plan of the basic structure of *Romeo and Juliet*:

1. Introduction to the situation – the feud between Montagues and Capulets.
2. Introduction to the characters – first of all Romeo and later Juliet.
3. Incident which provides starting point to play – Romeo meets Juliet.
4. Chaos and confusion – Romeo and Juliet have to keep their love and marriage a secret from everyone. Romeo kills Tybalt.
5. Things get worse – Juliet's parents try to force her to marry Paris. The Friar's plan with the potion. His message to Romeo fails to get through.
6. The climax of the play – Romeo kills Paris, then kills himself and Juliet kills herself.
7. The feuding Montagues and Capulets are brought together and the play ends in a spirit of harmony.

7.3 Opening scenes

LEARNING SUMMARY

After studying this section you should be able to understand:

● *why the opening is important*
● *techniques that Shakespeare used for opening his plays*
● *how these techniques are used in specific plays*

Why the opening is important

Opening the play at the right point in the action and in the right way is important to any play because it is vital to capture the audience's attention right away, but it is important for other reasons as well:

● Most of Shakespeare's openings **set the scene** in some way.
● They contain the seeds of what is going to **happen later** in the play.
● They do this in such a way as to **capture** the audience's **attention** and **interest**.

Techniques for opening plays

Shakespeare uses a number of techniques to make the opening of his plays more effective. Here are some ideas:

● The play opens in the middle of some kind of action – something has just happened or is about to happen.
● Often the play opens with minor characters speaking to describe to the audience the situation or what has happened.
● These characters often refer to a major character although, very often, the main character does not appear until a little later.
● A particular mood or atmosphere is established at the beginning of the play.

KEY POINT

Shakespeare uses a variety of techniques to make the opening of his plays more effective. Think about the play you are studying and see if you can recognise any of these techniques.

Opening scenes

Read the following opening from *Macbeth*.

SCENE I – *An open place*

Thunder and lightning. Enter three WITCHES

First Witch:	When shall we three meet again?
	In thunder, lightning, or in rain?
Second Witch:	When the hurly-burly's done,
	When the battle's lost and won.
Third Witch:	That will be ere the set of sun.
First Witch:	Where the place?
Second Witch:	Upon the heath.
Third Witch:	There to meet with Macbeth.
First Witch:	I come, Graymalkin.
Second Witch:	Paddock calls.
Third Witch:	Anon!
All:	Fair is foul, and foul is fair:
	Hover through the fog and filthy air.

WITCHES *vanish*

PROGRESS CHECK

What do you think are the important points about how Shakespeare opens this play? What do we learn from this scene?

- The stage directions *'Thunder and lightning'* suggest menace and violence.
- Witches are associated with evil.
- We learn a battle has taken place.
- The witches intend to meet Macbeth.

Here is part of a student's response to the question: 'Look at the opening scene of *Macbeth*. With reference to what happens later in the play, how effective do you find this opening?'

> The student pays attention to the stage directions, visualises what the effect on the stage would be and evaluates the dramatic effect of these.

> Comments on the creation of mood and atmosphere and connects this to the events that are about to happen.

> Focuses on the information that the scene conveys about what is happening.

> Identifies the significance of the mention of Macbeth and how this links him to the witches.

> Shows an appreciation of the significance of the witches in terms of the thematic development of good/evil in the play and creates a springboard to link the opening scene to later developments in the play.

The scene opens with thunder and lightning, which on stage would open the play in a dramatic way with loud noises and flashes of light. This would immediately capture the audience's attention and they would be focusing on the stage as the witches appear. The thunder and lightning create a frightening and menacing atmosphere and this sets the tone for the frightening, menacing and evil events that are about to unfold on the stage. The mood and atmosphere are set in this way but the effect of the scene is wider than simply the setting of mood and atmosphere. It also gives us information that is an important introduction to the events of the play. It seems that the play opens while a battle is raging and the three witches will meet again when it is all over. They seem to have fore-knowledge that that will be before the end of the day. The name of Macbeth is introduced and a connection is therefore established between themselves and Macbeth. Their closing lines:

"Fair is foul, and foul is fair:

Hover through the fog and filthy air."

give us a major clue to what the witches' objectives are. They find whatever is good, ugly and whatever is bad and ugly they find good. They seek, therefore, to turn goodness into evil and this directly links to the events concerning Macbeth that develop in the play.

The opening scene of *Macbeth*, then, prepares us for the tragedy that is to follow by creating a sense of evil and foreboding. The opening of the comedy, *Twelfth Night,* is quite different. Read the opening of it through carefully.

Enter Duke of Orsino, Curio, and other Lords; Musicians attending

Orsino:	If music be the food of love, play on;
	Give me excess of it, that, surfeiting,
	The appetite may sicken, and so die.
	That strain again! It had a dying fall:
	O, it came o'er my ear like the sweet sound
	That breathes upon a bank of violets,
	Stealing and giving odour! Enough, no more,
	'Tis not so sweet now as it was before.
	O spirit of love, how quick and fresh art thou!
	That, notwithstanding thy capacity
	Receiveth as the sea, nought enters there,
	Of what validity and pitch soe'er
	But falls into abatement and low price
	Even in a minute! So full of shapes is fancy,
	That it alone is high fantastical.
Curio:	Will you go hunt, my lord?
Orsino:	What, Curio?

Curio: The hart.
Orsino: Why, so I do, the noblest that I have:

O, when mine eyes did see Olivia first,
Methought she purg'd the air of pestilence!
That instant was I turn'd into a hart,
And my desires, like fell and cruel hounds,
E'er since pursue me.

Enter Valentine

How now, what news from her?
Valentine: So please my lord, I might not be admitted,
But from her handmaid do return this answer:

The element itself, till seven years' heat,
Shall not behold her face at ample view;
But, like a cloistress, she will veiled walk,
And water once a day her chamber round
With eye-offending brine: all this to season
A brother's dead love, which she would keep fresh
And lasting, in her sad remembrance.
Orsino: O, she that hath a heart of that fine frame
To pay this debt of love but to a brother,
How will she love, when the rich golden shaft
Hath kill'd the flock of all affections else
That live in her; when liver, brain, and heart,
These sovereign thrones, are all supplied and fill'd
Her sweet perfections with one self king!
Away before me, to sweet beds of flowers:

Love-thoughts lie rich, when canopied with bowers!

Exeunt

PROGRESS CHECK

Think about the ways in which this scene opens and make a note of the key points.

Here are some you might have noted:

- The lovesick Orsino is introduced.
- A perhaps excessively romantic atmosphere is created.
- It suggests something sentimental and self-indulgent about Orsino's attitude to love.
- It reveals that Orsino is in love with Olivia but his suit has been rejected.
- We are told that she intends to isolate herself and mourn her dead brother for seven years.

KEY POINT

When looking at the opening scene of the play you are studying, be aware of all its aspects – the giving of information, introducing characters, creating atmosphere and mood, establishing thematic ideas.

Now look at the opening scene of the play you are studying and make a note of how Shakespeare uses the scene to create an effective opening to the play.

7.4 Presenting characters

LEARNING SUMMARY

After studying this section you should be able to understand:
- *how Shakespeare creates characters*
- *soliloquies and asides*

The creation of characters

Characters are the central feature in any play. An essential part of your study will be to see how Shakespeare creates and presents his characters and how they function in the play. Shakespeare gives his audience an impression of the characters in a play in various ways.

Here are some ways we get a picture of a character:

- What the character **looks** like (physical appearance, clothing etc.). When a play is seen on the stage then much of this will be visual, although characters sometimes comment on another character's appearance in the dialogue. Don't forget to look at the stage directions too when studying from a text.
- What a character **says** and **how** it is said.
- What the character **thinks** (often we learn about this from a character's soliloquies).
- How the character **acts** – watch out for reaction to different situations.
- How the character's words **match** their actual **deeds** or their underlying **motives**.
- What other characters **say about a character**.
- How a character **changes** as the play goes on.

KEY POINT

There are several ways that we formulate impressions of characters. Make sure you take them all into account when considering a character.

Soliloquies and asides

Make sure you are familiar with all the soliloquies given by the characters in the play you are studying. Be clear in your mind as to what these soliloquies reveal about the characters.

In his plays, Shakespeare makes full use of the **dramatic devices**, **asides** and **soliloquies**, as a means of revealing to the audience what is in the mind of a character. It is as if the character is speaking aloud to the audience and no one else on stage can hear them. Asides are usually quite short and are often spoken while other characters are on stage.

For example, in *The Merchant of Venice*, Shylock is a moneylender and Antonio needs to borrow some money from him. Look at this extract.

Shylock [Aside]: How like a fawning publican he looks!
I hate him for he is a Christian;
But more for that in low simplicity
He lends out money gratis, and brings down
The rate of usance here with us in Venice.

	If I can catch him once upon the hip,
	I will feed fat the ancient grudge I bear him.
	He hates our sacred nation; and he rails,
	Even there where merchants most do congregate,
	On me, my bargains, and my well-won thrift,
	Which he calls interest. Cursed be my tribe
	If I forgive him!
Bassanio:	Shylock, do you hear?
Shylock:	I am debating of my present store,
	And, by the near guess of my memory,
	I cannot instantly raise up the gross
	Of full three thousand ducats. What of that?
	Tubal, a wealthy Hebrew of my tribe,
	Will furnish me. But soft! how many months
	Do you desire? [*To Antonio*] Rest you fair, good signor;
	Your worship was the last man in our mouths.

The Merchant of Venice Act I, scene iii, lines 37–57

PROGRESS CHECK

What does this aside reveal and why do you think Shakespeare uses it here?

It reveals that Shylock hates Antonio and relishes the idea of getting a hold over him. Shakespeare uses it here to reveal Shylock's true feelings and therefore increase dramatic tension.

Some asides are much briefer than the one Shylock uses, but soliloquies tend to be longer and usually occur when no other characters are on stage.

In the following example from *Henry IV Part One,* King Henry's son, the Prince, has been a complete disappointment to his father and has been apparently living a wild life, drinking with a group of disreputable characters, in particular one called Falstaff. He spends most of his time in the tavern and the brothel. However, early in the play, the Prince, left alone on the stage, delivers the following soliloquy:

Prince:	I know you all, and will awhile uphold
	The unyok'd humour of your idleness:
	Yet herein will I imitate the sun,
	Who doth permit the base contagious clouds
	To smother up his beauty from the world,
	That when he please again to be himself,
	Being wanted, he may be more wonder'd at,
	By breaking through the foul and ugly mists
	Of vapours that did seem to strangle him.
	If all the year were playing holidays,
	To sport would be as tedious as to work;
	But when they seldom come, they wish'd for come,
	And nothing pleaseth but rare accidents.
	So, when this loose behaviour I throw off,
	And pay the debt I never promised,
	By how much better than my word I am
	By so much shall I falsify men's hopes;
	And like bright metal on a sullen ground,

King Richard:	What must the King do now? Must he submit?
	The King shall do it. Must he be deposed?
	The King shall be contented. Must he lose
	The name of king? O God's name, let it go.
	I'll give my jewels for a set of beads,
	My gorgeous palace for a hermitage,
	My gay apparel for an almsman's gown,
	My figured goblets for a dish of wood,
	My sceptre for a palmer's walking-staff,
	My subjects for a pair of carved saints,
	And my large kingdom for a little grave,
	A little, little grave, an obscure grave;
	Or I'll be buried in the King's highway,
	Some way of common trade where subject's feet
	May hourly trample on their sovereign's head,
	For on my heart they tread now whilst I live,
	And buried once, why not upon my head?

Richard II, Act III, scene iii, lines 143–159

Shakespeare uses iambic pentameter quite differently in this speech, where Othello, believing Desdemona to have been unfaithful, prepares to kill her.

Othello:	It is the cause, it is the cause, my soul,
	Let me not name it to you, you chaste stars:
	It is the cause, yet I'll not shed her blood,
	Nor scar that whiter skin of hers than snow,
	And smooth, as monumental alabaster;
	Yet she must die, else she'll betray more men.
	Put out the light, and then put out the light:
	If I quench thee, thou flaming minister,
	I can again thy former light restore,
	Should I repent me; but once put out thy light,
	Thou cunning pattern of excelling nature,
	I know not where is that Promethean heat
	That can thy light relume: when I have pluck'd the rose,
	I cannot give it vital growth again,
	It must needs wither; I'll smell it on the tree, [*Kisses her.*]
	O balmy breath, that doth almost persuade
	Justice herself to break her sword: once more:
	Be thus, when thou art dead, and I will kill thee,
	And love thee after: once more, and this the last,
	So sweet was ne'er so fatal: I must weep,
	But they are cruel tears; this sorrow's heavenly,
	It strikes when it does love: she wakes.

Othello Act V, scene ii, lines 1–22

My reformation, glittering o'er my fault,
Shall show more goodly and attract more eyes
Than that which hath no foil to set it off.
I'll so offend to make offence a skill;
Redeeming time when men think least I will.

Henry IV Part One

PROGRESS CHECK

**What does the Prince reveal in this soliloquy and w
has the character deliver it so early in the play?**

The soliloquy reveals that the Prince is only giving th
lifestyle but this is not his true nature. He knows th
reveals his true, noble nature, he will surprise and i
Through this soliloquy, Shakespeare allows us, the
nature of the Prince early on in the play. We can se
other characters can.

7.5 Shakespeare's

LEARNING SUMMARY

After studying this section you should be able to und
* *how Shakespeare uses poetry and prose*
* *what imagery adds to the play*

Poetry and prose

Shakespeare's plays are written mainly in poetry
prose too (ordinary writing not organised with
kind of verse form that Shakespeare uses is calle
verse is the form of verse that is closest in rhyth
the ideal form to use for dialogue.

Blank verse is verse that does not rhyme and w
'iambic pentameters'. An iamb is an unstres
syllable. Five iambs in a row make a line of iam
in Greek, as in 'pentagon' or 'pentathlon'). Thi
syllables, five stressed and five unstressed, as in

⌣ ⁄ ⌣ ⁄ ⌣ ⁄ ⌣ ⁄ ⌣
"But soft, what light through yonder window bre

However, where necessary for his effects, Shak
them longer in order to express his meaning,
where one line flows on into the next.

This speech from *Richard II*, where Richard resi
is written in regular iambic pentameter:

> My reformation, glittering o'er my fault,
> Shall show more goodly and attract more eyes
> Than that which hath no foil to set it off.
> I'll so offend to make offence a skill;
> Redeeming time when men think least I will.

Henry IV Part One, Act I, scene ii, lines 217–239

PROGRESS CHECK

What does the Prince reveal in this soliloquy and why do you think Shakespeare has the character deliver it so early in the play?

The soliloquy reveals that the Prince is only giving the impression of leading a wild lifestyle but this is not his true nature. He knows that when he 'reforms' and reveals his true, noble nature, he will surprise and impress people all the more. Through this soliloquy, Shakespeare allows us, the audience, to see the true nature of the Prince early on in the play. We can see him in a way that none of the other characters can.

7.5 Shakespeare's language

LEARNING SUMMARY

After studying this section you should be able to understand:
- *how Shakespeare uses poetry and prose*
- *what imagery adds to the play*

Poetry and prose

Shakespeare's plays are written mainly in poetry (verse) but he does use some prose too (ordinary writing not organised with rhymes or fixed line lengths). The kind of verse form that Shakespeare uses is called **'blank verse'**. This kind of verse is the form of verse that is closest in rhythm to natural speech. This makes it the ideal form to use for dialogue.

Blank verse is verse that does not rhyme and which is composed of lines called **'iambic pentameters'**. An iamb is an unstressed syllable followed by a stressed syllable. Five iambs in a row make a line of iambic pentameter ('pent' means five in Greek, as in 'pentagon' or 'pentathlon'). This means that each line has 10 syllables, five stressed and five unstressed, as in this line from *Romeo and Juliet*:

"But soft, what light through yonder window breaks?"

However, where necessary for his effects, Shakespeare may shorten lines or make them longer in order to express his meaning, or use **enjambment** (running on) where one line flows on into the next.

This speech from *Richard II*, where Richard resigns himself to giving up his crown, is written in regular iambic pentameter:

King Richard: What must the King do now? Must he submit?
The King shall do it. Must he be deposed?
The King shall be contented. Must he lose
The name of king? O God's name, let it go.
I'll give my jewels for a set of beads,
My gorgeous palace for a hermitage,
My gay apparel for an almsman's gown,
My figured goblets for a dish of wood,
My sceptre for a palmer's walking-staff,
My subjects for a pair of carved saints,
And my large kingdom for a little grave,
A little, little grave, an obscure grave;
Or I'll be buried in the King's highway,
Some way of common trade where subject's feet
May hourly trample on their sovereign's head,
For on my heart they tread now whilst I live,
And buried once, why not upon my head?

Richard II, Act III, scene iii, lines 143–159

Shakespeare uses iambic pentameter quite differently in this speech, where Othello, believing Desdemona to have been unfaithful, prepares to kill her.

Othello: It is the cause, it is the cause, my soul,
Let me not name it to you, you chaste stars:
It is the cause, yet I'll not shed her blood,
Nor scar that whiter skin of hers than snow,
And smooth, as monumental alabaster;
Yet she must die, else she'll betray more men.
Put out the light, and then put out the light:
If I quench thee, thou flaming minister,
I can again thy former light restore,
Should I repent me; but once put out thy light,
Thou cunning pattern of excelling nature,
I know not where is that Promethean heat
That can thy light relume: when I have pluck'd the rose,
I cannot give it vital growth again,
It must needs wither; I'll smell it on the tree, [*Kisses her.*]
O balmy breath, that doth almost persuade
Justice herself to break her sword: once more:
Be thus, when thou art dead, and I will kill thee,
And love thee after: once more, and this the last,
So sweet was ne'er so fatal: I must weep,
But they are cruel tears; this sorrow's heavenly,
It strikes when it does love: she wakes.

Othello Act V, scene ii, lines 1–22

PROGRESS CHECK

Compare the different effects created by the ways in which Shakespeare uses iambic pentameter.

- The speech from Richard II is much more regular and most of the lines are end-stopped. The regularity of the rhythm pattern gives a solemn, ritualistic feel to the lines as Richard prepares to give up his crown.
- Othello's speech, although using elevated and emotional language, follows more closely the rhythm of speech. Shakespeare sometimes divides a line into two by a pause (a caesura) and many of the lines run on (enjambment) and, where necessary, his lines contain more than the 10 syllables.

As well as using blank verse, Shakespeare also uses **prose** in his plays. It is often said that, in his plays, blank verse is used by important characters of high standing and that the 'low' or comic characters use prose. This is often true but is not always the case. The real answer is that Shakespeare uses prose for a variety of purposes and in a variety of **contexts** and the key is what is happening in the text at that point.

It was the convention of the time that prose was used in:

- the reading aloud of letters, proclamations, challenges, accusations etc.
- circumstances where a character descends into madness or is losing control, e.g. Othello when he is overtaken by jealousy
- comic scenes, e.g. Sir Toby Belch and his associates in *Twelfth Night* (over half of *Twelfth Night* is in prose)
- situations where characters of low status, such as clowns, servants, drunks etc., are speaking

Look carefully at the play you are studying and be aware of which characters use verse, where in the play they use it and why.

However, it is important to note that these are not hard and fast rules and that Shakespeare was prepared to change his language according to circumstances. For example, the Nurse in *Romeo and Juliet* speaks in both prose and verse, as does Hamlet.

 KEY POINT

In order to decide why Shakespeare uses prose or verse, you need to look closely at the text and at who is speaking, what they have to say and in what context they are saying it.

In *Macbeth*, for example, the porter is both a low and a comic character. Appropriately, he speaks in prose when he is describing the effects of drink.

> *Porter:* Marry, Sir, nose-painting, sleep and urine. Lechery, Sir, it provokes and it unprovokes: it provokes the desire, but it takes away the performance. Therefore, much drink may be said to be an equivocator with lechery: it makes him and it mars him; it sets him on, and it takes him off; it persuades him, and disheartens him; makes him stand to, and not stand to: in conclusion, equivocates him in a sleep, and, giving him the lie, leaves him.
>
> *Macbeth Act II, scene iii, lines 27–35*

Even here, the prose has a pattern to it as the contrasts are balanced against each other.

However, a central and noble character such as Hamlet also speaks in prose on occasion. Here, for example, he talks about the effect that his melancholy has on him and how he has lost all interest in the earth and mankind.

> *Hamlet:*   King and Queen moult no feather. I have of late – but wherefore I know not – lost all my mirth, forgone all custom of exercises; and indeed it goes so heavily with my disposition that this goodly frame, the earth, seems to me a sterile promontory. This most excellent canopy the air – look you, this brave o'er-hanging firmament, this majestical roof fretted with golden fire – why, it appeareth no other thing to me than a foul and pestilent congregation of vapours. What a piece of work is a man. How noble in reason, how infinite in faculties. In form and moving how express and admirable, in action how like an angel, in apprehension how like a god. The beauty of the world. The paragon of animals. And yet, to me what is this quintessence of dust? Man delights not me – no, nor woman neither, though by your smiling you seem to say so.
>
> *Hamlet* Act II, scene ii, lines 301–317

PROGRESS CHECK

What do you notice about the nature of Hamlet's prose here?

Even though written in prose, it does have poetic qualities to it. The language is elevated and uses imagery to explore the extent of his disillusionment.

Shakespeare's use of imagery

Imagery involves the use of emotionally charged words and phrases, which create **vivid pictures** in the minds of the readers or listeners. Shakespeare's imagery often includes **metaphors** or **similes**. A simile compares one thing to another using 'like' or 'as'. For example, Juliet's words to Romeo:

'*My bounty is as boundless as the sea,*
My love as deep.'

A metaphor is also a form of **comparison** but, instead of using 'like' or 'as', it suggests that the thing being described, and the thing compared to it, are the same. Donalbain's warning to brother Malcolm in *Macbeth*:

'*There's daggers in men's smiles*'

Shakespeare often uses imagery to explore and add emphasis to a particular idea. In *The Tempest*, for example, Prospero compares the brief and temporary nature of the span of a human life with the impermanent nature of actors acting out a part in the theatre.

> *Prospero:* As I foretold you, were all spirits, and
> Are melted into air, into thin air:
> And, like the baseless fabric of this vision,
> The cloud-capp'd towers, the gorgeous palaces,
> The solemn temples, the great globe itself,
> Yea, all which it inherit, shall dissolve,
> And, like this insubstantial pageant faded,
> Leave not a rack behind. We are such stuff
> As dreams are made on; and our little life
> Is rounded with a sleep. Sir, I am vex'd;
>
> *The Tempest* Act IV, scene i, lines 148–158

In a play, there are often groups of **images** that are repeated and which build up a sense of the **themes** the play explores. For example, in *Othello* the evil Iago is frequently linked with the idea of hell through the imagery of the play.

Here are just a few examples:

● He swears by the '*divinity of hell*' (Act II, scene iii, line 341).
● He suggests to Roderigo that his wits are working with '*All the tribe of hell*' (Act I, scene iii, line 358).
● He explains how his untoward trustworthiness conceals his evil:

'When devils will the blackest sins put on,
They do suggest at first with heavenly shows
As I do now.'

(Act II, scene iii, lines 342–344)

On the other hand, the '*divine*' Desdemona is, from her first appearance in the play to the last, a figure of heavenly purity and goodness and this too is stressed through the repeated use of images that link her to the idea of heaven, as when Cassio welcomes her and prays that:

'*…the grace of heaven*
Before, behind thee, and on every hand,
Enwheel thee round.'

(Act II, scene i, lines 85–87)

The heaven and hell imagery is used to highlight and explore one of the key themes of the play – that of the contrast between good and evil.

KEY POINT

> **Apart from using imagery to enrich the descriptive qualities of the language, Shakespeare also uses it to highlight and develop key ideas and themes.**

Look for imagery in the play you are studying and see if you can spot any repeated patterns.

7.6 Endings

After studying this section you should be able to understand:

- *why the ending is important*
- *techniques that Shakespeare used for ending his plays*

The **ending** of any play is very important as it leaves the audience with the final impression of the drama they have just spent two or three hours watching. In order for the play to have maximum impact, it is important that the ending is effective.

The ending of the play:

- develops from the action of the play and forms a natural conclusion
- draws together all the threads of the plot
- resolves and sorts out problems, confusions and conflicts that have been developed through the course of the action
- creates a dramatic climax
- often has a sense of future happiness or reconciliation or a sense that a start is being made

> Have ideas about your response to the ending of the play. Exam questions sometimes ask you to write about the effectiveness of the ending of the play you are studying.

PROGRESS CHECK

Think about the ending of the play you are studying and tick the features it possesses.

a sense of happiness	☐	sense of a new start	☐
feelings of sadness	☐	reconciliation	☐
tragic consequences	☐	conflicts resolved	☐
confusions sorted out	☐		

Techniques used for ending plays

Put simply, Shakespeare's tragedies always end in the death of the central character and usually a number of other characters too – whereas, in the comedies, there are no deaths and things end happily.

In *Romeo and Juliet*, for example, this is what happens:

> Romeo (thinking Juliet is dead) goes to the Capulet vault.

> He encounters Paris and kills him.

> He finds the body of Juliet and drinks his poison to die with her.

> She wakes up from her drugged sleep to find the dead Romeo. Grief stricken, she stabs herself to death.

This tragedy ends with the deaths of three characters, including the central characters of Romeo and Juliet. However, Shakespeare does not leave the tragedy there. Tragic though the ending is, there is also a note of hope for the future in that the deaths of Romeo and Juliet have brought together the feuding Montagues and Capulets.

> *Prince:* A glooming peace this morning with it brings;
> The sun for sorrow will not show his head.
> Go hence to have more talk of these sad things;
> Some shall be pardoned, and some punished.
> For never was a story of more woe
> Than this of Juliet and her Romeo.
>
> *Romeo and Juliet* Act V, scene iii, lines 304–309

In a comedy, such as *Twelfth Night*, there are no such tragic deaths. Here is what happens in the final scene:

Viola is reunited with her twin brother, Sebastian, whom she thought had drowned at sea.

The confusion over Viola's disguise is sorted out and she and Orsino plan to marry.

Sebastian and Olivia love each other and they plan to marry.

Everyone is happy at the end, with the exception of Malvolio who is angry at having been tricked.

PROGRESS CHECK

Look carefully at the play you are studying and make a brief plan of the way in which Shakespeare brings it to an end.

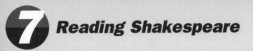

Sample GCSE coursework question

Write an analysis of the dramatic contribution that Friar Laurence makes to *Romeo and Juliet*.

We first meet Friar Laurence in Act II, scene iii, and it is immediately clear that he is a good friend to Romeo, as well as being his confessor and spiritual advisor. When Romeo arrives at his cell, the Friar is collecting herbs to make his medicines and potions. It is one of these potions that he will give to Juliet later. His words here are ironic as he talks of:

> "The earth that's nature's mother is her tomb:
> What is her burying grave that is her womb"
>
> Act II, scene iii, lines 9-10

These words are prophetic of what will happen to Juliet later in the play.

Romeo has gone to the Friar to tell him about his love for Juliet and to ask him to marry them. As well as being Romeo's friend and advisor, the Friar is also the spiritual advisor to Juliet. He has known them both since childhood and knows the family and their feud. Dramatically, and in terms of the plot, this is important because it is the idea that the love of Romeo and Juliet could bring an end to the Capulet and Montague feud that motivates him in agreeing to marry them.

He also has a key role in the plot because of the advice that he gives the two lovers. There are four key points here that add to the dramatic development of the plot. Firstly, the fact that he marries Romeo and Juliet causes problems later. Secondly, the idea of the potion is his and this brings tragedy later. Thirdly, it is he who instructs Friar John to take the message to Romeo and, because this is not delivered, Romeo buys poison. Finally, the fact that Friar Laurence is not at the tomb when Romeo arrives is dramatically necessary for the tragedy to take place. In other words, this character is dramatically important because he is responsible for a whole sequence of events that are essential to the development of the plot.

Dramatically, he also provides a sense of contrast that heightens the tragedy because, although his actions end in disaster, they are not done deliberately. He acts out of the best of intentions to try to bring good to everyone. He also contrasts with Romeo and Juliet because he is a steadying and calm influence and advises moderation when their love seems to overwhelm them.

Overall, then, the dramatic contribution that the Friar makes to the play is very important and, as a character in the play, he performs a number of functions.

Focuses clearly on the Friar.

Makes a very good point here, linking forward to events in the plot. Good identification of the irony here and clearly explained.

Quotation used to illustrate point.

Shows knowledge of plot and the Friar's position in relation to other characters.

Awareness of motivation.

Clear understanding of dramatic significance and explained in a clear and logical way.

Sums up ideas.

Provides other dramatic contributions. Perhaps some supporting quotations would be useful here to illustrate ideas.

Coursework practice question

What views of the nature of friendship and love are offered in *The Merchant of Venice*?

You should focus closely on TWO or THREE examples from the play to illustrate your answer.

....

....

....

....

....

....

....

....

....

....

....

....

....

....

....

....

....

....

Studying drama texts *(pre- and post-1914)*

The following topics are included in this chapter:

- **Approaching the text**
- **Opening scenes**
- **Presenting characters**
- **Issues and themes**

ENGLISH LITERATURE AQA A

8.1 Approaching the text

LEARNING SUMMARY

After studying this section you should be able to understand:

- **the nature of drama texts**
- **how to begin to study your text**

The nature of drama

Before you begin this section it is worth noting that much of what was discussed in Chapter 7, in relation to Shakespeare, also applies to the study of other drama texts. Drama texts were written to be seen rather than read and the full meaning and impact of many of them can only be fully appreciated when they are seen in **performance**. When studying your text, keep this in mind and recognise that you are dealing with a work that is very different from a novel or short story.

KEY POINT   Drama texts are written to be seen rather than read.

Approaching your text

Here are some suggestions of things you can do to familiarise yourself with a play before you look at it in detail:

Stage 1

1. **Read** the play all the way through. If you can read it with others, with people reading the parts aloud, this will help a great deal. Remember, drama is really a group activity.
2. See a live **performance** of the play if you can. If you can't, try to see a film or video version of it. If this is not possible, try to listen to it on audio tape or CD. (Your school, college or public library might be able to help in obtaining video or audio recordings.)

3. Make notes on any performance you see or hear. Keep a log book to record your initial impressions of characters, action etc.

Stage 2

You are now ready to start looking at the play in more detail. Here are some things you can do to help develop your understanding further:

1. Have ideas about the characters – look at the **key speeches**.
2. Look for various meanings or 'patterns' in the play – this will help you to identify **themes**.
3. Think about the **structure** of the play and the **dramatic effects** that are created.
4. Look carefully at the language of the play, focusing on key speeches, soliloquies, dialogue between characters etc.

Stage 3

If you are studying the text for an exam, you will need to make sure you have some detailed notes to revise from. It will help you a great deal if you adopt an organised and systematic approach to your note-making. Here are some suggestions:

It's a good idea to select specific references from the text to support the points you make.

1. Make a brief **summary** of what happens in each scene/act. It's a good idea to note any key speeches or events here – you can use the summary as a quick reference to locate particular things in the text.
2. Keep a separate **character log**. Make notes on:
   - each occasion where a character appears in the play
   - what they say and do and the significance of this
   - any important things they say or key speeches
   - what other characters say about them

Be aware of how all these elements link together in the play.

3. Keep notes on the **key ideas** (themes/issues raised in the play). Make notes on:
   - **themes** and how these are presented
   - how **language**, **images**, **symbols** etc. develop these ideas

8.2 Opening scenes

LEARNING SUMMARY

After studying this section you should be able to understand:
- *the dramatic function of an opening scene*
- *how some dramatists open their plays*

What opening scenes do

The way in which a play opens is very important because that is where the dramatist needs to capture the audience's interest and attention. There are many ways to do this, depending on the intended purpose of the scene and the effect the dramatist wants it to have on the audience.

An opening scene can have a number of purposes, in any combination. For example, it can:

- provide an **explanation** of what has happened before the play actually starts, giving background **information** that the audience needs to know in order to understand what is going on
- create a background **setting** against which the action of the play takes place
- create a particular **mood** or **atmosphere** that immediately captures the audience's attention
- introduce characters, perhaps revealing something of situations and relationships
- create a sense of intrigue or mystery that captures the audience's **attention** and makes them want to know more

 KEY POINT | The opening of a play can have a variety of purposes and achieve its effects in a number of ways.

How plays can open

Now let's have a more detailed look at how some dramatists open their plays.

Read the following opening of *She Stoops to Conquer* by Oliver Goldsmith, a comedy first performed on the stage in 1773.

Mrs Hardcastle	I vow, Mr Hardcastle, you're very particular. Is there a creature in the whole country but ourselves, that does not take a trip to town now and then, to rub off the rust a little? There's the two Miss Hoggs, and our neighbour, Mrs Grigsby, go to take a month's polishing every winter.
Hardcastle	Ay, and bring back vanity and affectation to last them the whole year. I wonder why London cannot keep its own fools at home! In my time, the follies of the town crept slowly among us, but now they travel faster than a stage-coach. Its fopperies come down, not only as inside passengers, but in the very basket.
Mrs Hardcastle	Ay, *your* times were fine times indeed; you have been telling us of *them* for many a long year. Here we live in an old rumbling mansion, that looks for all the world like an inn, but that we never see company. Our best visitors are old Mrs Oddfish, the curate's wife, and little Cripplegate, the lame dancing-master: And all our entertainment your old stories of Prince Eugene and the Duke of Marlborough. I hate such old-fashioned trumpery.
Hardcastle	And I love it. I love every thing that's old: old friends, old times, old manners, old books, old wines and I believe, Dorothy, (*taking her hand*) you'll own I have been pretty fond of an old wife.
Mrs Hardcastle	Lord, Mr Hardcastle, you're for ever at your Dorothy's, and your old wife's. You may be a Darby, but I'll be no Joan, I promise you. I'm not so old as you'll make me, by more than one good year. Add twenty to twenty, and make money of that.
Hardcastle	Let me see; twenty added to twenty, makes just fifty and seven.
Mrs Hardcastle	It's false, Mr Hardcastle: I was but twenty when I was brought to bed of Tony, that I had by Mr Lumpkin, my first husband; and he's not come to years of discretion yet.
Hardcastle	Nor ever will. I dare answer for him. Ay, you have taught him finely.
Mrs Hardcastle	No matter, Tony Lumpkin has a good fortune. My son is not to live by his learning. I don't think a boy wants much learning to spend fifteen hundred a year.
Hardcastle	Learning, quotha! A mere composition of tricks and mischief.
Mrs Hardcastle	Humour, my dear: nothing but humour. Come, Mr Hardcastle, you must allow the boy a little humour.

Hardcastle	I'd sooner allow him an horse-pond. If burning the footmen's shoes, frighting the maids, and worrying the kittens, be humour, he has it. It was but yesterday he fastened my wig to the back of my chair, and when I went to make a bow, I popt my bald head in Mrs Frizzle's face.

From *She Stoops to Conquer* by Oliver Goldsmith

PROGRESS CHECK

What is Goldsmith's purpose here and what effect do you think he wants this opening to achieve?

● Two characters, Hardcastle and his wife, Mrs Hardcastle, begin by exchanging information in order to give the audience certain important details.

● We learn some important details about the characters, such as the fact that Mrs Hardcastle has pretensions towards refinement and that she has a son by a previous marriage. This character, Tony Lumpkin, wastes his money on drink and is not very bright.

● The setting is revealed as the Hardcastles' house, which is provincial and old-fashioned. We also learn that it looks like an inn – a detail that is very important to the plot development later.

You will see from this text that Goldsmith manages to convey a good deal of important information to his audience in these opening lines. He does this while maintaining the interest of the audience through the humorous interaction between Mr and Mrs Hardcastle.

KEY POINT

Make sure you are aware of the techniques that the dramatist uses to start the play you are studying.

8.3 Presenting characters

LEARNING SUMMARY

After studying this section you should be able to understand:

● *the importance of characterisation*
● *how dramatists present characters*

The importance of characterisation

Characters are at the centre of all drama and the effectiveness and success of a play often depends on how successfully the dramatist creates and presents characters. When watching or studying a play, you can learn about characters in three main ways:

● through what they do, their actions on the stage
● through what they say
● through what other characters say about them

It is important to be aware that you must always look at all these aspects in the context of what is happening in the drama. For example, a character's words may not match what they actually do, or what one character says may not be the same as what another character says. Where this happens, the dramatist has created the effect deliberately for a particular purpose. You need to look carefully at all the evidence in order to reach your assessment of characters.

A useful way to gather information on characters is to keep a **character log** for each of the main characters in the play. Here is a brief example based on a character from *The Crucible* by Arthur Miller.

CHARACTER: John Proctor

Act/ Scene	Character point	Evidence e.g. what they say/do – others say about them	Supporting quotation	Lines/ Page
Act I	He is blunt and speaks his mind	Bluntly says that what is needed in Salem is common sense.	"I've heard you to be a sensible man, Mr Hale. I hope you'll leave some of it in Salem."	p31

 PROGRESS CHECK Work through the play you are studying and produce a table of key points for each character, together with supporting evidence.

 KEY POINT Each character has a role to play in the drama and the dramatist presents them in such a way as to fulfil that role.

How dramatists present characters

In examining the characters in a play, you should make sure you consider all the possible ways you can **interpret** them and the **role** they **perform** in the play, and support your ideas with evidence from the text.

Look at this extract from *An Inspector Calls* by J.B. Priestley – where Arthur Birling, a wealthy, self-made man gives his son and prospective son-in-law the benefit of his experience.

Birling   (*solemnly*) But this is the point. I don't want to lecture you two young fellows again. But what so many of you don't seem to understand now, when things are so much easier, is that a man has to make his own way – has to look after himself – and his family too, of course, when he has one – and so long as he does that he won't come to much harm. But the way some of these cranks talk and write now, you'd think everybody has to look after everybody else, as if we were all mixed up together like bees in a hive – community and all that nonsense. But take my word for it, you youngsters – and I've learnt in the good hard school of experience – that a man has to mind his own business and look after himself and his own – and –

From *An Inspector Calls* by J.B. Priestley

PROGRESS CHECK

Think about what we learn about Birling from what he has to say and note down your ideas.

CHARACTER POINT	EVIDENCE
Takes himself seriously	Stage direction '*solemnly*'
Aware that he lectures people – speaks down to them – patronising	'*I don't want to lecture you… young fellows. But what many of you don't seem to understand.*' '*youngsters*'
Believes that everyone has to look after himself and his own	'*…a man has to make his own way… to look after himself*'
Doesn't agree with people who believe in 'community'	Calls them '*cranks*' and calls it '*nonsense*'
He knows best	'I've learnt in the good hard school of experience'

KEY POINT

Even a short extract can reveal a good deal about the character and the ways in which the dramatist presents them.

In this extract from *A Streetcar Named Desire* we learn about one character's opinion of another. In this case, Blanche is talking to her sister, Stella, about Stella's husband, Stanley.

Blanche   Well – if you'll forgive me – he's common!

Stella   Why, yes, I suppose he is.

Blanche   Suppose! You can't have forgotten that much of our bringing up, Stella, that you just *suppose* that any part of a gentleman's in his nature! *Not one particle, no!* Oh, if he was just – *ordinary*! Just *plain* – but good and wholesome, but – *no.* There's something downright – *bestial* – about him! You're hating me saying this, aren't you?

Stella   [*coldly*]: Go on and say it all, Blanche.

Blanche   He acts like an animal, has an animal's habits! Eats like one, moves like one, talks like one! There's even something – sub-human – something not quite to the stage of humanity yet! Yes, something – ape-like about him, like one of those pictures I've seen in – anthropological studies! Thousands and thousands of years have passed him right by, and there he is – Stanley Kowalski – survivor of the Stone Age! Bearing the raw meat home from the kill in the jungle! And you – you here – waiting for him! Maybe he'll strike you or maybe grunt and kiss you! That is, if kisses have been discovered yet! Night falls and the other apes gather! There in the front of the cave, all grunting like him, and swilling and gnawing and hulking! His poker night! – you call it – this party of apes! Somebody growls – some creature snatches at something – the fight is on! God! Maybe we are a long way from being made in God's image, but Stella – my sister – there has been some progress since then! Such things as art – poetry and music – such kinds of new light have come into the world since then! In some kinds of people some tenderer feelings have had some little beginning! That we have got to make grow! And cling to, and hold as our flag! In this dark march toward whatever it is we're approaching… Don't – don't hang back with the brutes.

From *A Streetcar Named Desire* by Tennessee Williams

It is quite clear from the extract that Blanche does not think very much of Stanley. However, in studying the play you would need to think about whether her view is an accurate one in terms of the character or whether it is biased in some way.

 KEY POINT Consider all the evidence when you are making an assessment of characters.

8.4 Issues and themes

LEARNING SUMMARY

After studying this section you should be able to understand:

- *what themes are*
- *how to begin to study them*
- *how dramatists present and explore their themes*

Themes in plays

Almost all plays are concerned with certain **ideas** or **issues** that the dramatist **explores** throughout the course of the play. These ideas or issues are called **themes** and they are important because they make up the **message** that the dramatist wants to put across to the audience. Often the dramatist wants the audience to think about these issues or make them see things from a particular angle or point of view.

> Make sure you are aware of all the themes in the play you are studying but remember that some of them might be more important than others.

These themes can be about anything and there may be more than one presented in the play. However, the themes in a play often touch upon important issues to do with our lives. For example:

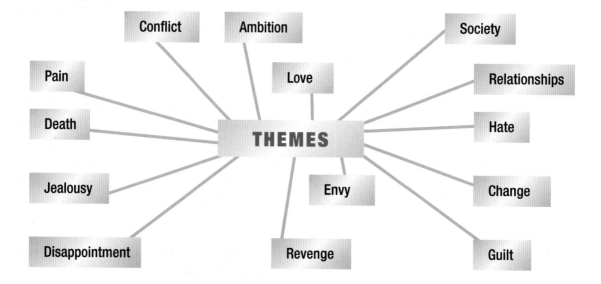

In studying the themes in your play the first thing you need to do is identify what they are. It can be useful to draw up a chart or a table to order your ideas.

Here is a student's plan of the themes of *The Crucible* by Arthur Miller.

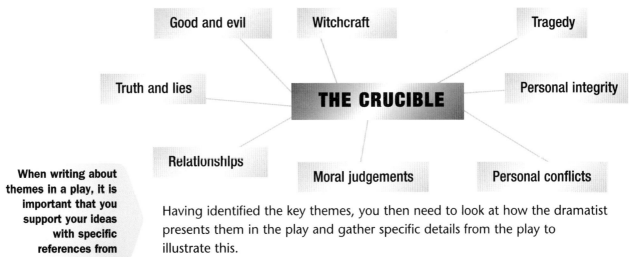

When writing about themes in a play, it is important that you support your ideas with specific references from the text.

Having identified the key themes, you then need to look at how the dramatist presents them in the play and gather specific details from the play to illustrate this.

How dramatists present and explore their themes

Dramatists present their themes in a variety of ways, often through a combination of various techniques. Some of the ways that they do this are through:

- the speeches in the play
- the dialogue
- the language and use of imagery and symbolism
- the setting and stage directions
- the actions of characters

Here are some examples of how dramatists use these techniques.

The speeches

We have already seen how, in *An Inspector Calls*, Arthur Birling is of the opinion that everyone should look after themselves and not bother about other people. The inspector, however, has rather different views after showing how each of the characters has been partly responsible for a young woman's suicide and he sums these up in his final speech before leaving the Birlings' house.

Inspector	(*taking charge, masterfully*) Stop! (*They are suddenly quiet, staring at him.*) And be quiet for a moment and listen to me. I don't need to know any more. Neither do you. This girl killed herself – and died a horrible death. But each of you helped to kill her. Remember that. Never forget it. (*He looks from one to the other of them carefully.*) But then I don't think you ever will. Remember what you did, Mrs Birling. You turned her away when she most needed help. You refused her even the pitiable little bit of organised charity you had in your power to grant her. Remember what you did –
Eric	(*unhappily*) My God – I'm not likely to forget.
Inspector	Just used her for the end of a stupid drunken evening, as if she was an animal, a thing, not a person. No, you won't forget. (*He looks at Sheila*)
Sheila	(*bitterly*) I know. I had her turned out of a job. I started it.
Inspector	You helped – but didn't start it. (*Rather savagely, to Birling*) You started it. She wanted twenty-five shillings a week instead of twenty-two and sixpence. You made her pay a heavy price for that. And now she'll make you pay a heavier price still.

Birling	(*unhappily*) Look, Inspector – I'd give thousands – yes, thousands –
Inspector	You're offering the money at the wrong time, Mr Birling. (*He makes a move as if concluding the session, possibly shutting up notebook etc. then surveys them sardonically.*) No, I don't think any of you will forget. Nor that young man, Croft, though he at least had some affection for her and made her happy for a time. Well, Eva Smith's gone. You can't do her any more harm. And you can't do her any good now, either. You can't even say 'I'm sorry, Eva Smith.'
Sheila	(*who is crying quietly*) That's the worst of it.
Inspector	But just remember this. One Eva Smith has gone – but there are millions and millions and millions of Eva Smiths and John Smiths still left with us, with their lives, their hopes and fears, their suffering and chance of happiness, all intertwined with our lives, and what we think and say and do. We don't live alone. We are members of one body. We are responsible for each other. And I tell you that the time will soon come when, if men will not learn that lesson, then they will be taught it in fire and blood and anguish. Good night.

From *An Inspector Calls* by J.B. Priestley

PROGRESS CHECK

Think about these questions:
1. **What is the main point that the Inspector is making here?**
2. **Find THREE quotations that support your ideas.**
3. **How does this speech reveal a theme of the play?**

1. He makes the point that we are all in this world together and that we should all look after one another (exactly the opposite of the message Birling gives out). How we live affects the lives of others.
2. '*We don't live alone*'
   '*...their suffering and chance of happiness, all intertwined with our lives.*'
   '*We are responsible for each other*'
3. A central theme of this play is that of social responsibility and that people **must** learn to accept that we have to live in this world together.

Setting and stage directions

As mentioned earlier, a play is meant to be seen rather than read and therefore the dramatist is able to control the audience's responses by vision and sound as well as language. This means that the stage set and other external factors, such as **lighting**, **sound effects** and **props**, can be exploited for dramatic effect, including suggesting or reinforcing themes in a play.

Look at the following extract, which is from the opening of *Death of a Salesman* by Arthur Miller. It describes the home of Willy Loman (the Salesman) who is the central character.

A melody is heard, played upon a flute. It is small and fine, telling of grass and trees and the horizon. The curtain rises.

Before us in the Salesman's house. We are aware of towering, angular shapes behind it, surrounding it on all sides. Only the blue light of the sky falls upon the house and forestage; the surrounding area shows an angry glow of orange. As more light appears we see a solid vault of apartment houses around the small, fragile-seeming home. An air of the dream clings to the place, a dream rising out of reality. The kitchen at the centre seems actual enough, for there is a kitchen table with three chairs, and a refrigerator. But no other fixtures are seen. At the back of the kitchen there is a draped entrance, which leads to the living-room. To the right of the kitchen, on a level raised two feet, is a bedroom furnished only with a brass bedstead and a straight chair. On a shelf over the bed a silver athletic trophy stands. A window opens on to the apartment house at the side.

Behind the kitchen, on a level raised six and a half feet, is the boy's bedroom, at present barely visible. Two beds are dimly seen, and at the back of the room a dormer window. (This bedroom is above the unseen living-room.) At the left a stairway curves up to it from the kitchen.

The entire setting is wholly or, in some places, partially transparent. The roof-line of the house is one-dimensional; under and over it we see the apartment buildings. Before the house lies an apron, curbing beyond the forestage into the orchestra. This forward area serves as the back yard as well as the locale of all Willy's imaginings and of his city scenes. Whenever the action is in the present the actors observe the imaginary wall-lines, entering the house only through its door at the left. But in the scenes of the past these boundaries are broken, and characters enter or leave a room by stepping 'through' a wall on to the forestage.

From *Death of a Salesman* by Arthur Miller

- Notice how the play opens, with music that is suggestive of the countryside '*of grass and trees and the horizon*'.
- The setting contrasts with this in that it is very urban.
- The kitchen with refrigerator etc. suggests a domestic setting.
- The athletic trophy suggests past successes.
- The description of '*an air of dream clings to the place, a dream rising out of reality*' is important.
- The description itself is concerned with Willy Loman, who, at sixty, is bewildered by the failure and futility of his life. He has avoided confronting this truth, though, by false dreams about his family and his wife. This opening setting, then, suggests some of the thematic ideas that Miller goes on to explore and develop in the play.

PROGRESS CHECK

Think about the play you are studying and see if you can identify any connections between setting, stage directions and themes.

The dialogue

Harold Pinter's play, *The Caretaker*, examines a number of themes, which are interlinked.

Loneliness/isolation   **Communication (or lack of it)**

Survival in a hostile world

Relationships

These themes are developed and explored primarily through the dialogue of the play. Much of this appears futile and ineffective, and therefore reveals a lack of ability to communicate on a real level. Much of Davies' language is an attempt to avoid the truth, that he is alone and has no-one, nowhere to go.

Here, for example:

Davies	(*with great feeling*). If only the weather would break! Then I'd be able to get down to Sidcup!
Aston	Sidcup?
Davies	The weather's so blasted bloody awful, how can I get down to Sidcup in these shoes?
Aston	Why do you want to get down to Sidcup?
Davies	I got my papers there!
	Pause
Aston	Your what?
Davies	I got my papers there!
	Pause
Aston	What are they doing at Sidcup?
Davies	A man I know has got them. I left them with him. You see? They prove who I am! I can't move without them papers. They tell you who I am. You see! I'm stuck without them.
Aston	Why's that?
Davies	You see, what it is, you see. I changed my name! Years ago. I been going around under an assumed name! That's not my real name.
Aston	What name you been going under?
Davies	Jenkins. Bernard Jenkins. That's my name. That's the name I'm known by, anyway. But it's no good me going on with that name. I got no rights. I got an insurance card here. (*He takes a card from his pocket*) Under the name of Jenkins. See? Bernard Jenkins? Look. It's got four stamps on it. Four of them. But I can't go along with these. That's not my real name, they'd find out, they'd have me in the nick. Four stamps. I haven't paid out pennies. There's been other stamps, plenty, but they haven't put them on, the nigs, I never had enough time to go into it.
Aston	They should have stamped your card.
Davies	It would have done no good! I'd have got nothing anyway. That's not my real name. If I take that card along I go in the nick.
Aston	What's your real name, then?
Davies	Davies. Mac Davies. That was before I changed my name.
	Pause
Aston	It looks as though you want to sort all that out.
Davies	If only I could get down to Sidcup! I've been waiting for the weather to break. He's got my papers, this man I left them with, it's got it all down there, I could prove everything.
Aston	How long's he had them?
Davies	What?
Aston	How long's he had them?
Davies	Oh, must be… it was in the war… must be… about near on fifteen year ago.

From *The Caretaker* by Harold Pinter

PROGRESS CHECK

What is Davies obsessed with here?

Through the dialogue, Davies reveals his central concern and a key theme of the play – that of the search for identity – and emphasises Davies' rootless and aimless existence.

KEY POINT   Dramatists can explore their themes through a variety of methods.

Sample GCSE coursework question

Examine Mrs Birling's role in the play, *An Inspector Calls*. Write about:

- her reactions to the Inspector
- her part in Eva Smith's fate
- her role as a parent
- her relationship with Birling

It is clear from the start of the play that Mrs Birling is not a character that we will warm to. She is portrayed as being cold and snobbish and we are told that she is "...about fifty, a rather cold woman and her husband's social superior". She is obviously from a higher class background than her husband and she knows it.

Clear focus right from the start with appropriate quotation to support comments.

Like Mr Birling, she exhibits a smug self-satisfaction and it is clear that she is very pleased with herself and her own importance. However, it soon becomes apparent that she has little understanding of either her offspring or the world around her. For example, she is completely surprised by the discovery that her son is a heavy drinker and has been for two years. She is also surprised by the revelation that Alderman Meggarty is a "...notorious womaniser as well as being one of the worst sots and rogues in Brumley."

Sound evaluation of characters.

Appropriate textual reference.

She shows a similar complete lack of understanding of her children. It seems that she has never really listened to or understood them. Her son, Eric, says of her "You don't understand anything. You never did. You never... even tried." It is obvious that her daughter, Sheila, is on a completely different wavelength from her mother too.

Provides clear evidence to support comments.

She likes to think that she knows what is going on, and the fact that she is "a prominent member of the Brumley Women's Charity Organisation" shows how she likes to feel important and feed her own ego. Ultimately it is she who seals the fate of Eva Smith when she rejects her pleas for help. Her treatment of Eva Smith shows that even though Eva was pregnant, Mrs Birling still had no qualms about turning her away – she really is the "cold" woman that Priestley describes at the beginning of the play.

Sound knowledge of the text on which to base assessment of character.

Effective conclusion.

Coursework practice question

In Act IV of *Pygmalion* by George Bernard Shaw, Higgins and Pickering discuss the day's events:

Pickering   [*Stretching himself*] Well, I feel a bit tired. It's been a long day. The garden party, a dinner party, and the reception! Rather too much of a good thing. But you've won your bet, Higgins. Eliza did the trick, and something to spare, eh?

Higgins   [*fervently*] Thank God it's over!
Eliza flinches violently; but they take no notice of her; and she recovers herself and sits stonily as before.

Pickering   Were you nervous at the garden party? *I* was. Eliza didn't seem a bit nervous.

Higgins   Oh, she wasn't nervous. I knew she'd be all right. No: it's the strain of putting the job through all these months that has told on me. It was interesting enough at first, while we were at the phonetics; but after that I got deadly sick of it. If I hadn't backed myself to do it I should have chucked the whole thing up two months ago. It was a silly notion: the whole thing has been a bore.

Pickering   Oh come! The garden party was frightfully exciting. My heart began beating like anything.

Higgins   Yes, for the first three minutes. But when I saw we were going to win hands down, I felt like a bear in a cage, hanging about doing nothing. The dinner was worse: sitting gorging there for over an hour, with nobody but a damned fool of a fashionable woman to talk to! I tell you, Pickering, never again for me. No more artificial duchesses. The whole thing has been simple purgatory.

Pickering   You've never been broken in properly to the social routine. [*Strolling over to the piano*] I rather enjoy dipping into it occasionally myself: it makes me feel young again. Anyhow, it was a great success: an immense success. I was quite frightened once or twice because Eliza was doing it so well. You see, lots of the real people can't do it at all: they're such fools that they think style comes by nature to people in their position; and so they never learn. There's always something professional about doing a thing superlatively well.

Higgins   Yes: that's what drives me mad: the silly people don't know their own silly business. [*Rising*] However, it's over and done with; and now I can go to bed at last without dreading tomorrow.
Eliza's beauty becomes murderous

Pickering   I think I shall turn in too. Still, it's been a great occasion: a triumph for you. Goodnight. [*He goes out*]

Compare the characters of Higgins and Pickering both here and elsewhere in the play.

Studying novels and short stories (pre- and post-1914)

The following topics are included in this chapter:

- **Approaching novels and short stories**
- **Openings**
- **Developing characters**
- **Setting and context**
- **Exploring themes**

9.1 Approaching novels and short stories

After studying this section you should be able to understand:

- **some of the features of novels and short stories**
- **how to approach the study of novels and short stories**

Features of novels and short stories

Novels and short stories are in many ways very similar, both in their basic purpose and in the ways they set out to achieve it. Here are some of the things they often have in common:

- They tell stories.
- They seek to interest and entertain the reader.
- They usually contain characters.
- They usually use dialogue.
- They often explore ideas or themes.

There are ways that short stories differ from novels, though. Here are some ideas:

- Short stories are obviously shorter than novels. This fact can make a significant difference to the ways in which they are written.

- The story may be much narrower in style than a novel and perhaps deal with a single idea rather than a range of ideas, or perhaps cover a much shorter time span than a novel. For example, many short stories focus on a single incident, moment in time or experience.
- Because the writer does not have the space to develop many characters, short stories often contain fewer characters than novels.
- The action usually focuses on the main plot and the story does not deal with secondary or sub-plots.

Approaching the text

Whether you are studying a novel or short story, the first thing you must do is to **read** the text in order to get a clear idea of the **plot** or storyline.

Here are some ways in which you can approach your text and help to develop your understanding of it quickly:

Keep a notebook o a 'log' for your work on the text. Jot down your ideas on plot, setting, characters, style etc. as you go along.

Read the text through from beginning to end to get an overall picture of the story.

Write a brief summary outlining the key points of the plot and the key characters.

Now go back and look over the story again.

Gain an overview – you will need to have a clear understanding of the plot and key ideas, the structure of the story, how events relate to each other etc.

Think about the narrative viewpoint – who tells the story – is it told in the first person ('I') or the third person ('He', 'She')?

Know the characters – who they are, what they do, how they relate to other characters, their function in the story etc.

Be aware of the setting and context of the story, e.g. where it is set, when it is set etc.

Have ideas on the ways in which the writer uses language and style and of the effects that are created.

9.2 Openings

LEARNING SUMMARY

After studying this section you should be able to understand:

● *why openings are important*
● *narrative viewpoint*
● *some ways in which writers open their novels and stories*

The opening of a novel or short story is very important because it is here that the writer must **capture the interest** of the reader and make them want to read on. A writer often begins the story by presenting important situations, characters or themes right from the start.

Here are the openings from a novel and a short story. Read them through carefully and think about what you learn from each and what **effect** is created.

You might like to think about:

● who the narrator is
● which characters are introduced and what you learn about them
● what setting or context is created
● what you notice about the writer's style
● whether it makes you want to read on, and why

It is a truth universally acknowledged, that a single man in possession of a good fortune, must be in want of a wife.

However little known the feelings or views of such a man may be on his first entering a neighbourhood, this truth is so well fixed in the minds of the surrounding families, that he is considered as the rightful property of some one or other of their daughters.

'My dear Mr Bennet,' said his lady to him one day, 'have you heard that Netherfield Park is let at last?'

Mr Bennet replied that he had not.

'But it is,' returned she; 'for Mrs Long has just been here, and she told me all about it.'

Mr Bennet made no answer.

'Do not you want to know who has taken it?' cried his wife impatiently.

'You want to tell me, and I have no objection to hearing it.'

This was invitation enough.

'Why, my dear, you must know, Mrs Long says that Netherfield is taken by a young man of large fortune from the north of England; that he came down on Monday in a chaise and four to see the place, and was so much delighted with it that he agreed with Mr Morris immediately; that he is to take possession before Michaelmas, and some of his servants are to be in the house by the end of next week.'

'What is his name?'

'Bingley.'

'Is he married or single?'

'Oh! single, my dear, to be sure! A single man of large fortune; four or five thousand a year. What a fine thing for our girls!'

'How so? How can it affect them?'

'My dear Mr Bennet,' replied his wife, 'how can you be so tiresome! You must know that I am thinking of his marrying one of them.'

From *Pride and Prejudice* by Jane Austen

The pond in our park was circular, exposed, perhaps fifty yards across. When the wind blew, little waves travelled across it and slapped the paved edges, like a miniature sea. We would go there, Mother, Grandfather and I, to sail the motor-launch Grandfather and I made out of plywood, balsawood and varnished paper. We would go even in the winter – especially in the winter, because then we would have the pond to ourselves – when the leaves on the two willows turned yellow and dropped and the water froze your hands. Mother would sit on a wooden bench set back from the perimeter; I would prepare the boat for launching. Grandfather, in his black coat and grey scarf, would walk to the far side to receive it. For some reason it was always Grandfather, never I, who went to the far side. When he reached his station I would hear his 'Ready!' across the water. A puff of vapour would rise from his lips like the smoke from a muffled pistol. And I would release the launch. It worked by a battery. Its progress was laboured but its course steady. I would watch it head out to the middle while Mother watched behind me. As it moved it seemed that it followed an actual existing line between Grandfather, myself and Mother, as if Grandfather were pulling us toward him on some invisible cord, and that he had to do this to prove we were not beyond his reach. When the boat drew near him he would crouch on his haunches. His hands – which I knew were knotted, veiny and mottled from an accident in one of his chemical experiments – would reach out, grasp it and set it on its return.

The voyages were trouble-free. Grandfather improvised a wire grapnel on the end of a length of fishing line in case of shipwrecks or engine failure, but it was never used. Then one day – it must have been soon after Mother met Ralph – we watched the boat, on its first trip across the pond to Grandfather, suddenly become deeper, and deeper in the water. The motor cut. The launch wallowed, sank. Grandfather made several throws with his grapnel and pulled out clumps of green slime. I remember what he said to me, on this, the first loss in my life that I had witnessed. He said, very gravely: 'You must accept it – you can't get it back – it's the only way,' as if he were repeating something to himself. And I remember Mother's face as she got up from the bench to leave. It was very still and very white, as if she had seen something appalling.

From *Chemistry* by Graham Swift

These are two very different openings but in both the writer wants to capture the attention of the reader. In order to do this, various **techniques** are used. Let's compare these techniques and the effects they create.

Pride and Prejudice	Chemistry
Austen writes in the third person and combines description, dialogue and comments from the narrator to achieve her effects.	The story is written in the first person and the narrator describes a memory from his past.
Introduces key themes – the idea of marriage and money.	The key characters are introduced – i.e. the narrator, Grandfather and Mother.
Dialogue is used, which brings the scene to life and tells us something about the characters.	Very little dialogue is used but the only words spoken are given more significance because of this. They touch on a key theme of the story – the 'acceptance of loss'.
The reader is given background information and the beginnings of the plot through the dialogue.	The story opens with the sinking of the model boat, which is described in detail. It is emphasised how much the narrator enjoyed sailing the boat and therefore what a loss it was.
The opening creates interest and makes the reader want to find out if Mrs Bennet will be successful in marrying off one of her daughters to Mr Bingley.	The reaction of the Mother intrigues the reader, particularly the reference to her white face and *"as if she had seen something appalling."*

 KEY POINT — **Writers use various techniques, which combine to make the openings of their stories effective.**

PROGRESS CHECK

Now look at the particular text you are studying and make notes on **how** the writer begins the story and **what effects** it creates on the reader.

Look at:

- the narrator
- the description
- the characters
- the use of dialogue
- methods of arousing interest
- the overall style

Who is telling the story?

When examining your novel or short story, it is important that you establish at the start what kind of **narration** the writer has chosen. Here are the opening paragraphs from two stories.

> I still have the brooch but I can hardly wear it. I thought of throwing it away once, but it is so very pretty. I don't think it is valuable but I have never dared to take it into a jeweller's to find out. It is a very awkward position.
>
> I might have sent it back to the people who owned it, in fact I ought to have done that, but if ever it was traced to me who would believe my story?
>
> From *The Lieabout* by Margery Allingham

> Charlie Stowe waited until he heard his mother snore before he got out of bed. Even then he moved with caution and tiptoed to the window. The front of the house was irregular, so that it was possible to see a light burning in his mother's room. But now all the windows were dark. A searchlight passed across the sky, lighting the banks of cloud and probing the dark spaces between, seeking enemy airships. The wind blew from the sea, and Charlie Stowe could hear behind his mother's snores the breaking of the waves. A draught through the cracks in the window-frame stirred his nightshirt. Charlie Stowe was frightened.
>
> From *I Spy* by Graham Greene

What do you notice about who is telling the story in each of these extracts?

1. Margery Allingham tells the story from the point of view of one character. The narrator is also a character in the story and so the reader sees things through the eyes of the narrator. This kind of narration is called **first-person narration**.

2. Graham Greene tells his story as if he is able to observe everything that is going on and even knows how Charlie Stowe feels. The narrator is all seeing and all knowing. This kind of narration is called **third-person narration**.

KEY POINT

Different kinds of narration achieve different effects. First-person narration is more personal and the character is able to direct the reader's attention and invite them into the experience. Third-person narration can give the reader an insight into what characters are thinking and why they act as they do but is more distanced from them.

9.3 Developing characters

After studying this section you should be able to understand:

● *how writers reveal characters*
● *introductory characters*
● *how characters are developed*

A good deal of the interest in a novel or short story comes from the characters that the writer creates, the things they do and the things that happen to them. We often respond to these characters as if they were people with whom we can **empathise** or who we disapprove of. However, we must remember that these characters are just that. They are the **creations** of the writers and they do not have lives outside the pages of the novel or short story. If we find the characters **convincing**, then it is the writer's skill that has made us feel like this. In studying a novel or short story, it is important to be aware of the ways in which writers **present** the characters and the methods they use to reveal them to us.

Writers can use a number of methods to present their characters:

● **Description** – writers can describe their characters, telling us what they look like, physical appearance, dress etc.
● **Dialogue** – what the characters say can give important information about a character. It is also important to take into account what other characters say about a character in building up your picture.
● **Actions** – how the characters behave and react in particular situations will contribute to your view of them.
● **Thoughts and feelings** – the writer can reveal, either through a character's own words or thoughts or through the narrator's, the character's innermost thoughts and feelings.
● **Imagery and symbols** – writers sometimes describe characters using metaphors or similes or link them with something symbolically. For example, in *Wuthering Heights*, Emily Bronte often links Heathcliff with fire or the colour black, which is symbolic of his temperament.

Keep a 'log' to record key passages and quotations for each important character and build this up as you work through the text.

KEY POINT

When examining characters look at:
• their actions
• what they say
• what others say about them
• their relationship with other characters
• the ways in which the writer uses language to describe and present them

Development of characters and relationships

One of the things you might be asked to do when studying a novel is to **explore** the way in which a character is **presented** and how they **change** and **develop** during the course of the story. In order to do this, it can help if you:

● choose a few passages or episodes from different parts of the novel in which the character you are examining plays a key part

- make sure these passages show different things about the character or the way they develop
- look at descriptive passages, dramatic moments or episodes where the character is faced with a decision, is in conflict with others, is experiencing emotional turmoil etc.

In your notes or reading log it can help if you build up a record of key moments, episodes etc. from the novel where each of your main characters appears.

In *Lord of the Flies* by William Golding, an airline carrying schoolboys has crashed on a tropical island. No adults have survived and the boys have to survive by fending for themselves. One of the characters, Jack Merridew, quickly shows his desire to be 'chief' of the boys. The character of Jack changes a great deal during the course of the novel, moving from a rather surly schoolboy to a savage prepared to kill others. Here are some of the key moments illustrating this change.

Jack – the leader of the choir shows his authority. Keen on exploring. Wants to hunt and lead.

Tries to kill a pig but fails – 'killing' is still taboo.

He is the first boy to appear like a savage but feels his weakness in being unable to kill a piglet.

He kills the pig – a key point in the novel.

Becomes more brutal still and is capable of harming the boys.

Shows no remorse at Piggy's and Simon's deaths – wants to and tries to kill Ralph.

Now let's look at how Golding presents this character at various points in the novel. Here is the point where we first meet Jack.

Within the diamond haze of the beach something dark was fumbling along. Ralph saw it first, and watched till the intentness of his gaze drew all eyes that way. Then the creature stepped from mirage on to clear sand, and they saw that the darkness was not all shadow but mostly clothing. The creature was a party of boys, marching approximately in step in two parallel lines and dressed in strangely eccentric clothing. Shorts, shirts, and different garments they carried in their hands: but each boy wore a square black cap with a silver badge in it. Their bodies, from throat to ankle, were hidden by black cloaks which bore a long silver cross on the left breast and each neck was finished off with a hambone frill. The heat of the tropics, the descent, the search for food, and now this sweaty march along the blazing beach had given them the complexions of newly washed plums. The boy who controlled them was dressed in the same way though his cap badge was golden. When his party was about ten yards from the platform he shouted an order and they halted, gasping, sweating, swaying in the fierce light. The boy himself came forward, vaulted on to the platform with his cloak flying, and peered into what to him was almost complete darkness.

"Where's the man with the trumpet?"

Ralph, sensing his sun-blindness, answered him.

"There's no man with a trumpet. Only me."

The boy came close and peered down at Ralph, screwing up his face as he did so. What he saw of the fair-haired boy with the creamy shell on his knees did not seem to satisfy him. He turned quickly, his black cloak circling.

"Isn't there a ship, then?"

Inside the floating cloak he was tall, thin, and bony: and his hair was red beneath the black cap. His face was crumpled and freckled, and ugly without silliness. Out of this face stared two light blue eyes, frustrated now, and turning, or ready to turn, to anger.

"Isn't there a man here?"

Ralph spoke to his back.

"No we're having a meeting. Come and join in."

The group of cloaked boys began to scatter from close line. The tall boy shouted at them.

"Choir! Stand still!"

From *Lord of the Flies* by William Golding

How does Golding mark Jack out as being different from the others? What is revealed about him through the dialogue?

- They are all dressed in black (which gives a menacing feel) but Jack stands out from the others with his golden cap badge. Golding also tells us that Jack is the one who controls them.
- When Jack speaks, we can see his commanding attitude through the sharp questions he fires at Ralph and ending with his shouted order 'Choir! Stand still!'

Now look at this next passage, from later in the novel, where Jack kills a pig.

Here, struck down by the heat, the sow fell and the hunters hurled themselves at her. This dreadful eruption from an unknown world made her frantic; she squealed and bucked and the air was full of sweat and noise and blood and terror. Roger ran round the heap, prodding with his spear whenever pigflesh appeared. Jack was on top of the sow, stabbing downward with his knife. Roger found a lodgement for his point and began to push till he was leaning with his whole weight. The spear moved forward inch by inch and the terrified squealing became a high-pitched scream. Then Jack found the throat and the hot blood spouted over his hands. The sow collapsed under them and they were heavy and fulfilled upon her. The butterflies still danced, preoccupied in the centre of the clearing.

At last the immediacy of the kill subsided. The boys drew back, and Jack stood up, holding out his hands.

"Look."

He giggled and flinked them while the boys laughed at his reeking palms. Then Jack grabbed Maurice and rubbed the stuff over his cheeks. Roger began to withdraw his spear and the boys noticed it for the first time. Robert stabilized the thing in a phrase which was received uproariously.

"Right up her ass!"

"Did you hear?"

"Did you hear what he said?"

"Right up her ass!"

This time Robert and Maurice acted the two parts; and Maurice's acting of the pig's efforts to avoid the advancing spear was so funny that the boys cried with laughter.

At length even this palled. Jack began to clean his bloody hands on the rock. Then he started work on the sow and paunched her, lugging out the hot bags of coloured guts, pushing them into a pile on the rock while the others watched him. He talked as he worked.

"We'll take the meat along the beach. I'll go back to the platform and invite them to a feast. That should give us time."

Roger spoke.

"Chief–"

"Uh–?"

"How can we make a fire?"

Jack squatted back and frowned at the pig.

"We'll raid them and take fire. There must be four of you; Henry and you, Bill and Maurice. We'll put on paint and sneak up; Roger can snatch a branch while I say what I want. The rest of you can get this back to where we were. We'll build the fire there. And after that–"

He paused and stood up, looking at the shadows under the trees. His voice was lower when he spoke again.

"But we'll leave part of the kill for…"

He knelt down again and was busy with his knife. The boys crowded round him. He spoke over his shoulder to Roger.

"Sharpen a stick at both ends."

Presently he stood up, holding the dripping sow's head in his hands.

"Where's that stick?"

"Here."

"Ram one end in the earth. Oh – it's rock. Jam it in that crack. There."

Jack held up the head and jammed the soft throat down on the pointed end of the stick which pierced through into the mouth. He stood back and the head hung there, a little blood dribbling down the stick.

From *Lord of the Flies* by William Golding

PROGRESS CHECK

How is Jack presented here?

Jack takes the lead role – he '*…was on top of the sow*' and his viciousness is stressed '*…stabbing downward with his knife.*' It is Jack who cuts the animal's throat and rubs the blood over Maurice's cheeks.

In this final extract from near the end of the novel, Jack's descent into savagery is complete as he tries to kill Ralph.

The rock struck Piggy a glancing blow from chin to knee; the conch exploded into a thousand white fragments and ceased to exist. Piggy, saying nothing, with no time for even a grunt, travelled through the air sideways from the rock, turning sideways as he went. The rock bounded twice and was lost in the forest. Piggy fell forty feet and landed on his back across that square, red rock in the sea. His head opened and stuff came out and turned red. Piggy's arms and legs twitched a bit, like a pig's after it has been killed. Then the sea breathed again in a long slow sigh, the water boiled white and pink over the rock; and when it went, sucking back again, the body of Piggy was gone.

This time the silence was complete. Ralph's lips formed a word but no sound came.

Suddenly Jack bounded out from the tribe and began screaming wildly.

"See? See? That's what you'll get! I meant that! There isn't a tribe for you any more! The conch is gone –"

He ran forward, stooping.

"I'm Chief!"

Viciously, with full intention, he hurled his spear at Ralph. The point tore the skin and flesh over Ralph's ribs, then sheared off and fell in the water. Ralph stumbled, feeling not pain but panic and the tribe, screaming now like the Chief, began to advance. Another spear, a bent one that would not fly straight, went past his face and one fell from on high where Roger was. The twins lay hidden behind the tribe and the anonymous devils' faces swarmed across the neck. Ralph turned and ran. A great noise as of sea-gulls rose behind him. He obeyed an instinct that he did not know he possessed and swerved over the open space so that the spear went wide. He saw the headless body of the sow and jumped in time. Then he was crashing through foliage and small boughs and was hidden by the forest.

The Chief stopped by the pig, turned and held up his hands.

"Back! Back to the fort!"

Presently the tribe returned noisily to the neck where Roger joined them.

The Chief spoke to him angrily.

"Why aren't you on watch?"

Roger looked at him gravely.

"I just came down –"

From *Lord of the Flies* by William Golding

 PROGRESS CHECK

What do you find striking about Golding's presentation of Jack here?

The death of Piggy is a symbol that all the restraining influences of 'civilised' behaviour have gone. Immediately Jack tries to kill Ralph. The emphasis on the word 'Chief' and the fact that Golding from now on refers to Jack as *'the Chief'* rather than 'Jack' shows that his dominance is now complete.

 KEY POINT

When writing about a character, focus on specific details from the text that show important aspects of that character and the ways in which it develops.

9.4 Setting and context

 LEARNING SUMMARY

After studying this section you should be able to understand:
- *the importance of setting and context*
- *how writers create atmosphere*

Setting and context

The imaginary 'world' within which a novel or short story is set can be an important element for several reasons:

- It forms the **backdrop** against which the action of the story takes place.
- It can be closely linked to the characters and experiences and can reflect these.
- It can also perform a **symbolic** function to develop ideas the writer wants to put across to the reader.
- It can present a world within which a character is a misfit or that they are in **conflict** with.

For example, the action in Barry Hines' *Kes* takes place in a northern industrial town. Here's how Hines describes the setting of the main character Billy Casper's home background.

It was still dark outside when he got up and went downstairs. The living-room curtains were drawn, and when he switched the light on it was gloomy and cold without the help of the fire. He placed the clock on the mantelpiece, then picked up his mother's sweater from the settee and pulled it on over his shirt.

The alarm rang as he was emptying the ashes in the dustbin. Dust clouded up into his face as he dropped the lid back on and ran inside, but the noise stopped before he could reach it. He knelt down in front of the empty grate and scrunched sheets of newspaper into loose balls, arranging them in the grate like a bouquet of hydrangea flowers. Then he picked up the hatchet, stood a log of wood on the hearth and struck it down the centre. The blade bit and held. He lifted the hatchet with the log attached and smashed it down, splitting the log in half and chipping the tile with the blade. He split the halves into quarters, down through eighths to sixteenths, then arranged these sticks over the paper like the struts of a wigwam. He completed the construction with lumps of coal, building them into a loose shell, so that sticks and paper showed through the chinks. The paper caught with the first match, and the flames spread quickly underneath, making the chinks smoke and the sticks crack. He waited for the first burst of flames up the back of the construction, then stood up and walked into the kitchen, and opened the pantry door. There were a packet of dried peas and a half bottle of vinegar on the shelves. The bread bin was empty. Just inside the doorway, the disc of the electricity meter circled slowly in its glass case. The red arrow appeared, and disappeared. Billy closed the door and opened the outside door. On the step stood two empty milk bottles. He thumped the jamb with the side of his fist.
"It's t' same every morning. I'm going to start hiding some at nights."

From Kes *by Barry Hines*

The novel also has another setting – that of the neighbouring countryside to which Billy often goes. Here is one of Hines' descriptions of this setting:

The sun was up and the cloud band in the East had thinned to a line on the horizon, leaving the dome of the sky clear. The air was still and clean, and the trilling of larks carried far over the fields of hay, which stretched away on both sides of the path. Great rashes of buttercups spread across the fields, and amongst the mingling shades of yellow and green, dog daisies showed their white faces, contrasting with the rust of sorrel. All underscored by clovers, white and pink and purple, which came into their own on the path sides where the grass was shorter, along with daisies and the ubiquitous plantains.

A cushion of mist lay over the fields. Dew drenched the grass, and the occasional sparkling of individual drops made Billy glance down as he passed. One tuft was a silver fire. He knelt down to trace the source of light. The drop had almost forced the blade of grass to the earth, and it lay in the curve of the blade like the tiny egg of a mythical bird. Billy moved his head from side to side to make it sparkle, and when it caught the sun it exploded, throwing out silver needles and crystal splinters. He lowered his head and slowly, very carefully, touched it with the tip of his tongue. The drop quivered like mercury, but held. He bent, and touched it again. It disintegrated and streamed down the channel of the blade to the earth. Slowly the blade began to straighten, climbing steadily like the finger of a clock.

Billy stood up and walked on. He climbed over a stile and followed the path through a herd of cows. The ones grazing lifted their heads slowly, chewing their cud. The ones lying in the grass remained motionless, as solid as toy cows set out on a toy farm. A covey of partridges got up under his feet, making him jump and cry out. They whirred away over the field, their blunt forms travelling as direct as a barrage of shells. Billy snatched a stone up and threw it after them, but they were already out of sight over the hedges. The stone flushed a blackbird, and it chattered away along the hedge bottom, disappearing back into the foliage further along.

He reached the stile which led into the woods, climbed on to it and looked back. Fields and fences and hedgerows. The sun was in the sky, and the only sound was the continuous relay of bird song.

From Kes *by Barry Hines*

These two **settings** are important to the novel for a number of reasons:

- They set the social context within which the action of the novel takes place – the harsh, hard-living lifestyle of Billy's brother and mother.
- They contrast with each other – Billy lives within the first setting but the countryside provides him with a place that he can escape to and find peace in.
- The rural life of the country contrasts against the grimy industrialisation of the town.

In Charles Dickens's *A Christmas Carol*, the **social and historical context** of the novel is important. In this extract, two gentlemen call on the main character, Scrooge, who is a miser at the start of the novel. It is Christmastime and these two gentlemen are collecting donations for the poor:

They were portly gentlemen, pleasant to behold, and now stood, with their hats off, in Scrooge's office. They had books and paper in their hands, and bowed to him.

"Scrooge and Marley's I believe," said one of the gentlemen, referring to his list. "Have I the pleasure of addressing Mr Scrooge, or Mr Marley?"

"Mr Marley has been dead these seven years," Scrooge replied. "He died seven years ago, this very night."

"We have no doubt his liberality is well represented by his surviving partner," said the gentleman, presenting his credentials.

It certainly was; for they had been two kindred spirits. At the ominous word "liberality", Scrooge frowned, and shook his head, and handed the credentials back.

"At this festive season of the year, Mr Scrooge," said the gentleman, taking up a pen, "it is more than usually desirable that we should make some slight provision for the poor and destitute, who suffer greatly at the present time. Many thousands are in want of common necessaries; hundreds of thousands are in want of common comforts, sir."

"Are there no prisons?" asked Scrooge.

"Plenty of prisons," said the gentleman, laying down the pen again.

"And the Union workhouses?" demanded Scrooge. "Are they still in operation?"

"They are. Still," returned the gentleman, "I wish I could say they were not."

"The Treadmill and the Poor Law are in full vigour, then?" said Scrooge.

"Both very busy, sir."

"Oh! I was afraid, from what you said at first, that something had occurred to stop them in their useful course," said Scrooge. "I'm very glad to hear it."

"Under the impression that they scarcely furnish Christian cheer of mind or body to the multitude," returned the gentleman, "a few of us are endeavouring to raise a fund to buy the Poor some meat and drink, and means of warmth. We choose this time, because it is a time, of all others, when Want is keenly felt, and Abundance rejoices. What shall I put you down for?"

"Nothing!" Scrooge replied.

"You wish to be anonymous?"

"I wish to be left alone," said Scrooge. "Since you ask me what I wish, gentlemen, that is my answer. I don't make merry myself at Christmas, and I can't afford to make idle people merry. I help to support the establishments I have mentioned: they cost enough: and those who are badly off must go there."

"Many can't go there; and many would rather die."

"If they would rather die," said Scrooge, "they had better do it, and decrease the surplus population. Besides – excuse me – I don't know that."

"But you might know it," observed the gentleman.

"It's not my business," Scrooge returned. "It's enough for a man to understand his own business, and not to interfere with other people's. Mine occupies me constantly. Good afternoon, gentlemen!"

From *A Christmas Carol* by Charles Dickens

This novel was written in the mid-nineteenth century.

PROGRESS CHECK

What do you learn from the extract about the social and historical context in which it was written?

Here are some ideas:

- Thousands of people were '*poor and destituted*'.
- Workhouses existed to accommodate the poor.
- These were terrible places as '*many would rather die*' than go there.
- Some people were hard-hearted and felt that if people died then there would be fewer poor people (Dickens has Scrooge express this sentiment).
- Some people adopted an attitude that as long as they were alright they didn't care about others. Again, Scrooge represents this idea.

KEY POINT

The setting and context of a novel or short story is important and often links with a story's themes and ideas.

Creating atmosphere

Closely associated with the setting of a novel or short story is the **atmosphere** that the writer creates. In order to create a sense of atmosphere, writers often use **description**. In studying your own novel or story, you need to be aware of how the writer uses language to create a particular atmosphere.

Look carefully at these extracts from *I'm the King of the Castle* by Susan Hill. Kingshaw has been tormented by another boy, Hooper, and escapes to Hang Wood to be alone.

Kingshaw held his breath. There was a continual soughing movement inside the wood, and the leaves rustled together like silk, directly overhead. They were very pale green, and almost transparent where the sun shone through, he could see all the veins. At his feet, in between the creeping foliage, were dead leaves, rusty-coloured and dry on top, but packed to a damp mould just below the surface.

Immediately ahead of him there was the trunk of a fallen tree. He sat down on it. The bark was covered with greenish-grey moss. It felt like moleskin under his fingers. There was fungus, too, issuing out of the cracks, and in the groin of a branch, in weird, spongy shapes.

He liked it here. He had never been anywhere like it, and it was not remotely what he had expected. He liked the smell, and the sense of being completely hidden. Everything around him seemed innocent, and he could see for some way ahead, it was all quite all right. The sun made even the dense holly and hawthorn bushes on the edge of the clearing look harmless.

Different birds kept on singing, though not very near to him, and he did not see any of them, except, now and again, a darting brown shape in the branches. There was a cooing from pigeons, right inside the wood. He saw a rabbit. It came out of the undergrowth, not far away from him, with an odd, bumping movement, and then sat down in a shaft of sunlight, and began to wash itself like a cat. Kingshaw held his breath.

From *I'm the King of the Castle* by Susan Hill

Here, Susan Hill creates a calm, peaceful and safe atmosphere. She does this through her description and the ways she uses language. Look at the positive images she uses here:

When writing about atmosphere, make sure you use specific examples with comments to illustrate how the writer uses language to create atmosphere.

- 'the sun shone through'
- 'it felt like moleskin'
- 'everything around him seemed innocent'
- 'birds kept on singing'
- 'there was a cooing from pigeons'
- 'He saw a rabbit'

All these **descriptions** and **images** create a pleasant, warm, soft, safe feel to the atmosphere.

However, in the next extract, Kingshaw finds that Hooper has followed him. The two of them get lost and Hooper is terrified of the wood.

There was a feeling of tension inside the wood, as the sky darkened. Every slight movement of the birds sounded very clearly, even if it was far away. Kingshaw was hot. He wanted the storm to break, he wanted rain and coolness. There was something unpleasant about this waiting, he felt everything around him to be holding back some kind of violence. But he was not afraid at all. He felt nothing. His brain was very clear and he could think everything out, he knew what they had better do. He remembered his mother. Perhaps they were in London, by now. He imagined her, clipping along in her high-heeled shoes and the smart green costume, at Mr Hooper's side. But that didn't matter, now, they didn't matter, he was going away, it was going to be all right.

The wood had made everything seem far off, not only removed in distance but in time, too. Here, he felt that he was shut away from all other people, from towns and cities and school and home. The wood had already changed him, enlarged his experience to a point where he felt that he was on the brink of discovering some secret, of whose existence, even, that other world did not know.

There was a great crash of thunder almost overhead, and a tearing noise, as though the sky had been ripped open. Hooper leaped to his feet, and looked about him, wild with terror.

"Come on," Kingshaw said, matter-of-factly, "we'd better make a shelter." He unzipped his anorak, and carried it over to one of the bushes. Hooper watched it, trembling slightly, rooted where he stood. Lightening came now, making the tree trunks white as it forked down.

Kingshaw draped his anorak carefully over the top of the bushes, spreading it out as much as possible. The bushes were very thick. He got down and crawled underneath.

"Come on," he said, "it's all right here, we might stay dry."

Hooper hesitated, and then came in beside him, crawling on his hands and knees. He went right back into the farthest corner, where it was dark, and curled up tightly, his hands held up towards his face. When the thunder boomed through the wood again, he stuffed his fingers in his ears, and ducked down.

"It's O.K.," Kingshaw said, "It's only a din."

Lightning flickered on the eyes of a bird, perched up somewhere in the branches ahead, and for a second, they shone yellow-green, like torches. The thunder came right on top ofthe lightning.

From *I'm the King of the Castle* by Susan Hill

PROGRESS CHECK

How does the atmosphere here contrast with that in the first extract? How does Hill create this atmosphere?

The peaceful atmosphere has gone and has been replaced with one of tension as the storm approaches. The fear of Hooper is reflected here through phrases like '*wild with terror*' in response to the '*great crash of thunder*', '*a tearing noise*', the sky '*ripped open*'. However, the coolness of Kingshaw is also present in the atmosphere here: '*He wanted the storm to break*' and his matter-of-fact attitude. The contrast of these very different attitudes to the situation serves to heighten the tense atmosphere further.

PROGRESS CHECK

Look carefully at the text you are studying and make notes on the significance of **setting**, **context** and **atmosphere** in it.

9.5 Exploring themes

LEARNING SUMMARY

After studying this section you should be able to understand:
- *why themes are important*
- *how to approach studying the themes in a text*

Why themes are important

Novels and stories often do more than simply 'tell a story'. Writers use their 'stories' to **explore** particular **themes** and **ideas** and to present ideas on them. When we talk about a **theme** we are really talking about the idea that lies behind the story as a whole and which the writer is interested in developing through the story. Often, novels contain several themes and the writer uses the story to make the reader think about these ideas or to put particular **messages** across to the reader.

For example, *Pride and Prejudice* explores a number of themes, which include:
- attitudes to money
- society and class
- marriage
- social conventions

Through her novel, Jane Austen explores all of these things, presenting the reader with characters and situations that show different views and ideas towards them.

KEY POINT

Be aware of the ideas that are explored in the text you are studying.

Approaching themes

Think carefully about the themes in the book you are studying – they are an important part of it.

When studying your novel or story it is a good idea to make a list of the main ideas or themes in the book. It can help you sort your ideas out in your mind if you draw a **diagram** or a **pattern note** that summarises each theme.

Here is one student's summary of the themes in *Kes* by Barry Hines.

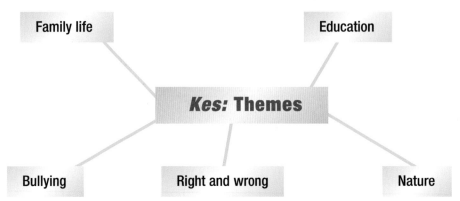

Having decided on the key themes in your text, you now need to think about each of them in turn, how each relates to the main storyline and what ideas the writer is exploring. Again, it can be useful to **summarise** your ideas in a pattern note. Here are the student's notes on the theme of education.

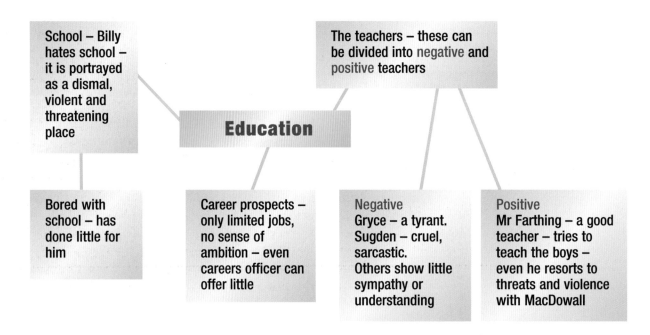

It can help if you include page references with your notes so that you can find particular sections easily.

Using your summary, you can now make more detailed notes on each theme. Make sure you include specific examples to support your points and comment on them.

PROGRESS CHECK

Now look at the novel you are studying and identify the key themes that it explores.

Sample GCSE question

Barry Hines' *Kes*

How is 'nature' an important element in the novel?

Billy's experiences are set against three quite distinct backgrounds in the novel. First of all, we gain an insight into his home life, which is clearly deprived and lacking in love. Secondly, we see him within the context of the school, which he finds equally unfulfilling. Thirdly, we see him experiencing nature with his hawk, Kes.

> *Good opening which sets the world of nature in context.*

This is the only part of his life that he really enjoys, where he learns something and feels that he has achieved something. Billy lives on a rough and grimy estate and the fact that it has little connection with nature is very evident through Hines' description of it. However, the tone of his writing changes whenever he describes the natural world when Billy is in the fields and woods beyond the estate. It is obvious from this description that Billy loves being in the country and has a genuine interest in wildlife.

> *Explains the importance of the natural world – shows an awareness of the creation of contrast here.*

> *Shows an understanding of how Hines varies his style to create effects.*

He has always loved animals, as we can see from what he has to tell Mr Farthing. He tells him about all the different kinds of birds he has had, such as magpies and jackdaws - and all sorts of other animals that he had too, even rearing a fox cub. He has obviously learned a lot from all this. His natural talent for animals is even more obvious when playing football (which he hates) and he is the only one who can get the dog off the football field.

> *Textual detail here. Some quotations would have been useful to support ideas.*

As Billy says to Mr Farthing, the creature that means most to him is Kes. He has hand-reared her, trained her and taught her to fly to the lure. The main thing about Kes, though, and the thing that makes her different from all the other animals he has kept, is her wildness. Even though she is trained, she is still wild and it is this link with the really wild things of nature that fascinates Billy.

> *A perceptive point showing a good level of understanding.*

The importance of nature in the novel, then, is to create a contrast between the harsh, cruel urban world of the estate and the school and a much more secure and less threatening environment where Billy feels he can be free. Kes is the link between this world and Billy's own - she provides his escape route into a world in which he can feel a sense of achievement and fulfilment.

> *A clear and sound conclusion.*

Coursework practice question

Harper Lee: *To Kill a Mockingbird*

Boo Radley is seen only as a shadowy figure and does not actually appear until the end of the book when he comes to the children's rescue. However, nearly the whole of the first part concerns the children's obsession with him.

What is his function in the novel?

....

....

....

....

....

....

....

....

....

....

....

....

....

....

....

10 Studying poetry

The following topics are included in this chapter:

- **Reading poetry**
- **Features of poetry**
- **Poetry in context**
- **Modern poetry**
- **Poems from different cultures**
- **Comparing poems**

10.1 Reading poetry

LEARNING SUMMARY

After studying this section you should be able to understand:

- *how to help improve your knowledge of different kinds of poems*
- *how to get the most out of reading poetry*
- *how to approach studying a poem*

If you are studying GCSE English, you will need to study poetry from other cultures at some point during your course. If you are studying English Literature then you will need to study a range of poetry written before and after 1914.

The first thing to recognise about poetry is that it comes in many **different forms** and it can be about any topic you can think of. Your work for GCSE will involve studying specific poems in some detail, but you can do a number of things to help yourself prepare for your poetry study. Here are some ideas:

- **Read** as many poems as you can to get a feel of the different forms poetry can take and the ways in which poets use language in different ways to explore their ideas.
- Keep a **reading 'log'** and make a **note** of any interesting ideas, images etc. that strike you as particularly effective.
- Read poems **aloud** (in the privacy of your own room if you prefer). Reading a poem aloud can often help you to understand it better and can also help you to get a feel of the **rhythm** and/or **rhyme** pattern.
- Ask yourself **questions** about the poems you read. These three questions are very important ones:
  - **What** is the poem about?
  - **How** does the poet use language in it?
  - **Why** does the poet use language in this way – why do they structure the poem in a particular way and what effect does he or she want to create?

This means that you consider:

CONTENT

STYLE

EFFECT

When studying specific poems as part of your course, it is important that you are clear in your mind what you are doing and what you want to achieve. Having a **planned** approach to studying your poems can help you. Here is a way of doing this:

When making your notes, always use specific examples to illustrate your ideas.

Read the poem through carefully several times (aloud if possible).

Write down your **initial** responses to it, making a note of any ideas that come into your head.

Write down your **thoughts** about the subject or theme of the poem.

Make a note of the ways in which the poet uses **language**, e.g. the vocabulary, metaphors, similes and images of the poem.

Describe what kind of **tone** or **atmosphere** the poem has and how this is created.

It can be useful to highlight or underline important words and phrases. You could colour code these to help identify particular ideas, images etc.

Make a note of other **effects** created in the poem, e.g. rhyme, rhythm, alliteration, onomatopoeia.

Sum up your **ideas** on the poem and how the poem 'works' as a whole.

PROGRESS CHECK

What three questions should you ask yourself when studying a poem?

- What is the poem about?
- How does the poet use language in it?
- Why does the poet use language in this way?

10.2 Features of poetry

LEARNING SUMMARY

After studying this section you should be able to understand:
- *how poets use language to create atmosphere, tone and mood*
- *what imagery is and how poets use it*
- *how rhyme and rhythm can affect a poem*

Tone, mood and atmosphere

The ideas of **tone** and **mood** are closely linked to the '**voice**' of the poem, in that it is the speaker's tone – whether it be happy, melancholy, bitter, regretful, angry, meditative etc. – that creates a sense of the mood or atmosphere a poem establishes.

The tone, mood and atmosphere of a poem are the product of many factors, such as:

- the poet's choice of words
- the imagery used
- the rhyme and rhythm patterns established
- the sound effects created through features such as alliteration and onomatopoeia
- the context or situation the poem describes

Now look at the following two poems. Both are concerned with the idea of death but the mood, tone and atmosphere created in each are very different. In the first poem, Thomas confronts the idea of his father's death.

Do Not Go Gentle Into That Good Night
Do not go gentle into that good night,
Old age should burn and rave at close of day;
Rage, rage against the dying of the light.

Though wise men at their end know dark is right,
Because their words had forked no lightning they
Do not go gentle into that good night.

Good men, the last wave by, crying how bright
Their frail deeds might have danced in a green bay,
Rage, rage against the dying of the light.

Wild men who caught and sang the sun in flight,
And learn, too late, they grieved it on its way,
Do not go gentle into that good night.

Grave men, near death, who see with blinding sight
Blind eyes could blaze like meteors and be gay,
Rage, rage against the dying of the light.

And you, my father, there on the sad height,
Curse, bless, me now with your fierce tears, I pray.
Do not go gentle into that good night.
Rage, rage against the dying of the light.

Dylan Thomas (1914–1953)

Here, Hardy reflects on his life and the prospect, ultimately, of his death.

Great Things

Sweet cyder is a great thing,
 A great thing to me,
Spinning down to Weymouth town
 By Ridgeway thirstily,
And maid and mistress summoning,
 Who tend the hostelry:
O cyder is a great thing,
 A great thing to me!

The dance is a great thing,
 A great thing to me,
With candles lit and partners fit
 For night-long revelry;
And going home when day-dawning
 Peeps pale upon the lea:
O dancing is a great thing,
 A great thing to me!

Love is, yea, a great thing,
 A great thing to me,
When, having drawn across the lawn
 In darkness silently,
A figure flits like one-a-wing
 Out from the nearest tree:
O love is, yes, a great thing,
 A great thing to me!

Will these be always great things,
 Great things to me? ...
Let it befall that One will call,
 'Soul, I have need of thee':
What then? Joy-jaunts, impassioned flings,
 Love, and its ecstasy,
Will always have been great things,
 Great things to me!

Thomas Hardy

PROGRESS CHECK

How do these poems differ in terms of the tone, mood and atmosphere created?

Do Not Go Gentle Into That Good Night has a fierce and bitter tone, which reflects Thomas' feelings of anger at the prospect of his father's death.
Great Things has a joyous and celebratory feel about it as Hardy reflects on the things he has enjoyed in life.

Now think about **how** the poets create these particular moods in their poems. Here are some ideas:

Do Not Go Gentle Into That Good Night

- **Vocabulary** – words such as '*burn*', '*rave*', '*rage*', '*fierce*' and phrases such as '*forked no lightning*', '*caught and sang the sun in flight*', '*blinding sight*', '*blaze like meteors*' are very colourful and contain violent connotations, which reflect the feelings of anger and frustration that Thomas feels about his father's death.
- The **rhythm pattern** of the poem and the rhyme scheme give the poem a solemn and serious feel, which helps to create the mood of the poem.
- The **repetitions** create an insistent tone, which emphasises both the message of the poem and the mood and atmosphere created.

Great Things

> When writing about how poets create particular moods or atmospheres, always use specific details from the poem and analyse the effects they have on the reader.

- **Words** such as '*revelry*', '*dancing*', '*love*', '*Joy-jaunts*' and '*ecstasy*' create a sense of enjoyment and happiness.
- The **rhythm pattern** of the poem creates a lively, upbeat tempo.
- The **repetitions** present a refrain, which emphasises the good things the poet has enjoyed in life, and that even death can never take away these experiences.

Imagery

Poets often use **imagery** in their poems. Imagery is where language is used in such a way as to help us form a kind of 'mental picture' of the thing that is being described or the idea that is being explored.

Images can work in a number of ways. For example, a poet can literally describe something, as Mary Ann Evans does at the beginning of her poem *In a London Drawing-room*.

'The sky is cloudy, yellowed by the smoke.
For view there are the houses opposite
Cutting the sky with one long line of wall'

In this example, Evans describes what she can see literally and so this is called a '**literal image**'. However, sometimes the thing that is being described is compared to something else in order to make the description more vivid. This kind of imagery is called '**figurative**'. Here are some examples of this kind of imagery.

Simile

You can spot **similes** easily because they usually make the **comparison** quite clear, often by using the words 'like' or 'as'. For example, in the poem you have just looked at, Evans continues her description using a simile:

'Cutting the sky with one long line of wall
Like a solid fog.'

Here she uses the simile of the fog to emphasise how the wall cuts out the light of the sky like a '*solid fog*' would do.

Metaphor

Metaphors are very similar to similes in that they also create a comparison, but instead of saying something is 'like' or 'as' something, it actually says it *is* that thing. For example, in his **sonnet** *Upon Westminster Bridge*, William Wordsworth describes London, which can be seen as the '*heart*' of the country, early in a morning saying, '*And all that mighty heart is lying still*'. Obviously, the city isn't literally a 'heart' but Wordsworth is using a metaphor to describe it.

PROGRESS CHECK

Look at the verse from Keith Douglas's *Vergissmeinnicht* in which he describes the body of a German soldier on the battlefield. He speaks of how the soldier's girlfriend –

'*....would weep to see today*
how on his skin the swart flies move;
the dust upon the paper eye
and the burst stomach like a cave'

Identify and explain:

- the metaphor Douglas uses
- the simile he uses.

The metaphor is '*the dust upon the paper eye*'. The eye of the dead soldier isn't actually made of paper but in death it has come to look like paper rather than alive and seeing.

The simile used is '*...the burst stomach like a cave*'. Here the poet compares the burst open stomach of the dead soldier to the dark opening of a cave.

Personification

Another form of imagery is created through the technique of attributing human qualities or feelings to something that is not human. For example, in this poem, James Stephens **personifies** the wind.

> ### The Wind
>
> The wind stood up, and gave a shout;
> He whistled on his fingers, and
>
> Kicked the withered leaves about,
> And thumped the branches with his hand,
>
> And said he'd kill, and kill, and kill;
> And so he will! And so he will!
>
> *James Stephens (1882–1950)*

PROGRESS CHECK

What effect does personification have on the poem?

It has the effect of bringing to the poem the sense that the wind is a living thing, therefore giving it a feeling of life.

Aural imagery

Apart from images created through words, poets often make use of images that are created through **sound**.

Alliteration involves the **repetition** of the same consonant **sound**, usually at the beginning of each word. For example, in Gerard Manley Hopkins' poem *The Windhover* he describes a kestrel hovering:

'I caught this morning morning's minion, kingdom of daylight's dauphin, dapple-down-drawn Falcon,'

Here there is alliteration of the 'm' and 'd' sounds.

Sometimes the alliteration can come at the end of words too, as in the line from another of Hopkins' poems *Spring*

'When weeds, in wheels, shoot long and lovely and 'lush','

Here the 'w', 'l' and 'sh' sounds are alliterated.

Students generally find alliteration easy to spot in a poem but the main thing is to be able to describe its effects, and this can be more difficult. There are certain things to look out for:

● The way that alliteration can help to affect and create the **tone** within a poem.
● The way that its regularity or irregularity can affect **rhythm**.

Assonance

Assonance is another kind of **aural** device involving **repetitions**. This time the repetition is of a **vowel sound** and again it is used to create a particular effect in a poem. For example, Sylvia Plath uses it in the opening line of her poem *Frog Autumn* –

'Summer grows old, cold-blooded mother'

Here the long, drawn out 'o' sounds create a slow, weary **tone** and give the impression of a loss of life and vitality as summer turns to autumn and winter approaches.

Onomatopoeia

Onomatopoeia is another kind of aural device in which the actual sounds of words reflect their meanings. Simple examples would be words like 'bang' or 'crash'. However, poets often use this device in more complex ways. Here, Wilfred Owen uses onomatopoeia to create a sense of the sound of gunfire in *Anthem for Doomed Youth* –

'Only the monstrous anger of the guns.
Only the stuttering rifles' rapid rattle
Can patter out their hasty orisons'

You might have noticed some alliteration here too.

KEY POINT The important thing is not to simply 'spot' features but to be able to explain and comment on the effects they create in a poem and what they contribute towards its overall effectiveness.

Rhyme and rhythm

Rhyme

Rhyme can make an important contribution to the overall **impact** of a poem and it is such a feature of poetry that often people expect poetry to rhyme, even though much of it doesn't. Like several of the other features that we have looked at, rhyme is quite easy to spot but it is rather more difficult to explain what effect it has on a poem. In order to establish this, each poem needs to be looked at individually.

Here are some possible effects to look for:

- The sound effects created, for example a 'musical' quality; a jarring, discordant effect etc.
- The emphasis that it places on certain words, giving them a prominence.
- It draws lines and stanzas together linking ideas and images.
- It creates a pattern.
- It can give a sense of ending or finality – the rhyming couplet is often used to give a sense of ending as in Shakespeare's Sonnett XVIII –
  'So long as men can breathe or eyes can see,
  So long lives this, and this gives life to thee.'

Philip Larkin, in his poem *Take One Home for the Kiddies* uses a straightforward rhyme scheme:

On shallow straw, in shadeless glass,	A
Huddled by empty bowls, they sleep:	B
No dark, no dawn, no earth, no grass –	A
Mam, get us one of them to keep	B
Living toys are something novel,	C
But it soon wears off somehow.	D
Fetch the shoebox, fetch the shovel –	C
Mam, we're playing funerals now	D

> In writing about the use of rhyme in a poem, you must comment on the effects it creates.

Here, Larkin uses an ABAB, CDCD rhyme scheme, in that alternate lines rhyme.

PROGRESS CHECK

What effect do you think this rhyme scheme has on the poem?

It is simple and straightforward, suited to the simple message of the poem. It also creates a cyclical pattern that reflects the events of the poem.

Rhythm

Another kind of pattern in poetry can be created through the **rhythm**, which consists of **patterns** of recurring **stresses** and **pauses**. The rhythm in a poem is, perhaps, more difficult to identify than some of the other features we have looked at. Often, it helps to read the poem aloud in order to get a feel for the rhythm pattern. Earlier in this Chapter we discussed how the rhythm pattern of a poem helps to create **mood** and **atmosphere**. Look back at pages 157–158 and re-read *Do Not Go Gentle Into That Good Night* and *Great Things* and note how the very different rhythm patterns affect the poems.

PROGRESS CHECK

The rhythm pattern of a poem has an important influence on the overall effect the poem creates.

10.3 Poetry in context

LEARNING SUMMARY

After studying this section you should be able to understand:

- *the importance of social, cultural and historical contexts*
- *how to analyse poetry written before 1914*
- *how to analyse modern poetry*
- *how to analyse poetry from different cultures*

Social, cultural and historical contexts

If you are studying English Literature, one of the things you must do is to "*relate texts to their social, cultural and historical contexts and literary traditions*". So the first question is, what does this mean? To understand this, it is important to recognise that texts, such as poems, are not created in a vacuum but are the product of many **influences** that affect the ways in which writers write and the ways in which we read and interpret their work. Becoming aware of this **background** information can help you to understand and appreciate the poetry texts you read and help you form your responses more effectively.

The 'social, historical and cultural' contexts can consist of a variety of factors. Here are some things you could consider in placing a text in '**context**':

- the life or **biography** of the poet
- **other works** that the poet has written
- the **historical period** in which that poem was written
- the **place** or **event** that gave rise to the poem
- the ways in which the **language** used in the poem reflects the period in which it was written
- the particular **culture** within which the poem was written
- the **social background** of the poet or the theme or setting of the poem

> Although any or all of these features can be important when writing about a poem, the poem itself should be at the centre of your discussion. Students often go wrong by writing more about the historical background or the life of the poet than about the poem itself.

Poetry written before 1914

'Poetry written before 1914' covers a wide range, encompassing the works of Chaucer, written in the thirteenth century, to the poems written in the year that World War One began. There is a huge **variety** of poetry covered by the period and you encounter features when studying it that you do not find in more modern poetry. For example:

- Some of the **language** used might be **archaic** (old-fashioned words and phrases that we don't use anymore) so you might have to look up the meanings of particular words. The language of Chaucer is an obvious example of this.

- The poem might be to do with **ideas** or **themes** that we no longer relate to in our own time.
- The poem might contain **references** that meant something to the reader at the time the poem was written but which you now need to look up to fully understand.
- The **style** in which the poet writes might be unfamiliar to you today.

 KEY POINT You sometimes need to work at a poem in order to begin to develop an understanding of it.

Some of these factors could apply to modern poetry too, but you are more likely to encounter them in poetry that was written some time in the past.

Now read the following poem, *On my first Sonne* by Ben Jonson in 1616.

> ### On my first Sonne
>
> Farewell, thou child of my right hand, and joy;
> My sinne was too much hope of thee, lov'd boy,
> Seven yeeres tho'wert lent to me, and I thee pay,
> Exacted by thy fate, on the just day.
> O, could I loose all father, now. For why
> Will man lament the state he should envie?
> To have so soone scap'd worlds, and fleshes rage,
> And, if no other miserie, yet age?
> Rest in soft peace, and ask'd say here doth lye
> Ben Jonson his best piece of poetrie.
> For whose sake, hence-forth, all his vowes be such,
> As what he loves may never like too much.

What immediately strikes you about Jonson's language here?

There are obviously some differences between Jonson's 1616 spelling and our modern spelling – '*sinne*' instead of 'sin' and '*yeeres*' instead of 'years', for example. However, for the most part, the language is little different to what we use today.

The occasion that gave rise to Jonson's poem, however, is a universal one, which we can relate to today just as much as Jonson did in his own time – he is writing about the death of his first son (in fact, none of Jonson's children survived into adulthood). This is the context of the poem.

Tichborne's Elegy is another poem in which the historical context in which it was written is closely linked to the content of the poem and the ideas it expresses.

Read the poem through carefully.

> ### Tichborne's Elegy
> #### Written with his own hand in the Tower before his execution
>
> My prime of youth is but a frost of cares
> My feast of joy is but a dish of pain;
> My crop of corn is but a field of tares,
> And all my good is but vain hope of gain.
> The day is past, and yet I saw no sun;
> And now I live, and now my life is done.
>
> My tale was heard, and yet it was not told,

My fruit is fallen, and yet my leaves are green;
My youth is spent, and yet I am not old,
I saw the world, and yet I was not seen.
My thread is cut, and yet it is not spun;
And now I live, and now my life is done.

I sought my death, and found it in my womb,
I looked for life and saw it was a shade;
I trod the earth, and knew it was my tomb,
And now I die, and now I was but made.
My glass is full, and now my glass is run;
And now I live, and now my life is done.

Chidiock Tichborne 1586

This poem is called an 'elegy', which is usually a poem that mourns the loss of something and is often sad or melancholy in tone. This poem is sometimes called *Elegy for Himself*, which gives you a major clue as to what it is about. Chidiock Tichborne (1558–86) and his father were devout Catholics. At that time, though, the Protestant Queen Elizabeth I was Queen of England and Catholics were regarded with much suspicion. In 1586, Tichborne became involved in a plot to replace Queen Elizabeth with her Catholic cousin, Mary (Queen of Scots). The plot was discovered and the conspirators arrested, Tichborne amongst them. He was imprisoned in the Tower of London and hanged on 20th September 1586. He is said to have written the poem on the night before his execution.

PROGRESS CHECK

Make sure you use specific details of language from the poem to support your ideas.

Make notes on your interpretation of the poem. Here are some questions to help you focus your ideas:

- What does Tichborne have to say?
- What tone does he create?
- How does he use language to create his effect?

Here are some ideas:

- He is lamenting the fact that his life is being cut short and feels the waste bitterly.
- Not surprisingly, the tone is melancholy and regretful as he dwells on the fact that he is not old but his life is over.
- His use of '*frost*' gives a sense of the cold of death – '*cares*', '*pain*', '*vain hope*' give a negative feel and helplessness that he no longer controls his fate.
- Repetition of '*yet*' balances what could have been against what will be.
- Imagery is used to suggest death and how this was destined to be.
- The repetition at the end of each stanza of '*...and now my life is done*' emphasises the overall message of the poem.

10.4 Modern poetry

After studying this section you should be able to understand:

- *that modern poetry often deals with modern themes and issues*
- *how the different elements of a modern poem work together*

Many things to do with life are universal and are not solely the preserve of modern poetry but, very often, modern poetry uses the kind of language with which we are more familiar and frequently deals with themes and issues relating to **modern life** and **experiences**.

Read the poem *Mid-Term Break* by Seamus Heaney.

Mid-Term Break

I sat all morning in the college sick bay
Counting bells knelling classes to a close.
At two o'clock our neighbours drove me home.

In the porch I met my father crying –
He had always taken funerals in his stride –
And Big Jim Evans saying it was a hard blow.

The baby cooed and laughed and rocked the pram
When I came in, and I was embarrassed
By old men standing up to shake my hand

And tell me they were "sorry for my trouble."
Whispers informed strangers I was the eldest,
Away at school, as my mother held my hand

In hers and coughed out angry tearless sighs.
At ten o'clock the ambulance arrived
With the corpse, stanched and bandaged by the nurses.

Next morning I went up into the room. Snowdrops
And candles soothed the bedside; I saw him
For the first time in six weeks. Paler now,

Wearing a poppy bruise on his left temple,
He lay in the four foot box as in his cot.
No gaudy scars, the bumper knocked him clear.

A four foot box, a foot for every year.

Many of Heaney's poems explore themes of family, relationships and loss. In this poem he explores a very personal memory of when his younger brother was killed in a road accident.

Make a note of your response to the poem and the ways in which Heaney explores his theme and creates his effects. Think about the **structure**, **theme** and **language** of the poem.

Here are some ideas:

Structure

- The poem is divided into seven stanzas, each of which develops the idea further:
  Stanza 1: describes Heaney sitting in the school sickbay all morning before being driven home by his neighbours
  Stanza 2: describes his father meeting him at home, crying.
  Stanza 3: describes his feelings of awkwardness at the behaviour of the adults. The baby is oblivious to what is going on.
  Stanza 4: adults tell him they are 'sorry' while he hears others telling strangers that he is the eldest.
  Stanza 5: the ambulance arrives with the body of his little brother
  Stanza 6: the following morning Heaney looks at the body of his brother laid out in his room.
  Stanza 7: he describes the body lying in the four-foot coffin
  Final line: tells us the the boy was only four years old

Themes

- The poet explores his feelings of bewilderment and loss at what has happened
- He presents the whole memory through the eyes of a child

Language

- The language used appears simple and straightforward, using ordinary words and phrases.
- This conceals the complexity of the feelings it explores.
- The language carries connotations of death and a sense of tragedy
- The language is descriptive as he notices specific things such as "bells knelling", the baby cooing, the attitude of the adults, the paleness of his brother's face, the "poppy bruise on his left temple."

 KEY POINT Think about the ways in which the different elements of the poem work together to create the overall effect.

Now read *Havisham* by Carol Ann Duffy.

Havisham

Beloved sweetheart bastard. Not a day since then
I haven't wished him dead. Prayed for it
so hard I've dark green pebbles for eyes,
ropes on the back of my hands I could strangle with.

Spinster. I stink and remember. Whole days
in bed cawing Nooooo at the wall; the dress
yellowing, trembling if I open the wardrobe;
the slewed mirror, full-length, her, myself, who did this

to me? Puce curses that are sounds not words.
Some nights better, the lost body over me,
my fluent tongue in its mouth in its ear
then down till I suddenly bite awake. Love's

hate behind a white veil; a red balloon bursting
in my face. Bang. I stabbed at a wedding-cake.
Give me a male corpse for a long slow honeymoon.
Don't think it's only the heart that b-b-b-breaks.

Writing down your initial thoughts and responses to a poem can help you to order your thoughts and plan your answer or analysis of the poem.

In this poem Duffy adopts the persona of Miss Havisham, a character in Charles Dickens's novel *Great Expectations*. Miss Havisham had been jilted at the alter on her wedding day and had spent the rest of her life bitter and resentful. In the poem Duffy explores how this character might have felt and the emotional torment that she suffered.

Here are some points to think about:

- What feelings does the persona experience in the first stanza?
- What do you think the phrase "Beloved sweetheart bastard" shows?
- Which words create a sense of violence?
- Note Duffy's use of metaphors and the effects they create.
- What is the effect of the ending of the poem?

10.5 Poems from different cultures

LEARNING SUMMARY

After studying this section you should be able to understand:

- *how and why non-standard language is used*
- *how symbols from another culture are used to explore ideas*

If you are studying English, you will need to study some poetry from different cultures. The idea of 'different cultures' is a very broad one, covering the tremendously diverse range of cultures in the world. Poems that find their roots in different cultures can have particular features that you might look out for and comment on.

Non-standard English and dialect forms

Some poetry from different cultures, rather than using Standard English, uses the **non-standard** English and/or **dialect** forms of the particular **cultural background** from which it comes. Read '*Unrelated Incidents*' by Tom Leonard. Here Leonard presents the news being read in a Glaswegian accent.

Unrelated Incidents

this is thi	widny thingk
six a clock	it wuz troo.
news thi	jist wonna yoo
man said n	scruff tokn.
thi reason	thirza right
a talk wia	way ti spell
BBC accent	ana right way
iz coz yi	ti tok it. this
widny wahnt	is me tokn yir
mi ti talk	right way a
aboot thi	spellin. this

trooth wia
voice lik
wanna yoo
scruff. if
a toktaboot
thi trooth
lik wanna yoo
scruff yi

is ma trooth
yooz doant no
thi trooth
yirsellz cawz
yi canny talk
right. this is
the six a clock
nyooz. belt up.

PROGRESS CHECK

- It is written in a language that captures the Glaswegian accent.
- It is written phonetically to convey the way the Glaswegian accent sounds.
- It creates a strong sense of the voice of the speaker.
- It clearly sets the poem in a culture other than that represented by 'Standard English'.

Sometimes a poet might use a mixture of **Standard English** and a **dialect form** in order to **emphasise** a particular idea. For example, in his poem *Half-Caste*, John Agard mixes West Indian patois with Standard English. Look at the following extract from the poem.

Half-Caste

Excuse me
standing on one leg
I'm half-caste

Explain yuself
wha yu mean
when yu say half-caste
yu mean when picasso
mix red an green
is a half-caste canvas?
explain yuself
wha yu mean
when yu say half-caste
yu mean when light an shadow
mix in de sky
is a half-caste weather?
well in dat case
england weather
nearly always half-caste

PROGRESS CHECK

Why do you think Agard mixes dialect form with Standard English in this poem?

By using this technique he emphasises the theme of his poem – that of being 'Half-Caste' – the half dialect, half Standard English emphasises this. It also gives a sense of the dual 'voice' that the poet possesses.

The use of symbols

A poet might also make use of the **symbols** of another culture to explore their ideas. In *Presents from my Aunts in Pakistan* by Moniza Alvi, the poet presents the idea of being caught between two cultures. She came to England as a baby and has grown up in the English culture but looks back to her roots in Pakistan, reflecting on the gifts that her aunts, still living in Pakistan, sent her as she was growing up:

> ## Presents from my Aunts in Pakistan
> *They sent me a salwar kameez*
>   *peacock-blue.*
>   *and another*
>   *glistening like an orange split open,*
> *embossed slippers, gold and black*
>   *points curling.*
>   *Candy-striped glass bangles*
>   *snapped, drew blood.*
>   *Like at school, fashions changed*
>   *in Pakistan —*
> *the salwar bottoms were broad and stiff,*
>   *then narrow.*
> *My aunts chose an apple-green sari.*
>   *silver-bordered*
>   *for my teens.*

All these gifts are **symbolic** of the Pakistani culture but the poet remembers that

'I longed
for denim and corduroy'

which symbolises the western culture she has grown up in. Ironically, even her aunts –

'...requested cardigans
from Marks and Spencer's.'

Throughout the poem, symbols are used to reflect the poet's feelings of being caught between two cultures and her feelings, ultimately of being –

'...of no fixed nationality.'

PROGRESS CHECK

Make a list of some of the features to look for when studying poetry from different cultures.

- The use of non-standard or dialect language forms.
- Imagery drawn from different cultures.
- The use of symbols that reflect different cultures.
- References or vocabulary that are rooted in different cultures.

10.6 Comparing poems

LEARNING SUMMARY

After studying this section you should be able to understand:

● *what features to look for in each poem*
● *how to plan and write your response*

As part of the GCSE English Literature course, one of the things you will need to do is to '*explore relationships and comparisons between text, selecting and evaluating relevant material*'. One of the ways in which you might be asked to do this is to compare two poems.

When comparing poems you need to look for all the features that you look for when studying a single poem. You need to look at the:

● **content** of the poem
● **tone** and **mood** of the poem
● **form** in which it is written and **structured**
● ways in which **language** is used

However, you also need to **compare** these features in both poems.

> When writing your response, avoid writing an examination of one poem and then the other and comparing them in a final paragraph. Integrate your comments on the poems throughout.

You will need to look at each poem individually to plan your response, but when writing your response you need to **integrate** your ideas on both poems.

Here's one way you could approach this task:

Planning your response

1. Read both poems through carefully and get an overall **sense** of what each poem is about and how the poets **handle** their topics.
2. Re-read poem 'A' and make **brief notes** either around the poem, if you are able, or on a separate sheet, noting key words, phrases, images etc. and your **response** to it. Do the same with poem 'B'.
3. Note down some **brief** quotations from each poem that you will use to illustrate your ideas. You could underline or circle these if you can write on the copy of the poem.
4. Make two lists – one headed **similarities** and one headed **differences** and list the main points under each heading.

Writing the response

It is important that you avoid writing an essay on each poem and then try to join them together. The best responses are those that **integrate** the ideas in **parallel** throughout the essay. Here's one way you could approach this:

INTRODUCTION

Introductory paragraph commenting on what each poem is about and capturing the 'flavour' of each.

MAIN BODY

Several paragraphs based on your detailed reading of the poems. It is a good idea to make a point about poem 'A' and then a point about poem 'B'.

It can help you structure your ideas in a logical way, e.g. one paragraph could compare the way each uses **imagery**, while another paragraph could focus on **structure** etc.

CONCLUSION

A concluding paragraph, summing up the main similarities and differences, saying which you find more effective and why, **if you are asked this**.

 KEY POINT Keep both poems at the centre of your focus and don't be tempted to write all about one and then the other.

Sample GCSE question

Compare how the poets explore the relationship between parents and their children in four of the poems you have studied from the anthology. Write about 'Digging' by Seamus Heaney and compare it with one poem by Gillian Clarke and two poems from the Pre-1914 Poetry Bank

The four poems chosen for discussion in this essay will focus on the often complex relationships and bonds that are formed between parents and their children.

In his poem 'Digging' Seamus Heaney presents the parent/child relationship from the point of view of the child (now an adult remembering the scene). Heaney's tone here when describing his father and grandfather is full of respect and he expresses what a pride they take in their work and how they are motivated by it through their 'hard-working attitudes. This tone contrasts markedly with that used by Gillian Clarke in 'Catrin', where she describes the conflicts, both emotional and physical created through the mother/child bond. Heaney's tone also contrast with that used by Ben Jonson in 'On my first sonne'. Here the physical bond between father and son has been broken by the death of his son and the pain and emotional conflicts the poet feels are clear. In 'The Song of the Mother' the tone is one of resentment and envy felt by the Old Mother for the childhood freedom experienced by her child.

In 'Digging' Heaney describes how his father and grandfather showed great skill in their work. His use of verbs such as 'rasping', 'digging' and 'slicing' create a sense of their task being hard and physically demanding. Although their work was hard, though, they both gained a great deal of satisfaction from it and found it both rewarding and fruitful in that the gathered the potatoes they had grown –

> 'To scatter the new potatoes that we picked
> Loving their cool hardness in our hands.'

Heaney also gives a strong impression of the pride his grandfather took in his work and that he could do his job better than anyone –

> 'My grandfather cut more turf in a day
> Than any other man on Toner's bog.'

We can see Heaney's determination to follow in their footsteps even though his work is very different to theirs. His tool is his pen –

> 'The squat pen rests.
> I'll dig with it.'

For Heaney the parent/child bond is something that he consciously chooses to maintain whereas in 'Catrin' Clarke struggles against this bond. Clarke views this bond much less positively than Heaney and much of the vocabulary she uses contains words with negative connotations creating a sense of this conflict, 'struggle', 'fierce confrontation', 'shouted'. There is a strong sense. of wanting to break free from the bond –

> 'We want, we shouted
> To be two, to be ourselves.'

However, Clarke also sees positive aspects of the parent/child bond reflected in the phrases 'rosy, defiant glare' and 'Trailing love and conflict'. In contrast to the life in Clarke's poem Jonson's 'On my first sonne' expresses a deep and intense sense of loss as the poet resigns himself to the death of his son –

> ' Farewell, thou child of my right hand...' the suggestion that his son was 'lent' to him
> gives the feeling that his death was inevitable.

Yeats also creates a sense of loss in 'The Song of the Old Mother' but in this case it is the loss of youth and freedom felt by the mother. Her life is full of toil and the monotony of her daily life is emphasised by the repetition of 'and' and the monosyllabic verbs used - 'I must scrub and bake and sweep.'

The different poets, then all present the parent/child bond in different ways. Heaney is proud of it and wants to maintain it, Clarke feels it is a frustrating, restricting but unbreakable link, for Jonson the breaking of the bond through death blights his own life and Yeats presents the feeling of envy felt by the mother for her child.

Clear focus on question right from start.

Compares with appropriate Clarke poem.

Brings in comparison with well-chosen pre-1914 poem.

Begins more detailed analysis of 'Digging'.

Focus on details of language use

Supports points with quotation.

Develops comparison with Clarke poem.

Again attention paid to details of language.

Appropriate supporting quotation.

Integrates comparison with pre-1914 poem.

Good supporting quotation.

Integration of comparison with fourth poem.

Analytical comments on language.

Short conclusion summarising views and reinforcing key ideas.

Exam practice questions

Compare the ways in which poets write about pain and suffering in four or more poems you have studied.

Write about 'The Affliction of Margaret', one poem by Simon Armitage, one poem by Carol Ann Duffy and one more poem from the pre-1914 Bank.

Remember to compare:

- what the poets write about
- how they present their ideas on pain and suffering
- how you respond to the poems

The Affliction of Margaret
By William Wordsworth

Where art thou, my beloved Son,
Where art thou, worse to me than dead?
Oh find me, prosperous or undone!
Or, if the grave be now thy bed,
Why am I ignorant of the same
That I may rest; and neither blame
Nor sorrow may attend thy name?

Seven years, alas! to have received
No tidings of an only child;
To have despaired, have hoped, believed,
And been for evermore beguiled, –
Sometimes with thoughts of very bliss!
I catch at them, and then I miss;
Was ever darkness like to this?

He was among the prime in worth,
An object beauteous to behold;
Well born, well bred; I sent him forth
Ingenuous, innocent, and bold:
If things ensued that wanted grace,
As hath been said, they were not base;
And never blush was on my face.

Ah! little doth the young one dream,
When full of play and childish cares,
What power is in his wildest scream,
Heard by his mother unawares!
He knows it not, he cannot guess:
Years to a mother bring distress;
But do not make her love the less.

Neglect me! no, I suffered long
From that ill thought; and, being blind,
Said "Pride shall help me in my wrong:
Kind mother have I been, as kind
As ever breathed:" and that is true;
I've wet my path with tears like dew,
Weeping for him when no one knew.

My Son, if thou be humbled, poor,
Hopeless of honour and of gain,
Oh! do not dread thy mother's door;
Think not of me with grief and pain:
I now can see with better eyes;
And worldly grandeur I despise,
And fortune with her gifts and lies.

Alas! the fowls of heaven have wings,
And blasts of heaven will aid their flight;
They mount – how short a voyage brings
The wanderers back to their delight!
Chains tie us down by land and sea;
And wishes, vain as mine, may be
All that is left to comfort thee.

Perhaps some dungeon hears thee groan,
Maimed, mangled by inhuman men;
Or thou upon a desert thrown
Inheritest the lion's den;
Or hast been summoned to the deep,
Thou, thou, and all thy mates, to keep
An incommunicable sleep.

I look for ghosts; but none will force
Their way to me: 'tis falsely said
That there was ever intercourse
Between the living and the dead;
For, surely, then I should have sight
Of him I wait for day and night,
With love and longings infinite.

My apprehensions come in crowds;
I dread the rustling of the grass;
The very shadows of the clouds
Have power to shake me as they pass:
I question things, and do not find
One that will answer to my mind;
And all the world appears unkind.

Beyond participation lie
My troubles, and beyond relief:
If any chance to heave a sigh,
They pity me, and not my grief.
Then come to me, my Son, or send
Some tidings that my woes may end;
I have no other earthly friend!

Exam practice answers

Chapter 1
- Your advice should be clear and logically organised.
- You should write about a range of ideas and aspects of your chosen hobby.
- Use an appropriate tone and vocabulary and avoid being too technical or using words or terms that your reader might not understand (if specialist terms are necessary, explain them).

Chapter 2
- Your writing should fit the title you have chosen from the selection.
- It should show careful planning and follow an effective structure.
- Your writing should engage the reader's interest and show good use of the imagination.
- A varied vocabulary should be used and the writing should be technically accurate.
- Your writing should have an effective ending.

Chapter 3
- Look at the content of the review.
- Examine the way in which the review is structured.
- Look at the use of illustrations and graphical features.
- Be aware of the message that the writer wishes to convey to the reader.

Chapter 4
- The careful selection of your topic is very important here.
- Your writing should give a real sense of the experience or the subject of your description to your reader.
- It is important to refer to details of what you thought and how you responded to events, if you are writing from personal experience.
- Make sure you stick to your chosen topic and don't wander off track.

Chapter 5
- You should look at the message the advert wishes to convey to the reader.
- Give your views on the illustrations.
- Comment on the effectiveness of the photographs.
- Examine the ways in which language is used in the text and the effects it produces.
- Have some ideas on the effectiveness of the advert.

Chapter 6
a)
- The film is famous but it may be less well known that it was filmed in New Zealand.
- The impressive photography of the film, which many of the readers of the article will probably have seen, will arouse their interest in terms of reading about the locations etc.

b)
- Discuss the vividness of the description.
- Discuss the use of the Tolkien quotation.
- Give specific examples of language use.
- Discuss the effects created through the language.
- Show how well suited this is to audience and purpose.

Chapter 7
- You should focus closely on the question.
- Make sure that you deal with both friendship and love.
- Relate the theme to appropriate characters.
- Illustrate the points you make with specific details from the text.
- Comment on the effects created by the details you select.

Chapter 8
- Begin by focusing on the extract from Pygmalion.
- You should spend time writing about each of the characters.
- You should broaden your discussion to bring in points from the rest of the play.
- Think about areas of similarity and difference in the characters.

Chapter 9
- Examine the effect that Boo Radley has on the other characters in the book.
- Think about the ways in which they respond to him.
- Discuss what his presence adds to the novel.

Chapter 10
- Select an appropriate poems to compare with *Tichborne's Elegy* – i.e. one that deals with the theme of relationships.
- Compare *Tichborne's Elegy* to your chosen poems. (Note: 'compare' here means look at both the similarities and differences.)
- Focus on the ways the poets use language – pick specific examples and comment on the effects they create.
- Look at the ways in which the poets explore their ideas.

Letts **Examining Group**

General Certificate of Secondary Education

English
Paper 1 Tier H (*Higher*)

Time: 1 hour 45 minutes

In addition to this paper you will require:
● loose-leaf sheets for your answers.

Instructions to candidates
● Write your name, centre number and candidate number in the boxes at the top of this page.
● Use blue or black ink or ballpoint pen.
● Answer both questions in **Section A** and one question from **Section B**.
● Spend about one hour on **Section A** and the rest of the time on **Section B**.
● Do all rough work in your answer book. Cross through any work you do not want marked.
● You must not use a dictionary in this examination.

Information for candidates
● The maximum mark for this paper is 54.
● Mark allocations are shown in brackets.
● You are reminded of the need for good English and clear presentation in your answers. All questions should be answered in continuous prose.

SECTION A: READING

- Answer **all** the questions in this Section.
- Spend about **60 minutes** on this Section.

Read **Item 1** (page 4 of this paper), the article from the *Guardian Unlimited*, entitled *I'm not sure it's my colour.*

You are being asked to distinguish between fact and opinion.

1 **(a)** Choose three opinions. Write each one down and explain how you know each is an opinion and not a fact. **[6]**

Read **Item 2** (page 6 of this paper), the article from the *Times Educational Supplement* (TES) entitled *Genie in your handset*.

You are now being asked to follow an argument and to select material appropriate to purpose.

(b) Explain how mobile phone technology 'could be harnessed for education'. **[3]**

You are now being asked to compare **Item 1**, *I'm not sure it's my colour* with **Item 2**, *Genie in your handset* and to identify similarities or differences.

(c) Compare:
- what they have to say
- the language used to say it. **[4]**

Read **Item 3** (page 7 of this paper), the web page by O2 on *Media Messaging* and **Items 1 and 2** as media texts.

2 **(a)** In **Item 1**, *I'm not sure it's my colour*, compare the ways meaning is conveyed in print and image. **[4]**

(b) How do the form, layout and presentation of **Item 2**, the article from the *TES*, help you understand what the writer is saying? **[4]**

(c) Compare **Item 2** with **Item 3**, the *TES* article with the O2 web page on *Media Messaging*.

You should write about:
- the different purposes of the two items
- the language used
- the way the material is presented. **[6]**

SECTION B: WRITING TO ARGUE, PERSUADE OR ADVISE

- Answer **one** question in this Section.
- Spend about **45 minutes** on this Section.
- You may use some of the information from Section A if you want to, but you do not have to do so.
- If you use any of the information do not simply copy it.

Remember:
- Spend five minutes planning and sequencing your material.
- You should not write more than about two sides of paper.
- Spend five minutes checking your:
  - ▸ paragraphing
  - ▸ punctuation
  - ▸ spelling.

EITHER

3 You are a journalist who reviews the latest technological products such as mobile phones and computers. Write a review for a new product and **argue** the merits and drawbacks that it may have for consumers. **[27]**

OR

4 Write a letter to your Headteacher to **persuade** him or her to either accept or ban the use of mobile phones in your school. **[27]**

OR

5 Write a set of instructions to **advise** Lower School pupils on how they can make the most effective use of computers or mobile phones. **[27]**

OR

6 Write an article for a teenage magazine. Consider how advertisers target the young and create peer pressure for owning new products. **Argue** the case whether young people should own 3G mobile phones. **[27]**

I'm not sure it's my colour

How your phone became more
important than your trainers
Jess Cartner-Morley
Monday November 11, 2002
The Guardian

ILLUSTRATION BY ROBYN NEILD

For a few years now, phones have been small enough to fit easily in a shirt pocket. Funny, that. Because walk into most trendy bars and you'd never guess it: at many tables, each occupant will have placed his – sometimes her, but usually his – mobile in front of him, next to his lager. Among all-male groups, each table looks uncannily similar: three men, three pints, three phones. And there is more than practicality at work here. Even those phones with vibrating alerts, which in a noisy bar can easily be felt in a pocket, are proudly paraded. The purpose of a modern mobile is to be seen, as well as heard.

The roots of mobile mania are technological; they have achieved their present ubiquity by being phenomenally useful gadgets. But for such a tiny, personal item they have a high visibility – on pub tables, with designer snap-on covers, trilling intentionally irritating ringtones. In embracing them as a fashion accessory, we have lifted mobiles above the strata of fax machines and tumble dryers.

Once every decade or so, the marketing men and women hit perfect pitch with a product that tallies precisely with the cultural aspirations of the moment. In the 1980s, the trainer became a key cultural accessory: the means by which the owner pronounced his or herself to be au fait with the modern world. Trainers embodied a new post-nine-to-five culture which embraced elements as disparate as rave culture and gym culture. They achieved this broad-brush appeal by being rooted in practicality, and therefore hard to dismiss. The right pair of trainers said something about you, lent a little style-mag airbrushing to your public image, while masquerading as a no-nonsense piece of kit.

Nike Air Max were very comfortable, but they didn't become a cult success at £100 a throw just by getting you from A to B without sore feet. Likewise, the cult of the mobile phone has been fed as much by cultural association and design innovation as by practicality. The mobile is the ultimate accessory for the Me generation. Just as Nike's most famous slogan, Just Do It, glamorised the individual's will and willpower, the mobile phone's epitaph could be It's For You – because with a mobile, it always is. After years of diminishing bulk, the mobile has settled around the size and weight of that other individual indulgence, a chocolate bar. A caller reaching you via your home or work landline is

What a mobile phone says is that you are too indispensable to the big, wide world to be allowed out of reach

● 16% of British kids have been bullied by text message.

identifying you with your family or company; even a car or a house may be a status symbol that you have to share. But a mobile phone is all about you.

What a mobile phone says is that you are too indispensable to the big, wide world to be allowed out of reach, but that you are "doing your own thing". You are independent, yet in demand; busy, but not tied down. In these days of competitive exhaustion, a ringing phone is both an albatross around the neck and a badge of honour. If the mobile has a predecessor in technology, it is the wristwatch, which spans the same territory between fashion accessory and functional item. Having an outsize diving watch was the precursor of having the newest, tiniest phone; the smart metallic phone cover has replaced the gold Rolex. Now that mobile phones display the time, wristwatches have been usurped in more ways than one.

As in all cultural phenomena, it's important to keep ahead of the game. This is where design comes in. As recently as seven or eight years ago, simply having a mobile phone marked you out as an early adopter; as they have become more common, it has been increasingly important to have not just any phone, but the right one. And in response, mobiles have moved on in design more in the past 10 years than landline telephones have in the past 30.

Whereas most cult fashion accessories are must-haves only to a relatively small number of shopaholic women, and most cult techno toys of interest only to a small band of men, the mobile has found a broad catchment area. Builders, taxi drivers, schoolchildren and politicians alike are suckers to the charms of the latest model; like trainers, mobiles have a rare unisex appeal. The increasingly tiny size has caught the imagination both of those who marvel over the technological sophistication, and those who just think they are cute. The most aspirational colour for a mobile? Silver, the colour of jewellery and expensive gadgets.

To keep the interest of women, designers have created ever more curvy phones. The latest phones have more in common, aesthetically, with a chic powder compact or elegant perfume bottle than with the awkward black bricks of a decade ago. The female market has also been the driving force behind the user-friendly technology developed by leading phone manufacturers, particularly Nokia. In contrast to the self-consciously techy, cliquey language of the video game, modern mobiles are deliberately user-friendly. And if the welcome notes and picture messages aren't touchy-feely enough, there is now a support industry to help you personalise your phone: from metallic covers to stickers and novelty ringtones.

Still, a mobile's most attention-grabbing characteristic is not how it looks, but how it sounds. The novelty ringtone, which began as a specialist subject for internet whizz kids, took off with the success of the Eminem "Stan" tune, and has become a premium-rate telephone line fixture, found in all the tabloid back pages. The ringing phone, in all its melodic guises, is now a soundtrack to bars, supermarkets and cinema foyers.

Twentysomethings who have grown up with mobile culture have developed a new style of Friday-night social life, in which meeting times and places are endlessly fluid, and constant changes of plans the norm. Among freelance thirtysomethings, the Starbucks-led concept of the "third place", a haven of deal-making over skinny lattes, would never have taken off without the mobile.

What the Finnish academic Timo Kopomaa called the "culture of interruption" created by the mobile is resented far more by older generations. Older age brackets are more likely to be censorious about "inappropriate" phone use than teenagers. To the traditionalist, the mobile fosters rude behaviour: it has eroded the art of making an arrangement and sticking to it; and breaking off a conversation to answer a ringing phone is the modern equivalent of looking over people's shoulders at cocktail parties. However, even among the apparently uncouth, mobile-obsessed young, there is an unspoken etiquette. Researchers have found that customers are far less likely to put their phone on the table in an establishment with tablecloths. Ubiquitous it may be, but the mobile divides generations; parents just don't understand. What more proof could you need to know that this is not a gadget, but a fashion accessory.

© The Guardian. Illustration © Robyn Neild.

- 2% of mobile phone users had their phones stolen last year – a theft every three minutes. The Metropolitan Police claim that mobile thefts account for 1/3 of all street robberies in London.

24   circuit

Genie in your handset

Forget laptops and handhelds, the mobile phone is the magic performer of portable technology and that may be good for teachers, discovers **George Cole**

It's strange to think that most of us carry in our pockets the sort of computing power that would have required a room full of computers in the 1960s. I am talking about a mobile phone, which eight out of 10 Britons now own.

It's easy to forget that a mobile is a highly sophisticated computer. All handsets contain a processor chip, memory and an operating system (some even use one developed by Microsoft). Many also use plug-in memory cards to expand their storage capacity and have web browsers. Some mobile phones are portable multimedia computers, with a colour screen and able to handle audio, text, graphics, animation, pictures and even video. Using these mobiles you can play games, listen to music and take (and send) digital photos. Some handsets offer an always-on internet connection for accessing email or websites.

Smart phones blur the line between mobiles and computers even more. For example, Sony Ericsson's P800 can view email attachments and exchange data with a PC. Later this year, Samsung will launch the SGH-1700, a phone that includes Microsoft *Pocket Office* (with *Word, Excel, Outlook, MSN Messenger* and *Internet Explorer*). Nokia's 9210 Communicator even has a Qwerty keyboard and the Orange SPV smart phone uses Microsoft *Smartphone* software. (Mind you, a friend's SPV tends to crash occasionally and has to be re-booted. Sorry, re-started.) Many mobiles are designed to connect to a PC and exchange data via a USB connector, infra-red link or Bluetooth wireless technology.

Now companies such as Motorola and NEC have launched handsets designed for the new "third generation" (3G) networks. These 3G phones offer faster data speeds than current phones so you can download larger files (such as video clips) in shorter times; I got hold of a 3G phone and was impressed by the video quality. And more and more phones now feature a built-in digital camera and allow picture messaging, enabling images to be sent to compatible handsets or a special website. The website allows those without a picture messaging phone to log on and view the images.

But enough about the technology. Far more exciting is how the mobile phone technology could be harnessed for education. Professor Stephen Heppell, director of the Ultralab learning research centre based at Anglia Polytechnic University, thinks teachers shouldn't confiscate mobile phones from their pupils but encourage their use for learning. He says mobiles offer a portability that can't be matched by conventional portable computing devices like laptops, tablet PCs and PDAs. Pupils also find them easy to use – ever watched a teenager enter text in a phone or personalise it with downloaded ring tones and graphics? This is a technology children are familiar and comfortable with and we should look at how it can be exploited in education. Several projects are tackling this.

Ultralab is involved in several educational projects that use mobile phones, including e-Viva, which delivers ICT assessments to ICT students at key stage 3 on a mobile phone. And the M-learning (mobile learning) project is a European-wide initiative aimed at people aged 16–24 who left school with few, if any, qualifications. It uses a variety of materials to help develop literacy and numeracy skills. There is also the DfES-funded Ingenium Project (formerly Classroom of the Future), which is designed to see how new and emerging technologies can be used in the classroom. Picture messaging is one area of interest – for example, pupils could go on a field trip and send back images to those in the classroom.

Heppell also notes that mobile phones are better at handling personal identity on the internet than a PC. If you log on to a website you have to type in your user name and password to identify yourself, but your mobile phone number can represent you.

Of course, there are many issues surrounding the use of this technology in education, not least cost. It currently costs around 50p to take and send a picture on a camera phone (although it costs nothing to take a photo and store it for display on the handset's screen).

Hopefully, the price of services like picture messaging and 3G will become more affordable. We also need to understand how the technology can be organised and managed and what tasks are ideal for mobile phones.

Even so, we should be seriously looking at the role mobiles could play in teaching and learning.

© *Times Educational Supplement*/George Cole

Item 3

Image reproduced courtesy of O2 Limited

 **Examining Group**

General Certificate of Secondary Education

English
Paper 2 Tier H (*Higher*)

Time: 1 hour 30 minutes

In addition to this paper you will require:
● loose-leaf sheets for your answers.
● A copy of the current *AQA Anthology* which you have been studying.

Instructions to candidates
● Use blue or black ink or ballpoint pen.
● Answer **one** question in **Section A** (*Poems from Different Cultures and Traditions*) and **one** question from **Section B** (*Writing to inform, explain or describe*).
● Spend about 45 minutes on each section.
● Write your answers in the answer book provided.
● Do all rough work in your answer book. Cross-through any work you do not want marked.
● You must not use a dictionary in this examination.

Information for candidates
● The maximum mark for this paper is 54.
● For Section A, candidates must have a copy of the current *AQA Anthology* in the examination room. This may be annotated, but candidates must not use any additional notes or materials.
● Mark allocations are shown in brackets **[27]**.
● You are reminded of the need for good English and clear presentation in your answers. All questions should be answered in continuous prose.

Section A: Reading

This section is linked to the *Poems from Different Cultures and Traditions* that you studied in Section 1 of the *2004 AQA Anthology*.

> Answer **one** question on this section of poems.
> Spend around **45 minutes** on this Section.

EITHER

1   Compare the ways in which the poets present people in 'Island Man' and **one** other poem from the *Poems from Different Cultures and Traditions*.   [27]

OR

2   Compare 'Love After Love' with **one** other poem and explore the theme of self-discovery in each of the poems.   [27]

Section B: Writing to inform, explain or describe

● Answer **one** question in this Section.
● Allow about **45 minutes** on this Section.

Remember:

● Spend five minutes planning and sequencing your material.
● You should not write more than about two sides of paper.
● Spend five minutes checking your:
  ‣ paragraphing
  ‣ punctuation
  ‣ spelling.

EITHER

3   You are a local councillor and the Council has decided to introduce new traffic calming measures in your area or ward.

Write a letter **informing** residents about the Council's decision in which you:
  • **inform** them of the Council's decision
  • tell them where the traffic calming measures will be
  • identify the measures that will be taken.   [27]

OR

4   There is a wide range of pressures on young people today.

Explain what you take to be the main pressures and how they affect you as well as people that you know.   [27]

OR

5   A room can say a great deal about the person who owns it.

Describe a room that you think does this and **explain** your choice.   [27]

OR

6   **Describe** a frightening confrontation or incident that you either witnessed or were involved in and **explain** how you felt about it afterwards.   [27]

Section A: reading assessment objectives

When answering Section A's reading questions you are expected to demonstrate the following skills:

(i) read, showing *insight* and *engagement*, making appropriate *references* to *texts* and *developing* and *sustaining interpretations* of them;

(ii) *distinguish between fact and opinion* and *evaluate* how information is presented;

(iii) show that you can *follow an argument*, identifying *what is implied* and pointing out *inconsistencies*;

(iv) select points and passages that are appropriate to their purpose, *collate material* from other sources and make *cross references* between *texts*;

(v) show that you can *evaluate how writers use linguistic and presentational devices to achieve their effects*, and comment on the *ways language varies and changes*.

Examiner's tips

To ensure that you fully understand what is expected of you, the chart below lists some key words and their meaning.

Key words	**Meaning**
Comment	Write remarks and explain your points when answering questions.
Collate material from different sources	Means 'bring together' similar points and ideas from two or more exam texts specified by the question.
Develop and sustain interpretations	Go into detail when making points in answering questions, usually giving evidence in the form of brief quotations.
Distinguish between fact and opinion	To identify facts that can be proved to be true as opposed to opinions that cannot. Sweeping statements and words such as 'can', 'may', 'perhaps', 'possibly', 'usually', etc. all hint at opinion. Facts can be proved from figures and looked up.
Evaluate how writers use linguistic and presentational devices to achieve their effects	*Linguistic devices*, means writers' various uses of language. For instance, check whether the writer uses the first, second or third person, rhetorical questions, alliteration, irony, similes, metaphors, puns, specifically selected vocabulary, sentence and paragraph length, etc. *Presentational devices* means the use of headings, subheadings, bullet points, italics, pictures, colour, how the writing or argument is set out (is it in two halves?), etc. *You need to point out whether the writers' use of linguistic and presentational devices aids or hinders the purposes of their texts.*
Follow an argument	Show that you have understood what the writer is saying on a particular topic by answering specific questions in your own words.
Inconsistencies	Are the writers' points and arguments consistent with their intention or purposes?
Insight and engagement	Show mental penetration and deep understanding in your answers when reading the texts.
How language varies and changes	Notice how language can vary within and between texts, for instance, formal and informal language, irony, literary-type language using metaphors, similes, contrasts in sentences and paragraphs, etc.
Cross references	Referring to similar points and ideas within and between texts.
Texts	Any form of writing, for example: article, letter, novel, essay, leaflet, etc.
What is implied	What is suggested or underlies the writers' points and ideas.

Answers for the Reading Section A

Use comments from the grade boundaries to help you mark each question.

Not all possible answers may be covered in this answer section. You should also reward answers that give appropriate evidence or reasoning for the questions.

1 a *Give 1 mark for each opinion and 1 mark for each explanation. Maximum 6 marks combined.*

Opinion	**Explanation**
Walk into most trendy bars and you'd never guess it: at many tables, each occupant will have placed his – sometimes her, but usually his – mobile in front of him, next to his lager.	This is a generalisation and sweeping statement that is grounded on the reader agreeing with the journalist.
Among all-male groups, each table looks uncannily similar: three men, three pints, three phones.	This is another generalised statement based on observation.
Even those phones with vibrating alerts, which in a noisy bar can easily be felt in a pocket, are proudly paraded.	This is a value judgement based only on observation.
The purpose of a modern mobile is to be seen, as well as heard.	This statement cannot be easily proved.
The mobile is the ultimate accessory for the Me generation.	While seemingly true this statement is not based on fact.

Examiner's tips
In most exam texts words such as *if, may, possibly, can, could,* etc. can be taken to indicate opinion. However, in the *Guardian* article, the writer's opinions are mainly expressed through sweeping statements that carry the ring of truth but are factually difficult to prove.

---

1 b *Give up to 3 marks*

The **content** of your answer is likely to include some of the following statements:
- Mobiles offer greater portability than more coventional computing devices such as laptops, PCs, and PDAs.
- Pupils find them easy to use and are familiar with the technology.
- Assessments could be delivered by mobile phone.
- Pupils can send picture messages back to their classrooms from field trips.

Marks and Grades	***Skills* shown in your answer**
U = 0 marks	Nothing written
D/E = 1 mark	• You may have included too much detail that obscures the answer. • You simply reproduced the order and language of the extract. • You attempted a relevant answer.
C/B = 2 marks	• You have made a clear attempt to follow the argument. • Your response is structured and the material has been understood and reshaped. • You have included more detail in some answers. • You have restated some of the order and language of the article.
A/A* = 3 marks	• Your answer is thoroughly competent and complete. • You have absorbed and summarised the argument. • You show a clear and full understanding of the question. • Your answer is as clear as one would expect from a sixteen-year-old pupil.

1 c   *Give up to 4 marks*

The **content** of your answer is likely to include some of the following statements:

Item 1
What it has to say:
- The purpose of modern mobiles is to be seen as well as heard.
- They are 'the ultimate accessory for the Me generation'.
- 'A mobile phone is all about you'.
- Having 'the right one' is important.
- They have 'rare unisex appeal'.
- The female market is the driving force behind its user-friendly technology.
- Their most attention-grabbing characteristic is how they sound.
- Mobiles have changed young people's social lives.
- 'The mobile divides the generations'.

Language used:
- Mostly to inform.
- It explains several changes.
- Third person.
- Some impersonal language used and quoted.
- Plain with no imagery.
- Title imitates direct speech.

Item 2
What it has to say:
- Mobiles are small, highly sophisticated computers.
- 'Smart phones blur the line between mobiles and computers'.
- 3G phones feature picture messaging but it is expensive.
- Mobile phone technology could be used in education.
- Pupils find mobiles easy to use.
- Mobiles are associated with personal identity.

Language used:
- Mostly to inform.
- Partly to persuade.
- First person but much of the article has the objective, essay-like feel of the third person.
- Conversational in places.
- Use of personal experience to make points, i.e. 'Ever watched a teenager enter text in a phone or personalise it with downloaded ring tones and graphics?'
- The only imagery used is in the article's heading.

Marks and Grades	*Skills* shown in your answer
U = 0 marks	Nothing written
D/E = 1 mark	• You simply paraphrased from the article without paying attention to the question. • The answer is unstructured; you simply copied and maintained each article's language. • You made a few attempts to compare each item.
C = 2 marks	• You have made an obvious attempt to compare the articles and answer the question. • Your answer is structured and it may have some added detail. • You have retained some of the articles' structure.
B = 3 marks	• You have given a competent response but it is not always centred on the texts' similarities and differences. • The information has been clearly understood and it is reordered in the answer. • There is also a sense of evaluation in your answer.
A/A* = 4 marks	• You have given a full answer that compares each text as fully as one would expect from a GCSE pupil. • You understood and refocused the material in a structured response. • You have given clear reasons for your points and shown judgement in your evaluation.

2 a   *Give up to 4 marks*

The **content** of your answer is likely to include some of the following statements for **uses of images and texts to convey meaning.**

Print

- Different fonts in the main article and the bulleted strip added to the bottom.
- Use of bold in headings.
- Bulleted added information that is not included in the article.
- Facts and opinions.
- Columns.
- Underlined subheading.
- Quotations.
- A large amount of text.

Image

- The image is linked to the main heading and it reflects how 'the female market has been the driving force' behind the design of mobile phones.
- It is a stylised drawing that is connected with fashion; the journalist is a fashion editor.
- The phone is also being compared with a compact in which the young woman examines her new hair colour, as if in a mirror. The mobile's small, accessory-like size also encourages this interpretation of it.
- The image is in black and white and therefore cannot carry any symbolism associated with colours.

Marks and Grades	*Skills* shown in your answer
U = 0 marks	Nothing written
G/F = 1 mark	• Your answer may be unclear because of too much detail or narrative. • Your comments are too general or descriptive. • You have shown little understanding of the differences between image and text.
D/E = 2 marks	• You tend towards paraphrase but there is an attempt to explain the differences. • Your answer is unstructured and mostly descriptive. • Some ways in which meaning has been conveyed in image and text have been given. • You have made a relevant attempt to answer the question.
C/B = 3 marks	• You have made a clear attempt to compare the images and texts, using media terms. • Your answer is structured with selected information and comments on the different aspects of the two texts. • You have given a clear explanation of how text and image is linked. • You show clear understanding and use of technical terms in answer.
A/A* = 4 marks	• You have written a clear and detailed answer comparing how meaning is conveyed by both print and image. • Your information is presented carefully and logically. • The texts have been absorbed and the answer has been shaped with a clear purpose. • Your use of critical terminology to describe media concepts is sophisticated and convincingly phrased.

2 b   *Give up to 4 marks*

The **content** of your answer is likely to include some of the following statements on the article's **choice of form, layout and presentation.**

Form:
- It is a newspaper with broadsheet type content.
- There are various expectations of the newspaper form.
- These are backed up by images, copy and subject matter.

Layout:
- It has lined columns.
- There is an image of a giant, blue genie to suggest the potential power that could be released by small mobile phones.
- The user in red could be anyone. The danger of misused power may also be suggested by the red user.
- The heading suggests the overlooked, educational potential of small mobile phones.
- The subheading is brown to set it off so that time-strapped readers can get the gist of the article before reading it.
- Most of the copy is wrapped around the main image.

Presentation
- The use of colour.
- The image is striking and central.
- Small headline.
- The white space beneath the article is probably intentional as it helps magnify the message and purpose of the article.

Of course, alternative analytical points/interpretations in each of these three areas may be raised in answers.

Marks and Grades	*Skills* shown in your answer
U = 0 marks	Nothing written
G/F = 1 mark	• Your answer is hidden by too much detail or descriptive comments. • Your answer is descriptive and too general. • There is no evidence in the answer that you know the difference between form, layout and presentation.
D/E = 2 marks	• There is a tendency to reword parts of the texts and you have attempted to explain effects. • The answer is descriptive and lacks structure. • You have stated some ways in which form, layout and presentation have contributed to the effects. • You have made an attempt to produce a relevant answer.
C/B = 3 marks	• You have made a clear and effective attempt to use media concepts. • It is a structured answer where various aspects of form, layout and presentation have been selected and commented on. • Some of the correct media terms have been used. • You have clearly explained the ways that form, layout and presentation contribute to effect. • You have used technical terminology effectively and with understanding.
A/A* = 4 marks	• You show a clear understanding of how form, layout and presentation contribute towards effects. • Your answer is careful and logical. • The information in each text has been fully understood and the answer shaped with clear purpose. • Your use of media terms is sophisticated and convincing and they are used in a critical manner.

2 c *Give up to 6 marks*

The **content** of your answer is likely to include some of the following points of comparison between the *TES* article and the O2 *Media Messaging* web page.

Item 2

Images:
- The main image is imposing and helps illustrate the purpose of the article.
- The image suggests that great power could be released from such a small object.
- Blue (a cold colour) may also signify teachers' current feelings about mobiles.
- Red could also signify danger (health, interrupted lessons, etc.).
- The red figure below could stand for anyone.

Text:
- The first half of the article explains the background to the technology; the second half argues the possible educational uses of mobiles.
- There are examples in the text.
- The writer uses the first person although the text is mostly in the third person as this gives it objectivity.
- The journalist uses plain language; the only imagery used is in the title.

Item 3

Images:
- In the box under the heading, *Media Messaging*, the image suggests an idea.
- The main image uses humour for its effect.
- The themed colour of the page, blue, suggests newness, innovation and possibly fresh ideas.
- The other images act as a kind of shorthand for the subheadings that they suggest. These light, fun-style images are aimed at a young, teenage to early 20s audience who might buy this service. They also act as hyperlinks for further information.

Text:
- The text explains, describes, informs and persuades.
- It is brief and lively with several command-like statements. (For example, *Get started with media messaging*.)
- There is an example of the type of comment that could accompany a media message.
- Some questions to engage the audience are asked and answered.
- Most of the text acts as entry points or hyperlinks for further information.

There could be a general point about the two articles being obviously linked.

Marks and Grades	*Skills* shown in your answer
U = 0 marks	Nothing written
G/F = 1 mark	<ul><li>You do not have much content in your answer.</li><li>Your answer is hidden under too much detail or descriptive comment.</li><li>Your answer is too general or descriptive.</li><li>There is little evidence that you understand the difference between image and text.</li></ul>
D/E = 2–3 marks	<ul><li>There is a tendency towards paraphrase but you have attempted to explain differences and engage with the question.</li><li>The answer is unstructured and is mostly descriptive.</li><li>You have indentified some ways in which meaning is made in image and text.</li></ul>
C/B = 4–5 marks	<ul><li>You have clearly attempted a comparison using media concepts and terminology.</li><li>Your answer has structure and comments on selected points.</li><li>The links between the image and texts is clearly explained.</li><li>Terminology is used with understanding.</li></ul>
A/A* = 6 marks	<ul><li>There is a detailed comparison of each item's text and images.</li><li>The answer is carefully written and organised.</li><li>The material has been fully understood and refocused in your answer.</li><li>Your use of critical terminology is convincing when describing media terms and ideas.</li></ul>

Section B: Writing to argue, persuade or advise

To mark your answer you will need to produce two sets of marks and then add the two marks together for your score. The first part, **Content and organisation**, is worth **18 marks** (of the 27 marks).

This section relates to Assessment Objective 2: Reading.

In this section you are generally tested on your ability to:

- communicate clearly and imaginatively, using and adapting written forms for different readers and purposes;

- organise ideas into sentences, paragraphs and whole texts using a wide variety of linguistic and structural features.

The second part of your score, **Sentence structures, punctuation and spelling**, is worth **9 marks** (of the 27 marks) and this is added to the first mark. This mark takes account of a single assessment objective that has three parts:

- the effective use of a range of sentence structures;

- accurate punctuation;

- spelling.

All relevant answers should be rewarded.
Remember also that test conditions apply and that they should also be taken into account.

Questions 3-6

Examiner's tip

To mark the question that you answered, look out for your question's key words: to advise, argue or persuade.

To achieve a *Grade D* answer (9–10 marks) you will need to show some of the following **content**:

- the answer has a range of reasons for and against if **arguing/persuading**;

- if asked to **persuade**, there is a range of methods in the answer;

- there is a range of reasons given with **advice**;

- there may be some personal experience and material from the articles supporting the answer;

- the register (tone of voice) is formal with an effort to manipulate tone: for example, confident, formal, humorous, playful, etc.

- points are organised into paragraphs that show some changes in **argument** or stages of **persuasion** or **advice**.

- there may be a range of rhetorical questions and discursive markers. For example, *as a result, consequently, for that reason, so* and *therefore*, etc. But these are not used with fluency and seem wooden.

To achieve a *Grade D* answer (9–10 marks) you will have shown the following **skills** in your answer:

- you have made a conscious effort to identify with the writing's purpose and audience;

- you have made an attempt to interest the reader.

To achieve a *Grade C* answer (11–12 marks) you will need to show some of the following **content**:

- your **argument** or method of **persuasion** is quite detailed and you have shown an awareness of other points of view;
- your **advice** is becoming quite detailed and you have shown an awareness of the needs of younger pupils;
- you have used tone consciously and have varied your tone in places for effect.;
- your paragraphs are coherently linked both by content and language;
- language devices such as anecdote (a brief story, incident or facts) and rhetorical questions are confidently used;
- discourse markers are increasingly used to clarify an **argument** or **persuade**. For example, *as a result, consequently, for that reason, so* and *therefore*.

To achieve a *Grade C* answer (11–12 marks) you will have shown the following **skills** in your answer:

- you have clearly identified your purpose and you are beginning to sustain a response from your reader;
- the structure of your writing is clear with paragraphs and selected vocabulary used effectively.

To achieve a *Grade B* answer (13–14 marks) you will need to show some of the following **content**:

- your writing is detailed and well developed. **Argumentative** and **persuasive** points are supported but not always convincingly;
- you have introduced some **abstract argument** but not always successfully;
- you are able to use **argument** and **counter argument**;
- if asked to **persuade** you have used **persuasive** techniques but not always convincingly;
- your **advice** is supported with reasons and evidence but they are not always convincingly carried through;
- your audience's possible response appears to be anticipated and thought through;
- your **arguments** for and against are convincing;
- you have used sophisticated vocabulary choices to **persuade** and influence the reader;
- your paragraphing is clearly linked;
- there is a more complex level of **argument** where the choice of vocabulary is selected to influence the reader;
- discursive markers (see C above) are clearly and competently integrated in the answer.

To a achieve *Grade B* answer (13–14 marks) you will have shown the following **skills** in your answer:

- the content, form and written style of your answer are generally suited to the writing's purpose and audience.
- your writing is well organised and paragraphs tend to emphasise meaning. There is growing complexity of vocabulary in your writing.

To achieve a *Grade A* answer (15–16 marks) you will need to show some of the following **content**:

- you are able to **argue/persuade** in a successful and convincing manner and draw on a variety of sources;
- if asked to **advise** you have done so convincingly by drawing on a variety of sources in a well-informed way;
- the tone of your writing shows growing subtlety of purpose and an ability to manipulate the reader;
- you are able to show emphasis through a range of literary devices: contrasts between short and long sentences, paragraphs, etc.;
- you have a fluent control of linguistic devices and discourse markers;
- there is evidence of a wide vocabulary in your writing.

To achieve a *Grade A* answer (15–16 marks) you will have shown the following **skills** in your answer:

- you have shown consistency in the way form, content and written style is suited to your writing's purpose and audience;
- your paragraphs and sentences are fluently structured and linked;
- the answer has been crafted and carefully written.

To achieve a *Grade A** answer (17–18 marks) you will need to show some of the following **content**:

- if you use ironic or satiric humour, it works well within your writing's context;

- you have shown ease when integrating a wide variety of complex sources and ideas. Your writing shows intellectual strength;

- your use of discourse markers is effortless and fluent throughout your writing;

- you may have used a creative approach to structure, language and punctuation.

To achieve a *Grade A** answer (17–18 marks) you will have shown the following **skills** in your answer:

- you display an assured use of form, content and style to suit your purpose and audience. Your writing style is distinctive and highly effective;

- your writing is controlled and your points and ideas are sustained and crafted. You have used a very effective and pleasing choice of vocabulary.

Sentence structures, punctuation and spelling

Examiner's tip
You now need to add a mark for **Sentence structures**, **punctuation** and **spelling** to complete your mark for SECTION B. This Section is the same for Papers 1 and 2.

To achieve a *Grade E/D* answer (4–5 marks) you will need to show some of the following **content**:

- syntax (the grammatical arrangement of words) that is sometimes used consciously but this is not always secure;

- some complex sentences that may include discourse markers, e.g. *alternatively, although, because, in contrast,* etc.;

- the correct spelling of commonly used words;

- the accurate use of capital letters and full stops.

To achieve a *Grade E/D* answer (4–5 marks) you will need to show the following **skills** in your answer:

- the ability to use a range of sentence structures;

- accurate spelling of more complex words;

- use of a range of punctuation.

To achieve a *Grade C/B* (6–7 marks) answer you will need to show some of the following **content**:

- discourse markers to help shape sentences and paragraphs.
  For instance, your writing may include some of the following for effect:
  first person
  adjectives
  adverbs
  syntactical lists (structured lists of points, arguments or ideas)
  imperatives (these are commands; for example, *Do not put your head out of the window!*, *Stop!*, *Go ahead*, etc.)
  modal verbs (modal verbs are irregular verbs; the most common include: *can, could, may, might, must, ought to, shall, should, will* and *would*)
  parallel sentences (parts of sentences that ought to match. This frequently happens when writers use paired words like *either – or* or *not only – but also* within their sentences.)
  contrasting sentences/paragraphs
  repetition
  rhetorical questions
  short sentences
  exclamations.

To achieve a *Grade C/B* answer (6–7 marks) you will need to show the following **skills** in your answer:

- you can use a variety of sentence forms for effect;

- your spelling is accurate and secure;

- you know how to punctuate to clarify your meaning and purpose.

To achieve a *Grade A/A** answer (8–9 marks) you will need to show some of the following **content**:

- writing that is clear and controlled; sentence structures have been manipulated to create effects;

- a wide range of discourse markers appropriately used;

- variation in syntax (the grammatical arrangement of words) in a number of ways for rhetorical reasons;

- sophisticated use of a range of punctuation; for instance, colons and semi-colons are effectively and appropriately used.

To achieve a *Grade A/A** answer (8–9 marks) you will need to show the following **skills** in your answer:

- you have a full range of sentence structures and you can use them in an appropriate way;

- you have demonstrated a high level of accuracy in spelling;

- you have shown a high degree of accuracy in your punctuation.

Important information

Although this specimen question paper and mark scheme have been prepared and carefully considered by Letts Educational, it must be emphasised that they have not been subjected to the normal rigorous review which takes place prior to the approval of material for use in an operational examination. In addition, in an operational examination, optional questions (and their mark schemes) will be written to be exactly comparable with each other.

A deliberately broad range of question types is included in this specimen material in order to show the variety that is possible.

Grade predictor

The grid below suggests the grades that you might expect to achieve on these papers.
Remember that the grade boundaries change from year to year at each Examination Board.

Add the grades for the two papers and divide by 2 for your final mark.

Grade E	19–24
Grade D	25–30
Grade C	31–36
Grade B	37–42
Grade A	43–48
Grade A*	49–54

Section A: Reading

How to work out your answer

The comments for each grade are intended to help you to mark the **skills** and **content** that will be typically found within each grade band. However, the grade statements will not necessarily cover every possible answer. If the answer strongly fits a particular grade boundary give a mark towards the upper end of the band. If the answer only just fits the grade boundary, you should give a mark at the lower end of the scale. For instance, if the answer only just gets into grade D give 13 marks for question 1 rather than 14 or 15 marks.

This Section engages with the Assessment Objective 2: Reading

When answering your question on this Section you will be generally tested on your ability to:

- read with insight and engagement by making appropriate references to texts;
- develop and sustain your interpretations of texts;
- select material that is appropriate for your purposes;
- collate (gather) your material from different sources to make cross-references between texts;
- understand and evaluate (judge) how writers use linguistic, structural and presentational devices to achieve their effects;
- comment on the way language varies and changes.

Each of the questions answered in section A and B should be marked out of 27.

Answers to Reading Section A (Higher Tier)

Use comments from the following grade boundaries to help you mark questions 1 or 2 on
Poems from Different Cultures and Traditions.

To achieve a *Grade D* answer (13–15 marks) you will need to show some of the following **content**:
- some focus on how people or the theme of self-discovery is presented/explored in the two poems;
- details from the two poems to support comments on how people are presented or the theme of self-discovery is explored;
- a relevant comparison of the methods by which people are presented or the theme of self-discovery is explored in the poems.

To achieve a *Grade D* answer (13–15 marks) you will need to show the following **skills** in your answer:
- make some supportive extended points;
- use evidence effectively to support your points;
- give textual evidence and ideas;
- give some comments on the effects created by the poets;
- show some awareness of feelings, attitudes and ideas.

To achieve a *Grade C* answer (16–18 marks) you will need to show the **skills** shown for Grade D and also some of the following **content** in your answer:
- effective use of textual evidence to support points;
- some cross-referencing of the texts with regard to shared ideas;
- an awareness of poetic technique and its purpose within the poems;
- an understanding of feelings, attitudes and ideas present in the poems.

To achieve a *Grade B/A** answer (19–27 marks) you will need to show some of the following **content**:
- each poet's methods of presenting people or exploring the theme of self-discovery is examined and analysed in the two poems;
- specific literary techniques and methods of presentation are examined/compared/explored for their effects and appropriateness;
- an integrated comparative analysis is made;
- a developing personal response is given.

To achieve a *Grade B* answer (19–21 marks) you are likely to show the following **skills** in your answer:
- textual evidence to support integrated, cross-referenced points;
- an understanding of poets' techniques (craft);
- an appreciation of the feelings, attitudes and ideas in the poems.

To achieve a *Grade A* answer (22–24 marks) you will need to show the following **skills** in your answer:
- integration of references to the poems within your argument;
- a range of analysis of each writer's techniques;
- empathy (mentally identifying with people's ideas and feelings) with each writer's ideas and attitudes.

To achieve a *Grade A** answer (25–27 marks) you will need to show the following **skills** in your answer:
- a conceptualised overview of how the poems are linked thematically;
- close textual analysis (i.e. point-evidence-comment);
- an imaginative interpretation of the poems that is convincing and consistent.

Section B: Writing to inform, explain or describe

To mark your answer you will need to produce two sets of marks and then add the two marks together to obtain your score. The first part, **Skills and content**, is worth **18 marks** (of the 27 mark question).

This section engages with the Assessment Objective 2: Reading.

In this Section you are generally tested on your ability to:
- communicate clearly and imaginatively, using and adapting written forms for different readers and purposes.
- organise ideas into sentences, paragraphs and whole texts using a wide variety of linguistic and structural features.

The second part of your score, Sentence structures, punctuation and spelling, is worth **9 marks** (of the 27 mark question) and this is added to the first mark. This mark takes account of a single assessment objective that has three parts:
- **the effective use of a range of sentence structures;**
- **accurate punctuation;**
- **spelling.**

All valid and relevant answers should be rewarded. Remember that test conditions apply and that they should also be taken into account.

Answers to Reading Section B (Higher Tier)

Use comments from the following grade boundaries to help you mark questions 3–6 that ask you to write to *inform*, *explain* or *describe*.

To achieve a *Grade D* answer (9–10 marks) you will need to show some of the following **content**:
- a relevant range of description/information/explanation to support your ideas;
- possibly more than one source for information;
- various aspects of the subject that may be described or explained in detail.

To achieve a *Grade D* answer (9–10 marks) you will need to show the following **skills** in your answer:
- you have made a conscious attempt to meet the needs of purpose and audience;
- you have begun to engage with the reader's response;
- your paragraphing is clear though unimaginative;
- you have tried to use some vocabulary for effect.

To achieve a *Grade C* answer (11–12 marks) you will need to show some of the following **content**:
- information that has been selected to interest the reader through description or explanation;
- a range of information gathered from different sources to inform or explain. Description is likely to cover a range of aspects, e.g. the senses, colour, etc.;
- the use of the first person to address the reader directly, giving a range of reasons for the subject;
- control and competence in questions and answers, use of emphasis, etc. Anecdotes, if used, are usually given in context;
- integrated discursive markers that shape how information is organised and described. For example, *firstly, secondly, on the other hand, to sum up*, etc.

196

To achieve a *Grade C* answer (11–12 marks) you will need to show the following **skills** in your answer:
- a clear identification with your purpose and audience;
- signs that you have the ability to sustain the reader's response;
- clear paragraphing to aid the structure of your writing;
- vocabulary that has been selected and used for effect.

To achieve a *Grade B* answer (13–14 marks) you will need to show some of the following **content**:
- writing that is clear, detailed and well developed;
- examples that help build descriptions or explanations;
- an understanding of how your audience may respond to what you have written;
- a range of devices to create variety and engage the reader's interest e.g. bullet points, question and answer, rhetorical questions, parallels, etc.;
- discursive markers that are consistently integrated;
- effective use of technical vocabulary where appropriate.

To achieve a *Grade B* answer (13–14 marks) you will need to show the following **skills** in your answer:
- your use of form, content and style is suited to the writing's purpose and audience;
- your answer is clearly structured; paragraphs tend to heighten meaning and have clear linkage;
- you have used increasingly complex vocabulary.

To achieve a *Grade A* answer (15–16 marks) you will need to show some of the following **content**:
- a focus on the topic with a wide variety of interesting points, description or explanations;
- increasing subtlety in both purpose and manipulation of the reader's response;
- a response that is structured and developed, using a variety of means to describe, make points or convey the chosen topic;
- devices and discourse markers that are integrated in a fluent, controlled way;
- a wide-ranging vocabulary.

To achieve a *Grade A* answer (15–16 marks) you will need to show the following **skills** in your answer:
- a consistency in the way that form, content and style are suited to the writing's purpose and audience;
- evidence that the writing has been consciously crafted;
- coherent structure with fluency in both sentences and paragraphing.

To achieve a *Grade A** answer (17–18 marks) you will need to show some of the following **content**:
- a style of writing that is strong, informative, personal or creative;
- an appropriate use of satire, irony, humour, etc., if it is in keeping with the writing's purpose and context;
- a wide range of details that have been integrated from a number of sources;
- stylistic techniques and discourse markers that are integrated and effective.

To achieve a *Grade A** answer (17–18 marks) you will need to show the following **skills** in your answer:
- your form, content and style are assuredly matched with the writing's purpose and audience;
- your answer is distinctive and effective;
- your writing is controlled and crafted in a sustained manner;
- your vocabulary is effective and skilfully chosen.

Sentence structures, punctuation and spelling

You now need to add a mark for **Sentence structures**, **punctuation and spelling** to complete your mark for **Section B** of Paper 2.

To achieve a *Grade E/D* answer (4–5 marks) you will need to show some of the following **content**:
- syntax that is sometimes used consciously but this is not always secure;
- some complex sentences that may include discourse markers, e.g. *alternatively, although, because, in contrast*, etc.;
- the correct spelling of commonly used words;
- the accurate use of capital letters and full stops.

To achieve a *Grade E/D* answer (4–5 marks) you will need to show the following **skills** in your answer:
- the ability to use a range of sentence structures;
- accurate spelling of more complex words;
- use of a range of punctuation.

To achieve a *Grade C/B* answer (6–7 marks) you will need to show some of the following **content**:
- discourse markers to help shape sentences and paragraphs.
  For instance, your writing may include some of the following for effect:
  first person
  adjectives
  adverbs
  syntactical lists (structured lists of points, arguments or ideas)
  imperatives (these are commands; for example, *Do not put your head out of the window!*, *Stop!*, *Go ahead*, etc.)
  modal verbs (modal verbs are irregular verbs; the most common include: *can, could, may, might, must, ought to, shall, should, will* and *would*)
  parallel sentences (parts of sentences that ought to match. This frequently happens when writers use paired words like *either – or* or *not only – but also* within their sentences.)
  contrasting sentences/paragraphs
  repetition
  rhetorical questions
  short sentences
  exclamations.

To achieve a *Grade C/B* answer (6–7 marks) you will need to show the following **skills** in your answer:
- you can use a variety of sentence forms for effect;
- your spelling is accurate and secure;
- you know how to punctuate to clarify your meaning and purpose.

To achieve a *Grade A/A** answer (8–9 marks) you will need to show some of the following **content**:
- writing that is clear and controlled; sentence structures have been manipulated to create effects;
- a wide range of discourse markers appropriately used;
- variation in syntax (the grammatical arrangement of words) in a number of ways for rhetorical reasons;
- sophisticated use of a range of punctuation; for instance, colons and semi-colons are effectively and appropriately used.

To achieve a *Grade A/A** answer (8–9 marks) you will need to show the following **skills** in your answer:
- you have a full range of sentence structures and you can use them in an appropriate way;
- you have demonstrated a high level of accuracy in spelling;
- you have shown a high degree of accuracy in your punctuation.

Grade predictor
The grid below suggests the grades that you might expect to achieve on these papers.
Remember that the grade boundaries change from year to year at each Examination Board.

Add the grades for the two papers and divide by 2 for your final mark.

Grade E	19–24
Grade D	25–30
Grade C	31–36
Grade B	37–42
Grade A	43–48
Grade A*	49–54

Sample answer

Question 2 **Compare 'Love After Love' with one other poem and explore the theme of self-discovery in each of the poems.**

The theme of self-discovery is equally important for the poem, 'Presents from my Aunts in Pakistan'. The poem's first person narrator discovers her identity through a series of reflections, images and senses when she considers the brightly coloured 'alien' clothes that she recalls her Aunts sending her from Pakistan; for example, the narrator's 'salwar kameez' is 'peacock blue', the 'embossed slippers' are 'gold and black' and the gift of the 'candy-stripped glass bangles' draws 'blood' when it snaps on her wrist. 'Blood' introduces the idea of the narrator's roots and with it a chain of clothes-induced memories that lead her to discover the Asian half of her identity.

The poem's style of narration has a sense of immediacy that is appropriate for the direct experience that is related in the poem. The poet's use of free verse is also effective as the poem's maze-like lines help embody the narrator's meandering sense of self-discovery as she reflects on a series of objects that enable her to 'discover' her roots.

The narrator's ornate 'presents' stimulate her imagination: she recalls through the 'glass circles' of the clothes' 'mirror-work' how she made the uncomfortable journey to England with her parents as a young child: an event that she would otherwise have been far too young to remember.

'Love after Love' also uses a number of strong visual images and the senses to explore the theme of self-discovery. Again, reflections and mirrors act as a catalyst for the imagination: 'You will greet yourself at your own door, in your own mirror'; however this poem's narrator addresses the audience more directly with the second person, 'you' as Walcott explores how we can become strangers to ourselves and how we ought to make an effort to rediscover who we once were. The narrator thinks that if the audience takes the trouble to do so then they will be rewarded, 'You will love again the stranger who has loved you.'

In Walcott's poem there seems to be a greater sense of distance between the narrator and the reader through the former's repeated use of the personal pronoun 'you'; paradoxically, this same pronoun could also be said to act as a linguistic focal point for the poem's central idea of reuniting the person you were with the person that you have become. The 'salwar kameez' in Moniza Alvi's poem seems to provide a similar function for her narrator.

The poets' selected form, free verse, is most appropriate for their reflective treatment of their shared theme: 'self-discovery'.

Examiner's comment

The answer appears to fit the upper band of A to A*. Textual evidence is skilfully used with integrated quotations; the writer has also taken care not to pepper his/her answer with too many quotations. Obvious comparative points between the poems have been selected, analysed and written about in a sustained, integrated manner where it has been appropriate to do so. The writer has demonstrated a clear understanding of each poet's shared literary techniques and methods of presentation, together with their effectiveness and appropriateness. There is evidence of a growing personal response and an overview of how the two poems are linked by a similar theme. However, the writer may be stretching a point in the second to last paragraph's comparison between the pronoun 'you' and the 'salwar kameez' acting as focal points for their respective narrators. The point is interesting, nonetheless.

All in all, an exceptional and relevant response within the time frame of 45 minutes.

Index

advertising 14, 15–16, 17, 71–7
advice, writing 19–22
alliteration 62, 161
analysis, writing 37–43, 44
arguing a case 9–14
asides 113–15
assonance 62, 161
atmosphere 126, 149–51, 157–9, 162
audience
    advice 21, 22
    analysis 42
    explanations 60
    informative writing 54, 57
    reviews 47–8
autobiographies 31–2, 93–5

biographies 93–5
blank verse 115–17

character logs 125, 128
characters
    drama 113–15, 127–30
    imaginative writing 25, 26, 28–9
    novels and short stories 137, 138, 142–6
    reviews 46
charities 14, 15–16, 17, 75–7
comment, writing 43, 44, 49–50
conclusion 9, 13
context 146–51, 163–5
coursework 8

description 27, 29, 30, 142, 149–51
descriptive writing 61–2
dialect 168–9
dialogue 83–5, 133–4, 137, 142
documentary writing 96–8
drama 105–23, 124–36

endings 9, 13, 18–19, 30–1, 120–1
enjambment 115, 117
entertaining writing 33–4
exams 7

explain, writing to 57–60
exploratory writing 31–3

facts
    arguing a case 11, 12
    newspapers 67
    non-fiction texts 90, 92, 99
    reviews 44
    writing to inform 54
films 78–85

iambic pentameters 115–17
ideas
    analysis 37, 39
    comment 49–50
    novels and short stories 149, 151–2
    poetry 156, 164
imagery 62, 118–19, 142, 150, 157, 159–61
imaginative writing 25–31
informative writing 53–7
interviews 81–3

journalism 31, 49–50, 65–70

language
    advertising 71–2
    advice 19–21
    analysis 37, 38–9, 42
    comment 49
    descriptive writing 62
    informative writing 54, 57
    non-fiction texts 93
    persuasive 15
    poetry 156, 159, 163, 168–9
    Shakespeare 115–19
literary non-fiction 98–100

magazine articles 90–3
media 65–88
metaphors 62, 118, 142, 160

narration 140, 141
narrative 25
newspapers 65–70
non-fiction texts 89–104
novels 137–54

onomatopoeia 62, 161
openings
    arguing a case 11
    drama 109–12, 125–7
    imaginative writing 26–8, 30
    novels and short stories 139–41
    persuasive writing 17–18
opinions 11, 44, 67, 90, 92

personification 160
persuasive writing 14–19
plot 25, 26, 46, 107–8, 138
poetry 31, 32, 155–72
previews 78, 79
prose 117–18
purpose
    advice 21, 22
    analysis 42
    informative writing 53, 54
    reviews 47–8
    writing to explain 60

reviews 44–9, 78, 80
revision 6
rhetorical questions 12, 13, 15, 17–18, 19
rhyme 162
rhythm 159, 161, 162

setting 25, 26, 126, 132–3, 146–51
Shakespeare, William 105–23
short stories 137–54
similes 62, 118, 142, 159
soliloquies 113–15
Standard English 168–9
structure 48, 54, 57, 58, 107–8
style 38–9, 48, 164
symbols 142, 170

themes
    drama 119, 125, 130–4
    novels and short stories 137, 149, 151–2
    poetry 164
tone 13, 156, 157–9, 161
travel writing 31, 95–6, 100